GOVERNMENT PURCHASING AND COMPETITION

The opinions expressed in this study are those of the author. The functions of the Bureau of Business and Economic Research are confined to facilitating the prosecution of independent scholarly research by members of the faculty.

Publications of the
Bureau of Business and Economic Research
University of California

GOVERNMENT PURCHASING AND COMPETITION

By

DICKSON RECK

UNIVERSITY OF CALIFORNIA PRESS
BERKELEY AND LOS ANGELES
1954

UNIVERSITY OF CALIFORNIA PRESS
BERKELEY AND LOS ANGELES

CAMBRIDGE UNIVERSITY PRESS
LONDON, ENGLAND

LIBRARY OF CONGRESS CATALOG NUMBER 54-12093

To My Wife

Acknowledgments

This study is the first project to be completed in the program of the Standardization Fellowship sustained by the Sarah Mellon Scaife Foundation at Mellon Institute in Pittsburgh, Pennsylvania. The generous financial support of the Foundation has made it possible to conduct the research required to complete the study, both through the Fellowship's program at Pittsburgh and through its continuation during the academic year at the University of California, Berkeley. The program at Berkeley is sustained by a grant to the University from the Foundation through the Mellon Institute and is administered by the Bureau of Business and Economic Research.

The data for the study were primarily obtained from the files of the Federal Supply Service of the General Services Administration in Washington; from conferences with buyers and officials of the Federal Supply Service and other government agencies; and from representatives of manufacturers and distributors who are suppliers to the government. Commissioner Clifton E. Mack of the Federal Supply Service and Director Willis S. Macleod of its Standards Division, through their understanding of the potential usefulness of the study and by introductions to members of their staffs, greatly facilitated the task of gathering the data. In addition, they and other officials of the Federal Supply Service provided many helpful comments.

Particular thanks are due to Professor Edward R. Hawkins of The Johns Hopkins University who contributed many ideas and suggestions. Constructive criticism of the manuscript by Professors Arthur Robert Burns and J. M. Clark of Columbia University and by Professors Frank L. Kidner and Robert A. Brady of the University of California prompted revisions and improvements. Others who read the manuscript and provided useful comments were Professors Maurice Moonitz, Delbert Duncan, John P. Carter, and David A. Revzan of the University of California, Professor Charles Abbott, formerly of Harvard University and now dean of the Graduate School of Business, University of Virginia, and Dr. William A. Hamor of Mellon Institute.

Publication has been made possible by the Bureau of Business and Economic Research of the University of California, whose director, Professor Frank L. Kidner, has guided the manuscript through its various stages of approval and publication. Mrs. Dorothy Haas and Miss Jean Trahan of the Bureau's staff typed the manuscript in its final version. The figures were prepared by Mrs. Reinhard Bendix and Mrs. Cole Eardley.

DICKSON RECK

Berkeley, 1954

Contents

FIGURES

TABLES

APPENDIX:

I

Introduction

The Problem and Its Significance

The policies established by Congress to guide the purchasing operations of the civilian agencies of the federal government have two dominant features: (1) the legal requirement that sealed bids be used in contracting, and (2) the delegation to the General Services Administration of the authority to centralize purchases and to unify the purchasing policies of all agencies. This study is planned to appraise these policies. While confined to an appraisal of government purchasing, the study is designed to contribute to an understanding of the effectiveness of the policies pursued by other large-quantity buyers.

This approach to the study of market operations opens relatively unexplored opportunities for research because investigators have, for the most part, focused their attention on the operation of sellers' policies. The emphasis on these is quite natural and appropriate. Most companies are more concerned with what they sell than with what they buy and, as sellers, take the initiative in establishing the market practices which determine contract prices. Sellers, furthermore, have been the principal targets of government regulation of market practices. For these reasons sellers' policies have offered a fruitful field for constructive research. While the business techniques of purchasing have been developed in the literature, the economic effects which buyers' policies and programs exert on sellers' policies have received scanty attention.

An improved understanding of the operation of buyers' policies is important. The success of the free-enterprise system depends in part on whether buyers actively develop and use rational policies and thus play an effective role in determining the composition and distribution of the national product. Large-quantity buyers are in a favorable position to play such a role. Each contract is an agreement between a buyer and a seller, and the volume buyer can shape his policies to cope with sellers' policies. Such buyers, in many markets where neither buyers nor sellers hold exceptionally strong monopsonistic or monopolistic positions, often are able to influence sellers to abandon the use of policies which lead to high prices, reduced outputs, and sometimes to the production of goods inadequately designed to meet the needs of users. To the extent that this is possible, the voluntary action of buyers can serve to increase the efficiency of markets without government intervention or legislation.

This study was prompted by the hypothesis that large-quantity buyers, such as governments, institutions, and large industrial and commercial firms, can substantially improve the effectiveness of their purchasing policies with consequent benefits not only to their organizations, but to the economy as a whole. Any rigorous examination of this hypothesis would require not one but a series of research projects. In this study the policies and programs of a single large-volume buyer, the federal government, are scrutinized, and the scope of the government programs included is limited.

Federal-government purchasing offers an effective approach to the study of market forces and purchasing policy. The government buys many products which are also used by private buyers, and although its total volume of purchases makes it the largest buyer in the country it seldom buys a sufficient quantity of any one product to make it a dominant factor in any market for civilian types of goods. It has adopted policies which are well defined, represent a consistently applied attempt to obtain the benefits expected from competition, and in important respects differ from the parallel policies typically employed in the same markets by private buyers.

Influence of Sellers' Policies

The markets for civilian goods include wide ranges of products which are to various degrees substitutes in the satisfaction of the same use and are offered at various prices. The prices at which these products are offered for sale and the qualities claimed for them are the principal data initially available to the buyer. They are determined, however, by the operation of sellers' policies, and the degree to which they can safely be used as the basis for formulating purchasing policies must be judged by the character of the sellers' price and product policies from which they result.

The price policies of sellers are different to some extent in each industry. From the government's point of view, the different price structures which result—involving, for example, list prices and discounts to classes of trade, formula pricing, or area pricing—play an important part in constructing invitations for bids. But the basically important differences are those which relate to the question of whether the policies result in competition for individual contracts or in the quotation of prices which are stable over time or uniform for rival suppliers. Typically, sellers declare their prices to prospective customers in printed form and attempt to maintain these prices. In some markets where the declared prices are backed by patent agreements, strong price leadership, or other devices, all sellers when quoting to the government adhere strongly to these prices; in many more markets at least some sellers will depart from their declared prices in quoting to the government; and in other markets such departures are general.

Sellers generally attempt to support their declared prices and increase sales by differentiating their products from those of their rivals. Policies of product differentiation result in claims of differences, which are either relevant or irrelevant in the government's judgment. For some industries the relevant differences between competitive products are great, while for others the products are functionally identical and the claimed differences irrelevant. By its very nature, product differentiation complicates rather than simplifies the buyer's problem of making direct comparisons of the characteristics of products which are substitutes for the same use. On the one hand the buyer is offered a greater range of products from which to select, while on the other hand some claimed differences only confuse and complicate the process of selection.

The government, and most other buyers who purchase for use and not for resale, attempt to maximize the utility received for each dollar spent. To do this, buyers must sort out the facts from the mixture of facts and fiction provided by sources of supply and supplement such information with any additional facts required to make rational judgments. The extent to which they maximize utility for each dollar spent depends on the success with which they are able to devise and apply rational policies to their purchasing.

If a purchaser must buy in small quantities, he can select the product which gives him the most utility per dollar from among the existing competitive offers, but he can do little to change sellers' policies. When purchasers are able to buy in large quantities, they need not assume that the markets they face are fixed structures of products, prices, and the sellers' policies that determine them. Large buyers, including the government, can adopt price and product policies to guide their purchasing programs with the intent of influencing sellers to change their policies.

Well-designed policies of large-quantity purchasers can often, where it is desirable to do so, open up wholesale instead of retail, or primary instead of intermediate, markets. They may also induce individual sellers to deviate from their established price policy when quoting on large-quantity contracts by encouraging independent competitive bidding for individual contracts unhampered by sellers' policies resulting in stable or uniform prices.

For important products large buyers can conduct research to uncover the significant characteristics of competitive products, shape their product policy to take advantage of relevant differences, ignore others, and encourage competition in important product differences. This may extend to the point of influencing suppliers to adjust or redesign their products to meet the particular needs of the buyer. Recognizing possibilities such as these, the federal government has formulated a set of policies and programs intended to maximize its gains from purchasing expenditures.

Purchasing Objectives and Policies

Purchasing is an integral part of the chain of activities by which needs for goods are satisfied. Purchasing policies and programs, therefore, can best be understood if their relation to the other activities in the chain, and to the broad objective of supply, are clarified.

Objectives and functions of supply.—The objective of supply policy is to help minimize the costs of government by maximizing the utility received for the dollars spent in procuring and consuming the goods it needs, and by minimizing any losses from shortages caused by untimely deliveries. The magnitudes of the utility-per-dollar ratios are finally determined only after the goods are consumed. The magnitudes depend on (1) the choice of the products, (2) the prices paid, (3) the administrative costs of purchasing and distributing, (4) the effectiveness with which the goods are utilized, (5) the utilization costs, such as maintenance and repair, and (6) the money value realized by the trade-in or other disposal of the goods. To minimize the losses in operating efficiency which result from shortages of goods, the proper performance of all supply activities is required.

The term "supply" thus includes all functions involved in providing goods to satisfy the government's needs from the time the demands are first made known until the goods are consumed or disposed of as scrap or surplus. More specifically, supply includes the following functions:

Survey of need and initial choice of product—the considerations by employees of government agencies which result in requisitions.

Property identification—the task of cataloging all goods to facilitate identification with respect to the need they can fill.

Specification—the establishment of standard purchase specifications for goods.

Centralization of purchase programs—the task of consolidating requirements to obtain economical order quantities for purchasing.

Invitation of bids and award of contracts—the direct negotiations with prospective suppliers.

Inspection—the comparison of goods received with purchase specifications.

Storage and issue—the storage of goods purchased in quantity and their issue against requisitions.

Traffic management—the negotiations with carriers and regulatory bodies regarding rates and classification for goods purchased on a delivered basis.

Utilization of existing property—the repair, maintenance, efficient use, and eventual disposal of goods.

Objectives and functions of purchasing.—The objectives of purchasing are the same as those of supply, that is, to maximize utility-per-dollar ratios and minimize the inefficiencies resulting from shortages, but the purchasing functions are only a part of those included in supply. The term "purchasing" is used with different meanings by different people, but as used by the government in the context "purchasing programs" it refers to the process of contracting with sources of supply for the quantities and types of goods requisitioned by the agencies or the employees who use these goods.[1] In this sense purchasing includes only the functions

[1] Some writers in the marketing field use the term "buying" to cover buying for use and buying for resale, and to include the functions of determination of what to buy, location of sources of supply, negotiations with sources, award of contracts, and approval of invoices for payment. Others use the term "purchasing" to mean buying for use and reserve the term "buying" to describe buying for resale. Still others prefer the word "procurement" in place of "purchasing" and in some cases use

of centralization of purchase programs, and invitation of bids and awards of contracts.

The purchasing policies of the government, however, extend a controlling influence over other supply programs, and their successful execution in turn depends on the performance of the other programs. The discussion of purchasing policies and their operation in this study, therefore, includes discussions of the supply programs most directly related to purchasing. Purchasing policies are classified below, for purposes of analysis, into internal policies which directly influence the decisions and activities of the agencies and employees of the government, and the policies of inviting bids, negotiating, and awarding contracts which directly influence the decisions of suppliers. The discussion of each of these classes of policies includes a listing of the relevant supply programs.

Internal policies.—The policies affecting purchasing which are applied within the government consist of plans of action covering the organization of requirements for goods, the choice of the kind and grade of goods to be purchased, and the methods by which the goods are delivered to fill the requirements. These are intimately connected with the supply programs of survey of need and initial choice of product, property identification, specification, centralization of purchase programs, and storage and issue.

Policies of inviting bids, negotiating, and awarding contracts.—The policies which extend outside the government organization to influence the decisions of suppliers consist of a product policy and a price policy.

The product policy incorporated in the sealed-bids and negotiating devices provides purchase specifications and methods of using them to compare the utility of competitive products offered in bids at the time contracts are awarded. This is a part of the broad product policies of the government which include also those applied internally for deciding what kind and grade of good to specify and what quantity to buy.

The price policy requires the use of sealed bids and in some situations permits direct negotiation of contracts; this policy is

---

"procurement" in a broader sense than "purchasing" to include control of inventories and obtaining supplies by manufacture as well as by purchasing them in markets for a money price. The government in the past increased the currency of the word "procurement" when it established the Procurement Division of the Treasury Department as its central purchasing agency, but subsequently adopted the terms "supply" and "purchasing" and now uses them with the meanings described in the text.

intended to encourage competitive pricing by suppliers, and also to provide methods for awarding contracts.

These product and price policies are intimately connected with the supply programs of specification and the invitation of bids and award of contracts.[2] The specification program also serves internally to choose the product and standardize demands on it.

SCOPE OF THE STUDY

Since the government buys goods with various objectives in mind, it is desirable to limit this study to those programs which are most closely related to private purchasing and therefore have the broadest interest and significance. With this in view, attention is confined to civilian goods which the government buys in direct competition with private buyers. This practice excludes purchases of strictly military items, because they involve special designs, secrecy, and urgency of supply and are therefore not directly comparable with ordinary purchases. For similar reasons purchases of strategic materials for stockpiling and purchases for foreign-aid programs are not considered. Purchases for price-support purposes are also excluded because they offer little information that is relevant for competitive purchasing. Goods included within the foregoing limitations are purchased by the military as well as the civilian agencies. The study has been focused on the purchase policies and programs of the civilian agencies because, compared with military purchasing, they are more closely related to private purchasing problems and are subject to less violent fluctuations.

Table 1 gives an idea of the volume and importance of the purchases which fall within this limited scope of government purchasing. Excluding strategic materials and purchases for foreign-aid programs, the volume of obligations for supplies, materials, and equipment by the civilian agencies in the fiscal year 1951 amounted to $865,000,000. The total obligations by civilian agencies for salaries of employees amounted to $4,003,000,000. Thus for every five dollars spent in salaries, more than one dollar goes for supplies,

[2] The following programs are so indirectly related to purchasing that they have been substantially excluded from consideration: utilization of existing property, which affects the replacement rate of goods but only indirectly affects purchasing through its influence on purchase specifications; traffic management, which is an important determinant of cost, but does not directly affect the awarding of contracts or purchase prices for the civilian types of goods under consideration; and inspection, which serves to determine satisfactory completion of contracts but needs to be considered only where its cost prevents the use of commodity specifications and the buying devices connected with them.

TABLE 1

OBLIGATIONS FOR PURCHASES AND OTHER OBJECT CLASSIFICATIONS BY CIVILIAN AGENCIES

(Fiscal year 1951)

Object classification[a]	Funds obligated (millions of dollars)
Printing and reproduction	71
Travel	120
Rents and utilities, and communication services	189
Transportation of goods	756
Other contractual services	835
Purchases of supplies, materials, and equipment	865
Lands and structures	1,890
Strategic materials	2,075
Personal services	4,003
Mutual security supplies, materials, and equipment	4,224
Interest, subsidies, pensions, refunds, investments, and other obligations	19,844
Total	34,872

SOURCE: Compiled from *Obligations by Objects for the Fiscal Years 1951, 1952, and 1953*, Bureau of the Budget, Washington.

[a] Object classifications 08 and 09 in the Bureau of the Budget report total $7,164,000,000. Of this the amount obligated for mutual-security programs of $4,224,000,000 is shown separately as is the amount obligated for strategic materials of $2,075,000,000, leaving a total of $865,000,000 which represents the remaining obligations for supplies, materials, and equipment made by the civilian agencies for other purposes.

materials, and equipment. The purchasing policies of the civilian agencies, however, also extend an influence over some unknown amount of purchases which the Department of Defense makes under contracts let by the civilian agencies, or which the Department of Defense itself contracts for on the basis of federal specifications which are developed by the civilian agencies. In all cases the goods are the same or similar to those purchased by private buyers and present similar policy and programing problems.

II

Historical, Organizational, and Legal Setting

The Government's Demands for Goods

To carry out successfully the many responsibilities set by the Constitution and federal law, the government requires goods of almost every conceivable description, some of them in huge quantities. The task of providing these commodities and services in a manner that permits the orderly flow of necessary government activity is unquestionably the most complex supply problem in the country, if not the world.

Character of demand.—It has been estimated that the government procures 3,750,000 different items, if each kind, grade, and size of each good is counted. Each item is significant because it must be purchased as a separate article distinct from every other. Sixty per cent of these are specialized items required by the military services, but an estimated 1,000,000 are used in common by the civilian and military agencies and another 500,000 by the civilian agencies alone.[1]

These goods range in size from pins to electric generators, are demanded in quantities from one to tens of thousands, and vary in unit price from a fraction of a cent to millions of dollars. Classified by end use, they cover the gamut of consumer, intermediate, producer, and capital goods, and run the range from the most perishable to the most durable of commodities. The requirements for these goods spring from the individual needs of more than 2,500,000 civilian employees,[2] the material requirements for the armed forces,

[1] For a discussion of the meaning of these figures and for sources see chap. iii, "Cataloging program."

[2] Civilian employment at the end of the fiscal year 1952 was 2,603,267, according to the Civil Service Commission.

and hundreds of production enterprises, repair shops, dams, warehouses, prisons, hospitals, schools, port facilities, office buildings, and construction projects. Geographically these requirements originate at thousands of points scattered all over the United States and in the cities of most foreign countries, wherever government personnel and projects are located. The biggest slice of this demand comes from Washington and the large cities where government agencies are thickly clustered, but streams flow from every state and county, and their sources reach back to trickles from the most remote village post office in the countryside and forest ranger in the Rockies.

All these demands are caused by the needs of employees in performing their work and by requirements resulting from constructing and maintaining facilities, institutions, and production enterprises. In translating these requirements into orders for specific commodities, therefore, the principal consideration is the contribution the commodities make to the productivity of employees and facilities, rather than the satisfaction of personal preferences of the individuals who consume the goods.

Legal and administrative limitations.—The basic law controlling purchasing by the federal government provides that, with certain exceptions for the Army, Navy, and Air Force departments, no purchase shall be made on behalf of the United States unless it is authorized by law or is under an appropriation adequate to its fulfillment.[3] Thus demand is made effective basically by the appropriation acts of Congress.

Appropriation requests are prepared in standard form by each agency, working with the Bureau of the Budget, which must review, approve, and consolidate the requests of the executive agencies before they are presented to Congress. Appropriations are made by object classifications covering broad categories of goods, the most important of which, from the viewpoint of purchasing, are "supplies and materials," "equipment," and "other contractual services." Funds may be legally transferred from one object classification to another according to need, but from a practical viewpoint budget estimates are reasonably accurate, and expenditures are substantially limited to the amounts appropriated in each classification. In addition, rental of buildings in the District of Columbia, purchases of passenger automobiles, of airplanes for use of civilian agencies, and of land must be specifically authorized in

[3] *U.S. Rev. Stat.* (1878), sec. 3732; 41 *U.S. Code* (1952), sec. 11.

appropriation acts or other laws.[4] Finally, the law imposes the general requirement that funds must be committed during the fiscal year for which they are appropriated. All unexpended appropriations revert to the Treasury at the expiration of each fiscal year.

The full effect, then, of the law is to channel demand into predetermined categories, and to make this demand potentially effective for the duration of the fiscal year beginning from the time the appropriation is approved.

In addition, of course, Congress may itself initiate a new program or eliminate an existing one and thus cause important changes in the effective demand for goods.

The result is a flow of demand for goods to satisfy the ordinary needs of continuing government activity. Periodically, however, great changes occur both in the volume and the kind of goods procured following swells in appropriations to meet the needs which arise from depressions, wars, national defense, and foreign aid.

Development of Centralized Purchasing

The character of the demand and the legal and budgetary procedures by which it is made effective leaves purchasing uncentralized in the individual agencies. Requisitions are characteristically initiated by persons or units within each agency, and the agency has the authority to expend its appropriated funds to purchase the requisitioned goods. To the executive heads of the agencies, who are typically in office for relatively short periods of time, procurement is a minor problem. As a result—with the exception of agencies such as the Army, Navy, and the Tennessee Valley Authority, for which procurement has been a major task—purchasing has historically been treated as a semiclerical procedure. The possibilities of savings through centralization have been recognized, but purchasing has been organized—with one early exception, noted below—according to the ideas of successive administrators of each agency. Only in the last few decades has centralized purchasing received close and concerted attention from the executive and legislative branches of the government.

Early attempts.—In 1792 the Congress provided for a centralized purchasing system under the Treasury.[5] The requirements of the government at that time were small and were mostly those of the military forces. The military were gradually able to encroach upon

[4] 60 *U.S. Stat. at L.* (1947), 810; 19 *U.S. Stat. at L.* (1877), 370; 40 *U.S. Code* (1952), sec. 34; *U.S. Rev. Stat.* (1878), sec. 3736; 41 *U.S. Code* (1952), sec. 14.

[5] 1 *U.S. Stat. at L.* (1845), 280.

the Treasury's authority, which became substantially ineffective with the establishment of the Quartermaster General's Office in 1812.[6] For a hundred years after this initial effort to centralize the planning and programing of purchasing the responsibility for procurement remained in the individual agencies where the organization and methods of supply grew without coördination. Aside from the requirements that contracts be awarded after advertising for bids and public opening of bids, which were first imposed in the 1860's, there was little or no central direction of purchasing policies.[7]

At the turn of the century two investigations sponsored by Congress gave publicity to the unsatisfactory results being obtained from the uncentralized and casually organized procurement systems then in effect.[8] The principal criticisms made by these commissions were the wide variety of prices paid by different agencies for the same item (in some instances to the same dealer at the same time), the failure to use effective specifications, and the failure to consolidate purchases to obtain the bargaining advantages of large-order quantities. As a direct result of these investigations, the General Supply Committee under the secretary of the Treasury was created in 1910 by act of Congress.[9]

The General Supply Committee.—The General Supply Committee's main task was to let contracts for the consolidated supply requirements of the government. To accomplish this it was empowered to prepare annual schedules of consolidated requirements, to standardize the demands of various agencies on common-use items, and to prepare specifications for the purchase of such items. In the first two decades of the Committee's existence its major accomplishments were the establishment of the Federal Specifications Board[10] and the development of time contracts with suppliers for common-use items under which the individual agencies could purchase their requirements in small quantities according to their needs.[11]

---

[6] C. E. Mack, *Federal Procurement* (Washington: Government Printing Office, 1943), p. 12.

[7] For further information concerning bidding procedure see the discussion in this chapter under "Inviting bids and awarding contracts."

[8] These were the Dockery Commission in 1893, and the Keep Commission in 1905. For discussion of their work see C. E. Mack, *op. cit.*, chap. iii.

[9] 41 *U.S. Code* (1946), sec. 7; 36 *U.S. Stat. at L.* (1911), 531.

[10] The Federal Specifications Board was created on October 10, 1921, by Budget Circular No. 42. See *Fourth Annual Report of the Budget*, 1925, p. 95.

[11] Contracts of this type are still widely used and are now known as the federal supply schedules. See chap. iii, "Federal supply schedules."

The advantages of large-quantity purchasing could be realized only partially by these time contracts because the quantities bought under them were determined finally by the sum of the small orders of many agencies and were indefinite at the time contracts were let. Definite-quantity contracts held the promise of fuller realization of the advantages of quantity purchases. These, however, required capital to finance the purchases and storage facilities to hold the goods until they were requisitioned by the using agencies. Congress responded to the need for clearing the way for bulk buying by enacting a law which authorized the General Supply Committee to make such purchases, authorized the construction of a warehouse in the District of Columbia, and provided a General Supply Fund of $300,000 to be used for bulk purchases.[12]

Although formally the work of the General Supply Committee marked the beginnings of centralized purchasing, the powers of the Committee were not comprehensive, and the authority for action rested in the members and the secretary of the Treasury, all of whom were only secondarily interested in the problems of supply. While the Committee did serve effectively to focus attention on the need for centralized responsibility, it was far short of being a fully effective device for improving the supply system of the federal government.

The Procurement Division of the Treasury.—In 1933 the first action which held real promise for effective rationalization of purchasing was taken in the establishment of the Procurement Division of the Treasury by executive order of the president under authority of the Reorganization Act of the same year.[13] The Procurement Division was provided with broad authority. It was authorized, after obtaining approval of the president, to centralize the actual procurement for all agencies in its own organization or in any other agency it designated, and also to determine the policies to be followed by other agencies which continued to procure their own goods.

In spite of this broad mandate the Procurement Division was

[12] 41 *U.S. Code* (1946), sec. 7a–7d; 45 *U.S. Stat. at L.* (1929), 1342–1343.

[13] The law was the Reorganization Act of March 3, 1933, 47 *U.S. Stat. at L.* (1933), 1517. This law authorized the president to reorganize the executive agencies by executive orders which were to be submitted to Congress and to become effective after 60 days in absence of congressional action to the contrary. Executive Order 6166 establishing the Procurement Division was issued by the president on June 10, 1933, and was unopposed by Congress. In effect, therefore, it had the force of law, a fact which was not fully appreciated by the other executive agencies and later served to weaken the Division's position.

TABLE 2

CENTRALIZED PURCHASE PROGRAMS; PROCUREMENT DIVISION, TREASURY DEPARTMENT

(Fiscal years 1941–1949)

Program	1941	1942	1943	1944	1945	1946	1947	1948	1949
	Millions of dollars								
Regular activities[a]	15.4	21.7	39.3	34.4	32.9	30.0	46.2	56.8	90.2
Emergency relief (WPA, NYA, etc.)	219.3	171.7	41.1	0.1	......	......	......	......	......
Defense housing (furniture, equipment)	5.4	15.4	15.9	[b]	......	......	......	......	......
Strategic and critical materials	29.4	6.5	4.8	7.0	......	......	68.9	252.9	420.6
Lend-Lease[c]	21.0	1,126.4	1,470.1	1,086.6	1,289.4	258.2	......	......	......
Foreign war relief (American Red Cross)[c]	18.4	17.1	2.6	4.3	7.6	0.8	......	......	......
UNRRA[c]	......	......	......	......	106.3	215.2	......	......	......
Special programs[c]	......	......	......	......	......	......	233.3	21.5	7.1
Total	308.9	1,358.8	1,573.8	1,132.4	1,436.2	504.2	348.4	331.2	517.9

SOURCE: Annual Reports of the Secretary of the Treasury. For 1947 and after, the figures are for the Bureau of Federal Supply.

[a] Includes direct purchases of supplies for other agencies and purchases of warehouse stock.

[b] Less than 1.

[c] Beginning 1947, foreign-aid and similar programs are combined as "special programs."

beset by difficulties in its effort to bring a greater measure of centralization of government purchasing. At the outset its activities were largely absorbed by purchasing for the work relief programs which were initiated in the 'thirties and did not terminate until well into the war years. From 1941 until after the close of the war, Lend-Lease purchases dominated its programs, and these were followed by substantial programs for UNRRA and the procurement of strategic materials for stockpiling. The "normal" functions of the Division never accounted for the predominant part of its activities. This is illustrated by the data shown in Table 2.

Nevertheless, beginning just before the war and particularly in the years following the close of the war, the Division, renamed the Bureau of Federal Supply in 1947, was able to make progress in solving the supply problems of the government.

The program, initiated by the General Supply Committee, of letting centralized contracts under which procuring agencies order locally was continued. Orders that amounted to approximately $90,000,000 were placed after the war, through 1949, under these contracts. The work of developing Federal Specifications was strengthened and speeded, and before the war an impressive start was made in developing a uniform Federal Commodity Catalog.

The Bureau made its most impressive progress in its stores and bulk-purchases programs. Warehousing and store facilities of the government throughout the country were in large measure consolidated. Twelve stores offering what amounted to a mail-order service to all agencies were established in the major cities where agencies are concentrated. Bulk purchases to fill combined requirements both through stores and by direct delivery to the using agencies were increased.

In addition to these accomplishments, the Bureau took a stronger lead in surveying government supply practice and regularizing supply policies in the various government agencies. This was accomplished in addition to the substantial contribution the Bureau made by performing the supply operations for the special programs mentioned above, such as stockpiling of strategic materials.[14]

[14] For discussions of these accomplishments of the Bureau of Federal Supply summarized here, see the testimony of C. E. Mack in the U.S. Congress, House, Committee on Appropriations, *Treasury Department Appropriation Bill for 1950,* Hearings, 81st Cong., 1st sess. (Washington: 1949), pp. 335–348, p. 389. Testimony of Harry M. Kurth, assistant director, Bureau of Federal Supply, in U.S. Congress, Senate, Committee on Expenditures in the Executive Departments, *Federal Property Act of 1948,* Hearings, 80th Cong., 2d sess., March 31–April 3, 1948 (Washington: 1948). Testimony

THE HOOVER COMMISSION FINDINGS

Despite these accomplishments, Congress, the officials of the Bureau of Federal Supply, and the purchasing executives of other agencies were of the opinion that a great deal remained to be done. These opinions were crystallized and given added force by the investigations of the Hoover Commission in 1948 and the issuance of its reports dealing with the federal supply system late in 1948 and early in 1949.[15]

The Commission agreed with the opinion current in the government that the supply policies and programs suffered from a lack of central direction, and that the need for legislative action was particularly pressing in view of the huge sums being expended in purchasing and supply. The picture as it was viewed by the Commission is outlined by the statistics presented below.

Volume of purchases.—Adequate figures for federal-government purchases are not compiled. Those shown in Tables 3 and 4 give an indication of the magnitude of purchases by the major agencies. They show the total obligations for supplies and materials, and equipment. On the one hand, these figures do not comprise all purchasing, because they do not include land and structures, fixed equipment, utilities services, and purchases which are contained in totals of other classifications but which cannot be segregated. On the other hand, the figures include an unknown amount of duplication resulting from the method of reporting the obligations. Still they provide a rough idea of the magnitude of federal-government procurement.

The obligations for supplies and materials, and equipment for agencies of the government totaled $8,610,000,000 in 1949. The civilian agencies were responsible for $1,345,000,000 of this or

---

of C. E. Mack in the U.S. Congress, Senate, Committee on Expenditures in the Executive Departments, *Federal Property Act of 1949,* Hearing, 81st Cong., 1st sess., on S. 990 and S. 859, April 14, 1949 (Washington: 1949). *Detailed Report on the Federal Supply System,* Submitted by the Federal Supply Project to the Commission on Organization of the Executive Branch of the Government (hereafter referred to as the Hoover Commission), Sept. 28, 1948, mimeographed. For a detailed discussion of the problem of centralization of procurement, see Dana Mills Barbour, *Interdepartmental Centralization in Federal Procurement* (Washington: 1948), typescript, available in the Bureau of the Budget Library, Washington.

[15] *Detailed Report on the Federal Supply System; Task Force Report on the Federal Supply System (Appendix B),* prepared for the Hoover Commission (Washington: 1949); Hoover Commission, *Office of General Services Supply Activities* (Washington: 1949).

TABLE 3

OBLIGATIONS FOR PURCHASES OF SUPPLIES, MATERIALS, AND EQUIPMENT; DEPARTMENT OF DEFENSE AND TOTAL FOR CIVILIAN AGENCIES
(Value in millions of dollars)

Agency	Dec. 1937 through Nov. 1938		Fiscal year 1947		Fiscal year 1948		Fiscal year 1949		Fiscal year 1950		Fiscal year 1951		Fiscal year 1952 (est.)	
	Value	Per cent	Value	Per cent	Value	Per cent	Value	Per cent	Value	Per cent	Value	Per cent	Value	Per cent
Department of Defense	485	53.1	5,508	88.6	6,675	83.1	7,265	84.4	6,229	67.7	33,151	81.5	55,562	87.9
Civilian agencies	428	46.9	712	11.4	1,359	16.9	1,345	15.6	2,975	32.3	7,523	18.5	7,661	12.1
Total	913	100.0	6,220	100.0	8,034	100.0	8,610	100.0	9,204	100.0	40,674	100.0	63,243	100.0

SOURCE: Dec. 1937 through Nov. 1938 figures are from the Temporary National Economic Committee, Report of the Procurement Division Group, Treasury Department Subcommittee, *Study of Government Purchasing Activities*, Part I, chap. ii. In addition to supplies, materials, and equipment certain services such as utilities, are included. The figures for 1947 through 1950 are the totals of the amounts in object classifications "08. Supplies and materials" and " 09. Equipment," given in *Summary of Obligations by Objects*, compiled yearly by the U.S. Bureau of the Budget. These figures include obligations for goods procured by one government agency for another on a reimbursable basis. Such obligations are included twice and cause an unknown, but substantial, duplication. For the fiscal year 1948 only, the reimbursable items were accounted for and amounted to $1,300 million of the total of $8,034 million. $1,227 million of the $1,300 million is for the Department of Defense and $73 million for the civilian agencies. Obligations for procurement of fixed equipment, land and structures, rents and utilities services and an unknown amount of commodities under the heading "other contractual services" are not included.

TABLE 4

Obligations for Purchases of Supplies, Materials, and Equipment by Civilian Agencies

(Value in millions of dollars)

Agency	Dec. 1937 through Nov. 1938		Fiscal year 1947		Fiscal year 1948		Fiscal year 1949		Fiscal year 1950		Fiscal year 1951		Fiscal year 1952 (est.)	
	Value	Per cent	Value	Per cent	Value	Per cent	Value	Per cent	Value	Per cent	Value	Per cent	Value	Per cent
Department of Agriculture..	46	10.7	32	4.5	29	2.1	33	2.5	31	1.0	29	0.4	27	0.3
Department of Commerce...	9	2.1	39	5.5	27	2.0	35	2.6	46	1.5	335	4.5	117	1.5
Department of the Interior.	56	13.1	54	7.6	68	5.0	69	5.1	88	3.0	103	1.4	96	1.3
Post Office Department....	18	4.2	27	3.8	36	2.7	62	4.6	48	1.6	50	0.7	56	0.7
Treasury Department[a].....	26	6.1	225	31.6	287	21.1	48	3.6	57	2.0	88	1.2	91	1.2
Federal Works Agency[b]....	196	45.8	9	1.3	13	1.0	...	.....	...	.....	...	.....	...	.....
General Services Administr.	...	.....	...	.....	...	.....	475	35.3	804	27.0	2,201	29.2	1,054	13.8
Atomic Energy Commission	...	.....	30	4.2	119	8.8	95	7.1	55	1.9	70	0.9	96	1.3
Federal Security Agency...	3	0.7	18	2.5	21	1.5	20	1.5	18	0.6	19	0.2	29	0.4
Maritime Commission......	3	0.7	13	1.8	19	1.4	184	13.6	...	.....	...	.....	...	.....
Veterans Administration...	21	4.9	135	19.0	124	9.1	111	8.3	120	4.0	138	1.8	148	1.9
All others................	50	11.7	130	18.2	616[c]	45.3	213	15.8	1,708[d]	57.4	4,490[e]	59.7	5,947[f]	77.6
Total................	428	100.0	712	100.0	1,359	100.0	1,345	100.0	2,975	100.0	7,523	100.0	7,661	100.0

Source: Dec. 1937 through Nov. 1938 figures are from the Temporary National Economic Committee, Report of the Procurement Division Group, Treasury Department Subcommittee, *Study of Government Purchasing Activities*, Part I, chap. ii. Certain services, such as utilities, are included. The figures for 1947 through 1950 are the totals of the amounts in object classifications "08. Supplies and materials" and "09. Equipment," given in *Summary of Obligations by Objects*, compiled yearly by the U.S. Bureau of the Budget. These figures include obligations for goods procured by one government agency for another on a reimbursable basis. Such obligations are included twice and cause an unknown amount of duplication. For the fiscal year 1948 only, the reimbursable items were accounted for and amounted to $73 million of the total of $1,359 million. Obligations for procurement of fixed equipment, land and structures, rents and utilities services, and an unknown amount of commodities under the heading "other contractual services" are not included.

[a] The Treasury Department totals show a substantial drop after 1948 as a consequence of the transfer of the Bureau of Federal Supply from the Treasury to the General Services Administration when the latter was formed on July 1, 1949.

[b] The figures in the first column are for the Works Progress Administration which became a part of the Federal Works Agency when the latter was formed in 1939. At the beginning of the fiscal year 1949 the Federal Works Agency was made a part of the newly formed General Services Administration.

[c] Includes $509 million of "Funds appropriated to the President."

[d] Includes $1,085 million of "Funds appropriated to the President."

[e] Includes $4,225 million under "Mutual Security."

[f] Includes $5,563 million under "Mutual Security."

15.6 per cent of the total. The balance of $7,265,000,000 or 84.4 per cent of the total was procured by the Department of Defense (Table 3). The volume of obligations was rather widely distributed among the civilian agencies as is shown in Table 4.

Table 4 does not present a picture of the degree to which procurement was centralized. The Federal Bureau of Supply, as the central purchasing agency of the government, entered into contracts which were made for and paid by other agencies. Such contracts are included in the figures for the agencies ultimately responsible for the contracts and not in the totals for the Federal Bureau of Supply.[16] The figures in Table 4 for the General Services Administration for 1949 and 1950, and for the Treasury Department for previous years, include mainly purchases for special programs, such as stockpiling of strategic and critical materials. Other estimates reveal that the Bureau of Federal Supply was responsible for the procurement of about 20 per cent of the total requirements of civilian agencies.[17] The remaining 80 per cent was procured by the using agencies through their offices in Washington and throughout the country.

Number of purchasing offices.—The number of purchasing offices operated by the government was an indication of the existing scattered organization for buying. A directory of such offices in the District of Columbia alone listed more than one hundred, most of which were headquarters for branches scattered throughout the country.[18] Members of the Hoover Commission pointed out that, while no accurate estimates were available, the known offices plus the many branches and subbranches brought "the total points at which purchasing operations are carried on for the Government into the thousands."[19]

[16] The Federal Bureau of Supply paid for such purchases with money from the General Supply Fund which was later reimbursed by the agency for which the purchase was made. Because the Federal Bureau of Supply did not make such payments from regularly appropriated funds, these purchases were not reported by it as obligations to the Bureau of the Budget. The same comment holds for the figures in Tables 3 and 4 for later years after the Federal Bureau of Supply had been transformed into the Federal Supply Service of the General Services Administration.

[17] Testimony of C. E. Mack in the *Treasury Department Appropriation Bill for 1950,* Hearings. The figure of 20 per cent referred to the fiscal year 1948. Mack estimated that this would increase to 25 per cent in the fiscal year 1950 because of new programs of consolidated purchases.

[18] U.S. General Services Administration, Federal Supply Service, *Directory of Federal Officials Purchasing under Federal Supply Schedules of the Federal Supply Service, Washington, D.C. Headquarters* (Washington: Dec., 1949).

[19] *Detailed Report on the Federal Supply System,* p. 77.

Size of orders.—Typically, the dollar value of individual orders placed through these many and scattered offices was very small. A study of 598,000 purchase orders totaling more than $100,000,000 issued by nineteen agencies in the fiscal year 1948 shows that 47 per cent or 280,000 orders were for less than $10 and accounted for only 1 per cent of the total value. Besides, 87 per cent or 520,000 orders were for less than $100 and accounted for only 10 per cent of the total value of the lot. Only 13 per cent were for

TABLE 5
DISTRIBUTION OF PURCHASE ORDERS BY SIZE
(February, 1947–June, 1948)

Size of order (dollars)	Orders		Value	
	Number	Per cent	Millions of dollars[a]	Per cent
.01– 10	280,000	47	1	1
10.01–100	240,000	40	9	9
More than 100	78,000	13	90	90
Total	598,000	100	100	100

SOURCE: Bureau of Federal Supply and the Bureau of the Budget surveys of nineteen agency supply facilities. Shown in the *Detailed Report on the Federal Supply System*, submitted by the Federal Supply Project to the Hoover Commission, September 28, 1948, p. 77, mimeographed.

[a] The report states that the value of the orders totaled "over $100,000,000," but does not give the exact amount nor its exact distribution by size of order; these figures are, therefore, approximations.

more than $100 in value and these accounted for 90 per cent of the total value. These data are summarized in Table 5.

Another study is available which supplements this analysis of the size of orders. It shows the total and average value of almost 800,000 orders classified by the seven agencies which issued them during the year ending June 30, 1948 (Table 6). The average value of all these was $256. If the Bureau of Federal Supply is excluded, however, the 750,000 orders placed by the remaining six agencies averaged $192. It is apparent from the data that the averages do little to describe the practices of individual agencies. The average value of orders by agencies ranged from $25 for the Office of Education to $1,250 for the Tennessee Valley Authority and $2,995 for the Washington office of the Bureau of Federal Supply. The Department of Agriculture issued more than 450,000 orders with an average value of about $70. The highest averages are at least partially explained by either the kinds of items required or by the character of the purchase transactions. For example, the

TABLE 6

NUMBER AND VALUE OF PURCHASE ORDERS ISSUED BY EIGHT TYPICAL CIVILIAN AGENCIES AND THE BUREAU OF FEDERAL SUPPLY
(July 1, 1947–June 30, 1948)

Agency	Number of orders	Total value (thousands of dollars)	Average value (dollars)
Post Office Department[a]	45,524	35,491	780
Department of Agriculture[a]	452,354	31,625	70
Department of the Interior[a]	197,247	34,120	173
Tennessee Valley Authority[a]	33,294	41,581	1,249
Federal Security Agency (Social Security Administration)[b]	7,524	990	132
Department of Justice[b]	14,400	400	28
Federal Security Agency (Office of Education)[b]	900	23	25
Federal Trade Commission[b]	500	27	54
Total eight agencies	751,743	144,257	192
Bureau of Federal Supply[c]			
Field offices	29,489	16,963	575
Washington	14,197	42,522	2,995
Total Bureau Fed. Supply	43,687	59,485	1,362
Total nine agencies	795,430	203,742	256

SOURCE: Compiled from data given in *Detailed Report on the Federal Supply System*, submitted by the Federal Supply Project to the Hoover Commission, September 28, 1948, pp. 42 and 77, mimeographed.

[a] Estimates, based on the fiscal year 1948 furnished by the agencies to the Federal Supply Project of the Hoover Commission.

[b] Surveys made by the Bureau of Federal Supply in cooperation with the Bureau of the Budget during the fiscal year 1948.

[c] Study made by the Bureau of Federal Supply.

Tennessee Valley Authority requires many items of expensive electrical equipment, and the Post Office Department requires many trucks and large volumes of standardized materials used in its mail equipment shops, while a large number of the orders placed by the Bureau of Federal Supply were purchases of consolidated requirements or stores items.

The size of orders of the Bureau of Federal Supply is of interest because it was the centralized purchasing agency. As would be expected, the average size of orders placed by the Bureau was much higher than the average for other agencies. Not only, as was pointed out above, is its average of $2,995 for the orders placed by the Washington office the highest for any agency, but the average for

TABLE 7

DISTRIBUTION OF BUREAU OF FEDERAL SUPPLY PURCHASE ORDERS BY SIZE
(July 1, 1947–June 30, 1948)

Value of order (dollars)	11 Field offices				Washington				Total			
	Number of orders	Per cent	Thousands of dollars	Per cent	Number of orders	Per cent	Thousands of dollars	Per cent	Number of orders	Per cent	Thousands of dollars	Per cent
Less than 10	1,657	6	10	[a]	694	5	4	[a]	2,351	5	14	[a]
10.01–100	9,198	31	556	3	1,593	11	88	[a]	10,791	25	644	1
100.01–300	9,476	32	2,133	13	3,817	27	875	2	13,293	30	3,008	5
More than 300	9,158	31	14,265	84	8,093	57	41,555	98	17,251	40	55,820	94
Grand total	29,489	100	16,964	100	14,197	100	42,522	100	43,686	100	59,485	100

SOURCE: Compiled from data given in the *Detailed Report on the Federal Supply System*, submitted by the Federal Supply Project to the Hoover Commission, September 28, 1948, p. 42, mimeographed.

[a] Less than .5 per cent.

all its offices, including those in the field, is $1,362 which is also higher than the average for any other agency (Table 6).

A Bureau of Federal Supply study of these 44,000 orders, covering a period roughly comparable to the one for 598,000 orders issued by 19 agencies (Table 5), shows the following distribution by value (Table 7): Only 5 per cent of the Bureau's orders were for less than $10 compared with 47 per cent in the 19 agencies; 30 per cent were for less than $100 compared with 87 per cent in the 19 agencies; 70 per cent were for more than $100 compared with only 13 per cent in the 19 agencies.

Establishment of the General Services Administration

The Hoover Commission concluded that the lack of an effective central coördinating agency had resulted in unplanned purchasing operations. As evidence of this it pointed to the fact that about half of the purchasing orders issued were for $10 or less, and that the cost of processing a purchase transaction was greatly in excess of $10.[20] It gave as causes for the deficiencies (1) the lack of widespread recognition of supply as an important executive function and the resultant failure to evolve an efficient government-wide system of supply, (2) the maze of laws, rulings, and regulations which encouraged routine buying rather than initiative and economy in purchasing, (3) the low salary scale of government buyers and the resulting lack of competence, and (4) the inadequacy of cataloging, specifications development, and inspection, as well as other specific elements of supply operations.[21]

The investigation of the Hoover Commission was conducted just at the time when Congress was concerned about military procurement and about the methods of handling the disposal of surplus war property. This concern of Congress spurred by the Commission's investigation and reports tipped the scales in favor of legislation. Two laws were enacted, one concerning military agencies and the other principally concerning civilian agencies. The military-agencies act, Public Law 436,[22] is not of direct interest for this study. Purchases of civilian types of goods, however, were affected in important ways by the passage of the Federal Property

[20] *Office of General Services Supply Activities*, pp. 25–27.

[21] A summary statement of these criticisms is given in the press release of the Commission on November 23, 1948, which is copied in the testimony of C. E. Mack in the *Treasury Department Appropriation Bill for 1950*, Hearings, p. 336.

[22] 82d Cong., 2d sess. (July 1, 1952).

and Administrative Services Act of 1949[23] which established the General Services Administration on July 1, 1949.

In the act Congress declared it intended, in establishing the General Services Administration (hereafter referred to as GSA), to provide an efficient system for (a) the procurement and supply of personal property and nonpersonal services, (b) the utilization of available property including real property, (c) the disposal of surplus property, and (d) records management. The act transferred to the new agency the affairs and personnel of the Bureau of Federal Supply, the Federal Works Agency, the National Archives, and the War Assets Administration.

With regard to purchasing, the act not only transferred the affairs of the Bureau of Federal Supply to the GSA, but it modified the law which defines the policy framework within which purchasing by the executive agencies, including the GSA, operates. An understanding of this legal framework is needed before the purchasing functions and organization of the GSA are described.

Legal Determinants of Purchasing Policies

Congress has established certain legal limitations within which the purchasing policies and programs of the executive agencies must be developed and in a few respects—notably regarding the invitation of bids and award of contracts—has specifically prescribed the policies which must be followed.

Internal policies.—The laws provide only broad limits to the formulation and execution of the internal policies by which products are chosen, demands standardized, and requirements consolidated for purchasing.

The only legal limits to choice are the appropriation acts which determine the amounts the agencies may spend and the laws limiting administrative discretion as to their expenditure. These have been summarized at the outset of this chapter.[24] Beyond the control of the amount available for purchases and the requirement of specific authorization for major purchases, the law leaves the executive agencies free to choose the products they judge will best fill their needs.

Demands are standardized by the executive agencies in large part through the operation of the commodity-cataloging and purchase-specifications programs. These have been a natural outgrowth of

[23] 63 *U.S. Stat. at L.* (1949), 377.

[24] See "Legal and administrative limitations."

the legal requirement of the use of specifications established to regularize contracting procedures, and described below, but they have also received specific congressional sanction through the laws establishing the General Supply Committee and the Procurement Division of the Treasury. In the Federal Property and Administrative Services Act of 1949 Congress went a step farther than it had previously and required all executive agencies to use the uniform Federal Supply Catalog system and the Federal Specifications which the General Services Administration was directed to develop. Centralized purchasing programs have been similarly endorsed by the same laws although the discretion to require the use of such programs is left with the GSA.

Centralized purchasing, which often uses time contracts, is restricted to some extent by the legal limitations on the time period for which contracts may run.

Unless otherwise provided by law, contracts for supplies may not be made for a longer term than one year. A further limitation is imposed by the general restriction that, unless authorization is provided specifically by law, no government agency may spend in any year more than the money appropriated to it for that year, nor may it obligate the government for more than the money appropriated for the year in which the commitment is made.[25] The test of legality of expenditure with respect to this law is whether or not the funds are committed during the fiscal year. Thus it does not prevent the letting of contracts for terms that extend beyond the end of the fiscal year.[26] Since the majority of contracts would, in any event, be for short terms or call for immediate delivery, these limitations only occasionally affect purchasing decisions.

Perhaps the most powerful legislative determinant of internal purchasing policies has been negative control of them through the appropriation process. Congressional committees at times have forced major changes in policies by denying funds for the execution of policies laid down by the executive agencies. For example, for years they imposed restraints on the development of stores facilities by limiting the amount of the General Supply Fund, and similarly prevented the development of an adequate supply catalog for civilian agencies.

Inviting bids and awarding contracts.—The laws governing methods of negotiating with suppliers and awarding contracts are

[25] 31 *U.S. Code* (1946), sec. 665.

[26] *U.S. Rev. Stat.* (1878), sec. 3690; 31 *U.S. Code* (1946), sec. 712.

much more specific and restraining than those governing internal purchasing policies. These prescribe the sealed-bids device for inviting bids and awarding contracts, stipulate its use for the greatest dollar volume of purchasing, and impose certain limitations on the sources of supply open to the government. The laws are brief in wording, but have been elaborated in detail by interpretations of the courts, the attorneys general, and the comptrollers general. Together, the laws and decisions have formed a rigid set of policies which restrict the latitude allowed administrators and buyers in their maneuvers to obtain the most favorable combination of price and product.

Sealed-bids requirement.—The basic law defining and requiring the use of sealed-bids is simple. It provides that, with certain exceptions, a purchase may be made only after advertising a sufficient time previously for proposals, and that the bids must be opened and recorded publicly at a previously announced time in the presence of any bidders who wish to attend the opening.[27] This requirement has been in force in essentially its present form since 1861.

The theory behind the law envisions the triple benefits of giving all persons an equal chance to obtain government business, preventing favoritism or fraud in the letting of contracts, and securing for the government the benefits arising from competition.[28] Interpretations of the law, made in the light of this underlying theory, have added to the two specific statutory requirements of advertising for bids and public opening, three equally important requirements. These five requirements provide a summary definition of the sealed-bids device as it is established by law.[29] They are: (1) advertising for bids sufficiently in advance of the opening to allow bidders to respond, (2) consideration of the bid of any bidder who has not been debarred from bidding, (3) public opening and recording of bids at a date announced sufficiently in advance to permit bidders to be present, (4) definition of the commodity or service by objective specifications unless this is technically not feasible, in which case the commodity may be identified with a brand or manufacturer's name, provided the words "or equal" are

[27] *U.S. Rev. Stat.* (1878), sec. 3709; *U.S. Rev. Stat.* (1878), sec. 3710; 60 *U.S. Stat. at L.* (1946), 809; 41 *U.S. Code* (1952), sec. 5–8.

[28] *United States v. Brookridge Farm, Inc.*, (1940), 111 Fed. Rept., 2d ser., 461 (C.C.A. Colo.), affirming *Brookridge Farm, Inc. v. United States* (1939), 27 Fed. Supp., 909 (Dist. Ct. Colo.); *Specifications—Restrictive Conditions—Bids* (1934), 13 Comp. Gen., 284.

[29] A definition of the sealed-bids device restated, in light of the administrative contracting procedures, to bring out its economic significance as given in chap. v, fig. 3.

added,[30] and (5) award of the contract to the lowest responsible bidder.[31]

Exceptions to sealed bids.—Certain exceptions to the sealed-bids requirement are provided for by law. In these exceptions the purchasing official is left free to negotiate the purchase by whatever method he deems will be most advantageous to the government. These are purchases where (1) the amount of the order does not exceed $500, (2) the public exigencies require the immediate delivery of the goods, (3) only one source of supply is available, and (4) services are required of a technical and professional nature or are performed under government supervision and are paid for on a time basis.[32]

The exception which is most important for the present discussion is that for purchases under $500. This exception exempts many small-value purchases from the sealed-bids requirement. The public-exigency exemption does not permit many orders to be negotiated because the term "public exigency" has been interpreted narrowly by the courts and comptrollers general to apply only to those occasions where the condition to be met is unforeseen, sudden, or particularly perplexing.[33]

General limitations on sources of supply.—There are three general limitations concerning sources of supply for government purchases which on occasion affect purchasing policy decisions. One is the Buy American Act[34] which requires the purchase of goods made in the United States substantially from materials produced in the United States unless the head of an agency determines this to be

[30] *Advertising—Acceptance of Other than the Lowest Bid—Quality* (1925), 5 Comp. Gen., 330; *Advertising—Acceptance of Other than Lowest Bid—Specifications* (1925), 5 Comp. Gen., 835; *Advertising—Acceptance of Other than Lowest Bid—Limitation of Authority of Government Contracting Officers* (1926), 6 Comp. Gen., 158; *Advertising—Acceptance of Other than the Lowest Bid* (1927), 7 Comp. Gen., 298; *Advertising—Bids—Specifications* (1931), 10 Comp. Gen., 555; *Advertising—Specifications—Particular Make* (1934), 13 Comp. Gen., 357; *United States v. Brookridge Farm, Inc., op. cit.*

[31] *Advertising—Acceptance of Other than the Lowest Bid—Quality* (1925), 5 Comp. Gen., 330; *Advertising—Bids—Acceptance of Other than Lowest— Alleged Superiority of Product of Higher Bidder* (1937), 16 Comp. Gen., 991; *Contracts—Awarding to Small Business Concerns at Higher Prices* (1943), 22 Comp. Gen., 1018; *Scott v. United States* (1909), 44 Ct. Cl. Repts., 524; *O'Brien v. Carney* (1934), 6 Fed. Supp. 761 (Dist. Ct. Mass.).

[32] 41 *U.S. Code* (1952), sec. 5.

[33] *Good Roads Machinery Co. of New England v. United States* (1937), 19 Fed. Supp. 652 (Dist. Ct. Mass.); *Contracts—Adequacy of Advertisement* (1934), 14 Comp. Gen., 364; *Personal Services—Stenographic Reporting Under Expired Contract—Textile Labor Relations Board* (1936), 15 Comp. Gen., 1095.

[34] 47 *U.S. Stat at L.* (1933), 1520; 41 *U.S. Code* (1952), sec. 10a.

inconsistent with the public interest or the cost to be unreasonable. Another requires provisions to be included in contracts stipulating compliance with the labor standards set forth in the Walsh-Healey Act of 1936.[35] The third is a statement of congressional policy rather than a requirement. A clause in the Federal Property and Administrative Services Act of 1949 states: "It is the declared policy of the Congress that a fair proportion of the total purchases and contracts for supplies and services shall be placed with small-business concerns."[36] The comptroller general, however, has ruled that awards may not be made to other than the low bidder solely on the basis that the bidder qualified as a small-business concern,[37] but has stated that the General Accounting Office would not question awards made to a small business firm where two or more bidders submitted identical low bids.[38]

Specific limitations on sources of supply.—The procurement of certain classes of goods from specified sources of supply is required by law. These are prison-made products which include the articles manufactured by the Federal Prison Industries, Incorporated, organized in the Department of Justice; blind-made products manufactured by organizations formed to give employment to blind people under quasigovernmental auspices; and certain products manufactured by the Government Printing Office. The schedules of articles available from the first two sources include such items as duck and canvas goods, cotton textiles, articles of clothing, mattresses, metal furniture, shoes, brushes, mats, processed foods, wood specialties, brooms, mops, huck towels, cotton bags, and pillow cases. The prices are set at competitive levels by government officials.[39] The Government Printing Office is a required source for all agencies for printing and binding, which includes forms, letterheads, pamphlets and manuals.[40] When procurement is for supplies to be used in the District of Columbia, paper, plain envelopes, and

[35] 49 *U.S. Stat. at L.* (1936), 2036; 41 *U.S. Code* (1952), sec. 35–45.

[36] 63 *U.S. Stat. at L.* (1949), 393, sec. 302b.

[37] *Contracts—Awards To Other Than Low Bidder—Armed Services Procurement Act of 1947* (1949), 28 Comp. Gen., 662.

[38] U.S. Congress, House, Select Committee on Small Business, *Progress Report,* 81st Cong., 1st sess. (Washington: 1949), p. 19.

[39] Federal Prison Industries Inc. was created by Executive Order 6197, Dec. 11, 1934, pursuant to 48 *U.S. Stat. at L.* (1934), 1211, which also included the requirement that government agencies procure from this source. The equivalent law covering blind-made products is 52 *U.S. Stat. at L.* (1938), 1196; 41 *U.S. Code* (1952), sec. 46–48.

[40] 28 *U.S. Stat. at L.* (1895), 622 and subsequent laws; 44 *U.S.Code* (1953), sec. 111, 111a, 111b.

selected stationery items must be procured from the Government Printing Office.[41]

The necessity of purchasing such goods from specified sources of supply removes those purchases from commercial supply sources. But the volume of these purchases is small, and they are therefore not considered further in this study.

Procurement by production.—The government, like private business, enjoys the unrestricted legal right to manufacture its own supplies.[42] It appears that no specific statutory authority is necessary for the government to enter production. In contrast to private business, however, a government agency normally has neither the facilities nor the capital ready at hand for such ventures. Funds appropriated for other purposes, such as for the purchase of supplies or for operation and maintenance, may not, according to the comptroller general, be used for the purchase of facilities.[43] Therefore, funds must be appropriated specifically for production, and thus would come under the scrutiny of the Congress. The Congress has on a number of occasions approved laws or appropriations for production, as for the Tennessee Valley Authority, arsenals, Navy yards, the Government Printing Office, and the Post Office for its Division of Mail Equipment Shops. Barring, however, a decided change in political atmosphere, it is very doubtful that Congress would countenance any move which would allow the government to manufacture its own supplies on any widespread scale.

Legal Determinants Applying Only to the GSA

The law outlined above applies to all executive agencies. In establishing the General Services Administration and vesting it with the authority to determine purchasing policies within the law for all executive agencies, however, Congress gave it somewhat wider discretion than is enjoyed by other agencies.

All elements of the sealed-bids procedure are left unchanged[44] with one exception: the way is open for the purchasing official to use more discretion in making awards than is possible under the

[41] 43 *U.S. Stat. at L.* (1924), 592; 44 *U.S. Code* (1928), sec. 225.

[42] *Perkins v. Lukens Steel Co.* (1940), 310 U.S. 127; 84 L. ed. 1114.

[43] *Purchase of Electric Power Plant from Appropriation for Electric Current* (1923), 2 Comp. Gen., 761; *Appropriations—Fiscal Year—Applicability of Maintenance, Repair, and Operation Provision to Substantial Property Improvements* (1939), 19 Comp. Gen., 333.

[44] 63 *U.S. Stat. at L.* (1949), 397, sec. 310 exempts the General Services Administration from *U.S. Rev. Stat.* (1878), sec. 3709 and associated laws, while 393, sec. 302c in effect continues the requirement of using the sealed-bids procedure.

current definition of the phrase "lowest responsible bidder." The law provides that "Award . . . shall be made . . . to that responsible bidder whose bid, conforming to the invitation for bids, will be most advantageous to the Government, price and other factors considered . . ."[45] The words "most advantageous to the Government, price and other factors considered" potentially have great importance because they ostensibly sanction awards based on product qualities offered above the minimum required by the purchase specification. During the first three years the law was in force, however, there was no indication that purchasing officials had taken advantage of the added latitude implied in the wording.

The law permits negotiation for 14 classes of purchases which are exempted from the sealed-bids requirement.[46] Nine of these cover special situations not of direct interest to the normal run of purchasing. The remaining five classes are: (1) medicines and medical supplies, (2) items for which procurement from specified sources is required to assure standardization and interchangeability, (3) items for which the administrator believes that bid prices after advertising are unreasonable or have not been arrived at in open competition, (4) supplies and services for which competition is impracticable, and (5) purchases which do not exceed $1,000.

The first four exceptions clarify the administrator's authority to resort to negotiation where monopoly elements make sealed bids inappropriate or ineffective. The fifth frees the hands of the General Services Administration buyers on a large number of contracts. Because the administrator is given the power to delegate his authority to negotiate contracts, any benefits which are found to accrue from negotiation may gradually be extended to other executive agencies, as experience is gained from the operations of the act.

Purchasing Functions of the GSA

The legal limitations and definitions of purchasing policies, then, leave considerable latitude for the exercise of discretion by the executive agencies. The establishment of the General Services Administration was the first positive expression of congressional opinion that a strong central agency is needed to coördinate the purchasing activities of the civilian executive agencies. The law

[45] 63 *U.S. Stat. at L.* (1949), 395, sec. 303b.

[46] *Ibid.* 393, sec. 302c.

gives to the administrator greater powers than had previously been held by the Bureau of Federal Supply of the Treasury Department.

The administrator's authority extends over all executive agencies, that is, departments, independent establishments, and any wholly owned government corporations. The secretary of defense, however, is given power to exempt the Department of Defense from any action unless the president overrides his decision to do so. The administrator's responsibility extends to providing his services on request to mixed-ownership corporations, establishments of the legislative and judicial branches including the Senate, the House of Representatives, and the municipal government of the District of Columbia.[47]

With respect to the supply policies and programs of the above agencies the law gives the administrator of the GSA the following powers:[48]

(1) To prescribe policies and programs for the purchase and supply of personal property and nonpersonal services in general, and specifically to establish a federal-supply catalog system (providing the administrator and the secretary of defense coördinate their cataloging efforts) and to prescribe standardized forms, procedures, and standard purchase specifications.

(2) To operate, consolidate, take over, or arrange for operation by any executive agency, supply facilities such as warehouses, supply centers, repair shops, and fuel yards.

(3) To procure and supply personal property and nonpersonal services for the executive agencies, and, for this purpose, to direct and control the use of the General Supply Fund for financing bulk purchases and other supply operations.

(4) To represent the executive agencies in negotiations with carriers and public utilities and in proceedings before federal and state regulatory bodies involving rates of carriers and public utilities.

To provide him with authority to carry out his responsibilities, the administrator is specifically authorized to make surveys of and obtain reports from executive agencies.[49] He is also specifically authorized to issue regulations necessary for carrying out his responsibilities and performing his functions under the act, and the heads of the executive agencies are required to issue the orders necessary to make such regulations effective.[50] The administrator

[47] *Ibid.* 383, sec. 201.
[48] *Ibid.* 383, sec. 201a.
[49] *Ibid.* 390, sec. 206a.
[50] *Ibid.* 390, sec. 205c.

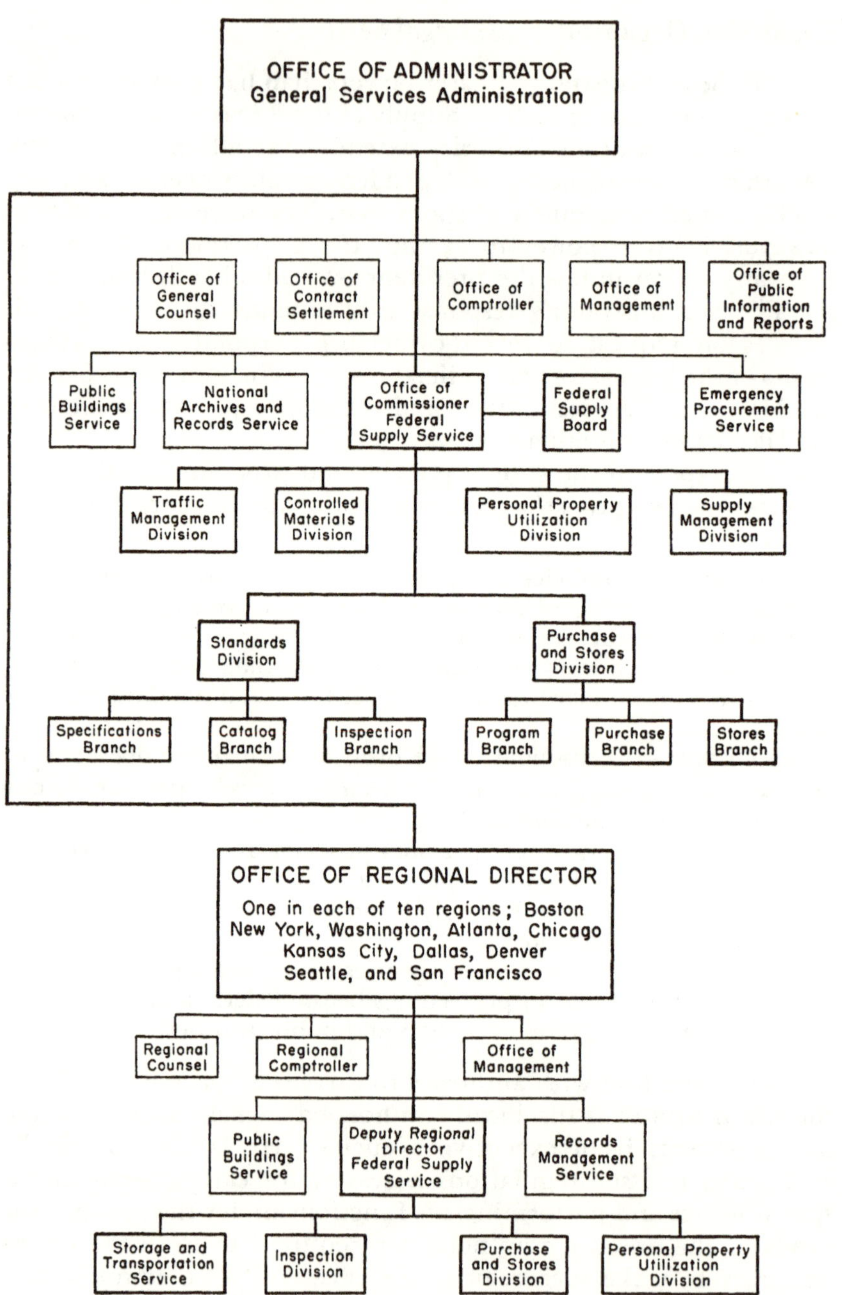

Fig. 1. Organization of the Federal Supply Service of the General Services Administration.

Source: General Services Administration, Administrative Orders, Nos. 26, 53 and supplements.

may not delegate his authority to issue regulations on matters of policy, but otherwise he may delegate and authorize redelegation of his authority to any official of his own organization or the head of any federal agency.[51]

Taken together these functions and powers are the most comprehensive that have been accorded an administrator of purchasing and supply in the government and follow closely the recommendations of the Hoover Commission. With respect to the organization of purchasing, the administrator of the General Services Administration is limited by little except his own imagination and the appropriations he is able to obtain to do the work.

Organization of the Federal Supply Service

After the establishment of the General Services Administration on July 1, 1949, the organization and programs of the Bureau of Federal Supply were continued unchanged under the new agency. The administrator of the GSA, however, immediately instituted plans to decentralize supply operations into regions and to centralize the supply activities of executive agencies within each region. The plan envisaged national determination of policies and regional execution of supply programs. Partly because of this policy, but also because the GSA had absorbed the organizations of the Federal Works Agency, the War Assets Administration, the National Archives, and the Bureau of Federal Supply, a new organizational arrangement was required for conducting supply activities. In the fall of 1949 the Bureau of Federal Supply was reorganized into the Federal Supply Service of the national office of the GSA, and regional GSA offices were established.[52] The broad outlines of this organization as it existed early in 1953 are shown in Figure 1.

In the central office of the GSA, the Federal Supply Service, directed by a commissioner, is responsible for the policy development, program planning, and coördination of programs administered by all regional offices. The two divisions under the commissioner of Federal Supply Service most directly concerned with purchasing are the Purchase and Stores Division and the Standards Division.

The Purchase and Stores Division is responsible for developing

---

[51] *Ibid.* 390, sec. 205d.

[52] The organization of the Federal Supply Service was established by GSA Administrative Order No. 26, Revision No. 2, August 14, 1950, and Administrative Order No. 53, September 25, 1950. The Federal Supply Board was estabilshed by GSA Circular No. 44, April 22, 1952.

the policies, regulations, programs, and procedures covering the purchase, storage, and distribution of supplies and equipment. It also determines the purchase assignments to the regional offices and recommends the delegation of purchasing responsibility to other executive agencies. The Standards Division is responsible for the development of Federal Specifications, the Federal Supply Catalog system, and inspection methods and procedures used both in the programs of organizing demand and of purchasing.

The responsibility for promulgating Federal Specifications and requiring their use rests with the administrator of the General Services Administration. From its creation in 1921, and until it was abolished in 1952, the Federal Specifications Board, composed of representatives of each major department of the government, supervised the work of technical committees which developed the specifications. With the intention of speeding the work, the responsibility for developing each specification is now assigned to the agency having a major interest in using it and the technical competence to develop it. The formal technical committees either have been abolished or are being abolished as the new plan takes effect. The function of the Federal Specifications Board of advising the administrator on specifications policies and designating technical representatives for the development work has been taken over by the Federal Supply Board which was created in April, 1952. The purpose of the Federal Supply Board is to promote, through its advice to the administrator, sound personal-property management practices in government, and this includes advice on the development of standards and purchase specifications. The personnel of the Standards Division of the Federal Supply Service assist the designated agencies in drafting specifications and coördinate the procedures by which they are developed and promulgated.[53]

There are ten regional offices of the General Services Administration, each with an organization parallel to that of the central office in Washington. These are located in Boston, New York, Washington, Atlanta, Chicago, Kansas City, Dallas, Denver, San Francisco, and Seattle. Each region has a Purchase and Stores Division which conducts all actual purchasing performed by the GSA in the region and operates the federal supply center in the area through which common-use items are distributed to the various executive agencies. Nationally centralized purchasing programs are conducted by the regional offices best located for the purpose.

[53] The procedure for developing Federal Specifications is explained in more detail in chap. iv, fig. 2.

III

Policies Affecting Administrative Costs and Contract Quantities

Within the limits imposed by law and by the organization of government agencies there remains considerable latitude for the development of specific policies and for a wide variation in the effectiveness with which they are applied. In carrying out the responsibilities given it by law the Federal Supply Service has formulated specific policies governing supply activities of the executive agencies.

The internal policies directly affecting purchasing cover the supply functions of (1) survey of need and initial choice of product, (2) the identification of items and specification of products which together serve to concentrate demands on the fewest varieties of goods which will adequately satisfy the needs, (3) the centralization of requirements for the goods on which demands have been concentrated, and (4) the development of storage and issue programs which facilitate large-quantity purchasing. The initial choice, identification, and specification of products serve both to concentrate demands on a specified list of goods for purposes of increasing contract quantities, and to define the characteristics of goods for purposes of inviting bids and awarding contracts. The latter effect is considered here because the emphasis is on the policies and programs which affect order quantities and administrative costs. The policies and programs which affect the utility of the goods are discussed in Chapter IV.

Centralized versus Uncentralized Purchasing

Maximizing the utility per dollar and minimizing costly shortages makes it necessary to balance centralized and uncentralized purchasing. Some degree of centralization is necessary not only to take advantage of the usually low prices of large-order quantities, but because it is obviously impractical and uneconomical for each government employee to purchase the goods he requires in his work. Conversely, some degree of local buying is necessary for the procurement of perishables, items rarely required, items which are urgently needed and can be procured more quickly locally than through centralized programs, and for goods which are immediately available from local sources at reasonable prices.

The policies and programs of the Federal Supply Service of the GSA have reflected an understanding of the need for a balance between centralized and uncentralized purchasing. The Federal Supply Service, therefore, has evolved policies aimed at facilitating local purchasing by reducing the administrative costs of requisitioning and contracting, and others aimed at facilitating economical centralized purchasing by standardizing demands, centralizing contracting, consolidating requirements, and establishing centralized stores for the use of all agencies. Both objectives are accomplished through centralized determination of purchasing policies which guide the decisions of the agencies.

Centralized Policy Determination

GSA regulations.—The General Services Administration is empowered by law to prescribe purchase policies, programs, standardized forms, and procedures for the executive agencies of the government. To carry out the responsibilities implied in this authority, the GSA has prepared and issued a book of regulations which provides policy guides, standardized procedures, and standard forms for the supply operations of the agencies.[1] These regulations are designed to increase the efficiency with which individual agencies conduct their uncentralized purchasing programs as well as to define the programs and procedures for centralized purchasing.

The regulations cover all phases of supply. Those which most directly affect purchasing are: criteria for determining the method of supply, interagency purchase assignments, methods of purchasing by sealed bids and by negotiation, establishment and maintenance of bidders' mailing lists, contract forms and special provisions, methods for making small purchases, the purchase of items under centralized programs, warehousing policies and procedures, the use of specifications and standards, commodity cataloging, and inspection and testing. The appendix contains a complete

[1] U.S. General Services Administration, *Regulations of the General Services Administration, Title 1, Personal Property Management* (Washington: 1952).

set of standardized forms required in supply operations with instructions regarding their preparation and use.

The regulations do not provide a complete substitute for similar regulations governing the purchasing programs of the individual agencies. The GSA regulations cover those policies and procedures which must be uniform because they are governed by federal law or by centrally determined policies and administrative procedures such as those of the General Accounting Office, the Treasury, and the GSA itself. They serve as guides for the bulk of the purchasing of most agencies, but the local purchasing and administrative problems which concern only the agency involved must be covered by each agency's own regulations.

These standard regulations serve three broad purposes: (1) to relieve the agencies of the administrative burden and expense of preparing policies, procedures, and forms which would satisfy the General Accounting Office; (2) to provide simplified procedures which minimize administrative expenses of purchasing; and (3) to prescribe detailed policies which, if followed, will enhance the agencies' chances of procuring goods at the most favorable prices, either through their own purchasing programs or through centralized programs.

Small purchases.—Since its establishment the Federal Supply Service of the GSA has introduced several changes in policy which are of considerable potential importance for the reduction of administrative expenses in small purchases. These efforts have been encouraged by the interest of the Committee on Expenditures in the Executive Departments of the House of Representatives which, through a task group headed by a GSA official, made a survey of the processes of making those purchases of less than $500 (in some agencies less than $1,000) which are exempt from the sealed-bids requirement in contracting.[2]

By the end of 1952 three important regulations had been issued to simplify the administrative work of making small purchases.

One regulation provides for the use of petty-cash funds for paying for purchases up to $50.[3] The use of these funds is intended for emergency, fill-in, occasional, or special purchases of articles or

---

[2] For the Committee's report, see U.S. Congress, House, Committee on Expenditures in the Executive Departments, *Survey of Procurement Process Part 2*, 82d Cong., 1st sess., H. Rept. 1224 (Washington: 1951).

[3] U.S. General Services Administration, Treasury Department, General Accounting Office, *Joint Regulation for Small Purchases Utilizing Imprest Funds* (Washington: March 10, 1952).

services, small-value repairs to equipment, and for perishable foodstuffs.

The second regulation provides that a simplified pocket-size form combining purchase order, invoice, and voucher shall be used for all purchases which are exempted from the requirement that sealed bids be used. This includes purchases under $500 for most agencies and under $1,000 for others. This purchase-order–invoice–voucher form can be used either for purchases paid for by check or by petty cash.

The third regulation exempts small purchases of $25 or less from mandatory provisions of supply schedules. This minimum was included by the GSA in 32 schedules during the fiscal year ending June 30, 1952.[4] Such small purchases may now be made by the combination purchase-order–invoice–voucher form and, on occasion, by use of petty cash, rather than by more elaborate procedures.

In combination, these three methods of making small purchases should substantially reduce the paper work of requisitioning and purchasing, cut administrative costs, and avoid many costly delays in procurement.

Standard forms.—The GSA regulations provide sample forms and instructions for using them for the documents most frequently required in purchasing. These include bidders' applications to be put on the mailing list; several types of supply-contract, invitation-to-bid, and certificate-of-award forms; purchase-order, invoice, and voucher forms; various bonding forms; and standard forms for domestic and foreign-delivery terms. The confusion of contract and other forms had long plagued the agencies and suppliers. Their simplification was difficult because of the necessity to take into account the various laws affecting contracting and the many interpretations of the laws by the comptrollers general and attorneys general. By dealing centrally with the legal problems, the Federal Supply Service was able to simplify the forms substantially and still meet the legal requirements, a job which each agency acting individually could not do. The result should be a reduction in the administrative costs of uncentralized contracting, and considerable simplification of the task of suppliers in submitting bids for government contracts.

In addition to providing the policies which guide uncentralized contracting procedures, standard forms for use in supply opera-

[4] U.S. General Services Administration, *Annual Report of the Administrator of General Services for the Year Ending June 30, 1952* (Washington: 1953).

tions, and simplified methods for small purchases, the regulations establish the policies and procedures by which demands are standardized for both uncentralized and centralized purchasing, and by which centralized purchasing programs are conducted.

Standardization of Demands

Standardization of its demands for goods has long been a difficult task for the government. The variety of goods it demands reflects the needs and to some extent the personal preferences of millions of users. These demands must be satisfied through a necessarily complex procurement organization operating at hundreds of locations in markets strongly influenced by product-differentiation policies of sellers. These characteristics of the demands and of market operations create both the need for and the obstacles to effective standardization of demands on the minimum necessary number of commodities.

The steps required to standardize demands are: item identification and cataloging; elimination of unnecessary variations of items serving the same or closely related needs; and the drafting, promulgation, and use of standard specifications to define the goods filling those needs.

Commodity cataloging.—An "item," from the viewpoint of supply, is a commodity or service which is unique with regard to a particular use, and which requires its own procurement decision. Thus each size of bolt, each different color of paint, each different size of can of the identical food, a chisel bought singly and the same chisel bought in a box of six would require different item numbers. Item identification describes the commodity in sufficient detail to define it clearly for purposes of purchasing and use. Item identifications brought together according to a standard classification compose a commodity catalog.

The listing of all items procured by the government according to their use serves to reveal and eliminate the duplications of identification. This alone provides some standardization of demand.

Concentration of demands.—The process of commodity cataloging not only automatically brings about a degree of standardization of demand by eliminating duplicate identifications for identical items, but also prepares the way for further simplification by arraying in convenient form the item descriptions of close substitutes for the same use or for closely related uses. The cataloging process makes it possible to weed out the unneeded items from among the million and a half used by the civilian agencies. With a catalog it is possible to make studies of related uses and the range of commodities currently being procured to satisfy them, and to concentrate procurement on the minimum number necessary to satisfy all real needs of efficient operations. When this is done, the catalog becomes a listing of all necessary items classified by use with each item described in sufficient detail to identify it as unique.

Relation of Federal Specifications to the Catalog.—The concentration of demand on the minimum number of commodities cannot be accomplished successfully without the specifications. Item descriptions which are sufficiently explicit to distinguish the item clearly from all others in the catalog seldom provide an adequate definition of the product's utility. Before close substitute products for a given use can be eliminated with impunity from the catalog the quality expected of the remaining products must be defined by specifications. For example, assume that cataloging has proceeded to the point where three kinds of tire chains are listed: standard duty, reinforced link, and heavy duty. The variation in quality between brands within each kind of chain may well be greater than the variation in the average quality of the kinds. The item description in the catalog distinguishes one kind from another, but does not define the quality of the chain. A test program of all brands of each of the kinds of chains reveals that among the good-quality chains which are standard with well organized manufacturers, the reinforced-link chain outwears either of the others and at current prices also gives substantially more utility per dollar. The only way that demand can be safely concentrated on the reinforced-link chain is by supplementing the item description with a reference to a quality specification which will confine procurement to the good-quality reinforced-link chain, and then eliminating the other chain items.[5]

The same specification which serves in the manner noted above to complete the program of standardizing demand is also necessary for buying. The item description may at times be sufficiently detailed for purposes of procurement, but normally it is not. It is a function of the specification to provide an objective commodity definition in sufficient detail to insure that quotations are received on comparable items and that the products delivered on contracts are of the quality contemplated when the contract was signed. This function of specifications is the subject of Chapter IV; it is men-

[5] Test data on tire chains are given in chap. iv, table 11.

tioned here only to clarify the relationship between the problem of defining quality levels and that of increasing order quantities by concentrating demand on a limited number of items.

Commodity cataloging may, as we have seen, serve a useful purpose by eliminating duplicate items when specifications are not available for all items. Similarly, specifications may be developed and used to standardize demand without a commodity catalog. A specification covering a group of items is often, in the absence of a complete catalog, a simplified item list as well as a definition of quality. If, however, there is no uniform catalog system and each agency has its own catalog, the procurement officer may have difficulty in deciding to which numbers in his catalog the specification applies. He may decide it applies to one item and not realize that it should also be used for other items which are close substitutes.

Ideally the development and use of a commodity catalog and of objective commodity specifications are complementary elements in the process of standardization of demand. Federal Specifications provide the logical extension of commodity cataloging which maximizes its effectiveness and links it to contracting procedures.

Cataloging program.—In a supply system as large and complex as the federal government's the programs necessary to develop satisfactory commodity-catalog and specifications systems assume the proportions of major tasks. Work on Federal Specifications has been in progress for three decades, and for two decades the construction of the Federal Standard Stock Catalog has been authorized by law. The books of Federal Specifications and the existing commodity catalogs in use in the government make an impressive array and represent substantial accomplishments. They are seriously deficient, however, when compared with the total program recognized to be necessary for an efficient procurement and supply system.

In 1929 Congress authorized the printing of a Federal Standard Stock Catalog and a board was established in that year to plan its development. A catalog was developed and for a time before the outbreak of World War II served an extremely useful purpose although it was never sufficiently comprehensive to serve adequately the needs of the government. After the outbreak of the war it rapidly became obsolete, and by 1949 there were seventeen major government commodity catalogs in use by various agencies.[6]

[6] Statement of W. S. MacLeod, deputy director in charge of the Standards Branch, Bureau of Federal Supply, Treasury Department in U.S. Congress, House, Committee on Appropriations, *Supplemental Appropriation Bill for 1948,* Hearings, 80th Cong., 1st sess. (Washington: 1947), p. 532.

The total number of items contained in these catalogs was more than 12,000,000, many of which were duplicates. In 1949 it was estimated that if duplications were eliminated, 3,000,000 items would remain, of which 1,000,000 would represent items in common use by the military and civilian agencies and another 500,000 items used by the civilian agencies only. New items, however, have been entering the supply system. In December, 1951, it was estimated that by June 30, 1952, 750,000 new items, largely for military combat, would have been added bringing the total to 3,750,000.[7]

The Federal Property and Administrative Services Act of 1949 made the General Services Administration responsible by law for developing the proposed standard federal-catalog system for all agencies, civilian and military, with a proviso that the administrator of the GSA and the secretary of defense coördinate their work on the program. Congress has never appropriated sufficient funds for the GSA to undertake the project. The Department of Defense, having funds available, and appreciating the importance of the task, has carried forward a major project in cataloging with which the Federal Supply Service, with the inadequate staff at its disposal, is attempting to coöperate to insure that the finished product meets the need of civilian as well as defense agencies. During the fiscal year 1952 the military agencies had about 3,700 employees working directly or indirectly on this cataloging project. In the civilian agencies, because of budget limitations, only 190 employees were engaged on the project.[8]

During the spring of 1952, Congress, impatient with the progress being made and in the throes of a preëlection economy mood, made two decisions which have had important effects. Congress completely eliminated the amounts requested by the GSA for cataloging work from the appropriation bill, and it passed the Defense Cataloging and Standardization Act[9] which gave the Department of Defense independent responsibility for cataloging the items it requires. Congress defined in unusual detail, for a public law, the manner by which the Department should proceed. As a result of these two actions the cataloging work of the civilian agencies virtually came to a standstill in the fiscal year 1953, and the mili-

[7] U.S. Munitions Board and General Services Administration, *Third Joint Report to Congress on the Federal Cataloging Program*, January 1 to December 31, 1951 (Washington: 1952), p. 6.

[8] Information supplied by the General Services Administration, Washington, D.C.

[9] 66 *U.S. Stat. at L.* (1952), 318.

tary program was directed by the Defense Supply Management Agency which was established by the provisions of the Defense Cataloging and Standardization Act.

By June, 1952, a total of 2,600,000 items had been identified and assigned federal item identification numbers by the Department of Defense.[10] This left an estimated 650,000 items to be identified before the military identification program would be on a current basis. After June, 1952, the emphasis of the program was shifted from the identification of items and assignment of numbers to the completion of specific sections of the Federal Supply Catalog, as the catalog developed under the new program was named.

A federal-supply classification has been established consisting of 74 groups, each including a number of classes. By the spring of 1953 the Defense Supply Management Agency had assigned the job of developing catalogs for these 74 groups to task forces composed of experts from the various military services. All federal item-identification numbers in each group of the classification are turned over to the relevant task group which, together with the research assistance of the Office of Standardization of the Defense Supply Management Agency, refines the data by eliminating duplications and unneeded close substitutes for the same end use. The items are then assigned federal stock numbers and are published as the Federal Supply Catalog for that group. The first catalog for Group 89, Subsistence, was issued in February, 1953. By June 30, 1953, catalogs had been published which included 53,513 items in 62 classes of the Federal Supply Catalog including subsistence, clothing, medical equipment and supplies, and bearings. The other groups and classes were in various stages of completion.[11]

An example will serve to clarify the process. In the case of subsistence each "supply element"[12] of the Department of Defense was assigned the task of describing the items in its system according to standard description patterns. The resulting item descriptions from all supply elements were filed, and a federal item-identification number was assigned for each item which, according to the descriptions submitted, was unique. After this preliminary refine-

[10] *Statement of Rear Admiral Joseph W. Fowler, Director, Supply Management Agencies, Munitions Board, Before the Senate Armed Services Subcommittee on S. 3023 and H.R. 7405, June 4, 1952,* Department of Defense, mimeographed.

[11] *Second Semiannual Report of the Defense Supply Management Agency, Department of Defense . . . on Progress of Department of Defense Cataloging and Standardization Programs . . . ,* 83d Cong., 1st sess. (Washington: 1953), p. 6.

[12] A "supply element" is any organizational unit which has responsibility for purchasing, storage, issue, or maintenance of supplies.

ment of the data there were, for subsistence, about 2,000 different items each with its number. These item descriptions were sent to the Quartermaster Corps as the responsible agency for this group of items. There, about 200 unnecessary items were eliminated, bringing the total to 1,800. These 1,800 were then turned over to the task group consisting of representatives of all interested supply elements, and this task group working with the staff of the Office of Standardization eliminated the unneeded close substitutes bringing the total of subsistence items to slightly more than 1,100. These were returned to the Quartermaster Corps and prepared for publication. The resulting Federal Supply Catalog was then sent to each supply element for its comments and plans for utilizing the catalog.

Such a Federal Supply Catalog is in effect a master catalog which will serve as the basis for printing specialized catalogs for each supply element. The specialized catalogs are necessary because the requisitioning procedures, prices, and other necessary information vary to some degree among different branches of the services and different geographical locations. Once the catalogs are issued there is, of course, a constant job of keeping them up to date by adding new items and eliminating obsolete ones.

The military program, then, was well under way early in 1953, and it appeared that it might well be brought to a current maintenance basis within two to three years. The program for the civilian agencies has not fared well because of the failure of Congress to provide adequate appropriations for its completion. The military agencies use 1,000,000 of the estimated 1,500,000 items used by the civilian agencies, and these items will have been cataloged by the Department of Defense. The same federal stock numbers will eventually be used by the civilian agencies, but, before that, it will be necessary for each supply element of the civilian agencies to write item descriptions for the items it uses, submit these to the Federal Supply Service for matching with the federal stock numbers and descriptions which have been prepared by the military. Where federal stock numbers then exist for the civilian items, they can be used, and where they do not—that is, where the items are used by the civilian agencies only—additional federal stock numbers will have to be assigned. Thus, while the military program will serve to speed the civilian program, the latter cannot be completed until Congress sees fit to approve the appropriations necessary to do the work. By December, 1951, the Federal Supply Service had been able, with its limited staff, to prepare about

170,000 item descriptions out of the estimated 1,500,000.[13] The work had not proceeded to the point where any sections of the civilian part of the Federal Supply Catalog system could be published and put to use.

Federal Specifications program.—On January 1, 1953, there were 2,719 Federal Specifications in effect (Table 8). This number falls short of being adequate to serve the needs of federal-government procurement. It gives, however, more coverage in purchasing than a simple comparison of the specifications with the estimated 1,500,000 items demanded for civilian use would lead one to believe. Each specification may include many items, that is, it may cover a number of varieties, classes, types, and sizes of the commodity or commodity group for which it is written. A study made by the Federal Supply Service disclosed that the minimum number of items covered by a single federal specification was five for one kind of white paint in five container sizes, while the maximum number was more than fifty thousand for photographic paper. The average number of items covered by each specification was estimated to be 155.

The number of 1,500,000 is an estimation arrived at after elimination of duplicate identifications for the same items, but does not reflect reductions which would result from elimination of close substitutes. In view of this possibility and also of the fact that many agencies have developed their own specifications for commodities that are used principally by them, it is estimated that specifications sufficient to cover about 1,000,000 items would be adequate. According to this reasoning, a little more than 6,000 Federal Specifications are required ultimately to serve the needs of government buying.[14]

These figures indicate that in 1953 Federal Specifications were available for less than one-half of the items where they were needed. But this statement requires qualification. Preference was given to the development of specifications for items which are frequently procured and which account for large dollar amounts. On the other hand, ease of development and the availability of suitable data were strong factors in programing the work of committees and were not necessarily related to the importance of the commodities. Also, while the use of Federal Specifications has been

[13] U.S. General Services Administration, *Annual Report of the Administrator of the General Services, for the Year Ending June 30, 1952* (Washington: 1953).

[14] This information on the relation of specifications and items was supplied by the Federal Supply Service from data in its files.

TABLE 8

DISTRIBUTION OF FEDERAL SPECIFICATIONS BY PROCUREMENT CATEGORIES

(January 1, 1953)

Category	Number
Instruments	266
Paints, Pigments, Varnishes and Products	197
Tools	163
Metals	162
Chemicals	154
Metal Products	117
Paper and Products	105
Rubber and Rubber Goods	100
Minerals and Products (nonmetallic)	99
Electric Apparatus	91
Textile Products	88
Brooms and Brushes	87
Insulating Materials	73
Furniture	68
Cleaning and Polishing Materials	62
Textiles (yardage)	60
Meats and Sea Foods	56
Pipe, Pipe Fittings, Plumbing Fixtures, etc.	52
Glass and Glassware	51
Hardware	49
Vegetable Products	48
Vegetables	47
Fruit Products	44
Machinery	44
Wood Products	43
Leather and Leather Goods	39
Animal Products	34
Petroleum and Products	34
Cellulose Products and Synthetic Resins	32
Fruits	31
Cereals and Products	30
Drugs and Medicines	25
Groceries	21
Knit Goods, Netting and Webbing	21
All other classes	126
Total all classes	2,719

SOURCE: Compiled from *Index of Federal Specifications and Standards.*

mandatory, complete application to purchasing transactions has not been possible in the absence of a standard Federal Supply Catalog system, because it has been difficult to tell easily whether or not a given specification applies to a particular transaction. In any event it was clear that Federal Specifications were far from adequate to cover the need.

Results of standardization.—The application of cataloging and specification programs to a complex supply system in any large organization inevitably results in substantial savings. A few examples will illustrate the importance of such standardization to the government.

One important design element common to equipment with moving parts is antifriction bearings. At one time the number of items of antifriction bearings carried in the records of the Navy Department totaled 225,000. As a part of its cataloging and subsequent standardization program the Navy was able to reduce this number to 8,500 without eliminating any bearing that was required to fill a need. The previous duplication not only had caused unnecessary repetition of contracts for identical items with a corresponding reduction in purchase quantities, and increased the costs and problems of storing these vital parts, but had resulted in costly confusion in supplying the needs of the Navy. On one occasion a ship was diverted 500 miles to obtain a replacement bearing, only to find, when it reached port, that the identical part was in the ship's inventory under a different item number.

To give another example: One common antifriction bearing, which was dimensionally and functionally interchangeable regardless of which manufacturer produced it, was carried under 207 different identification numbers in the government-catalog records where only one number was required.[15]

This confusion in the government system derives directly from the policy of product differentiation which is such a common element in sellers' policies today. The explanation of the 207 numbers for one bearing is this: Although all manufacturers make their bearings interchangeable, each one sells his brand under his individual catalog number which conveys no information that it is standard. Suppliers of assemblies or completed equipment using this bearing, purchase it from one or more manufacturers and in turn each uses his individual identification for the bearings as

[15] Testimony of W. S. MacLeod and C. E. Mack in U.S. Congress, House, *Treasury Department Appropriation Bill for 1950*, Hearings, 81st Cong., 1st sess. (Washington: 1949), p. 358.

repair parts. They may include each bearing under as many numbers as there are manufacturers from whom they buy. Dealers in spare parts who may bid successfully for government business also use their own numbers. When this compounding of numbers in private industry is further multiplied by the government as a result of procurement from different sources and the different cataloging practices of various procuring agencies, the result is considerable unnecessary duplication—in this example 207 numbers for one item. This confusion resulting from efforts of sellers to profit through product differentiation is characteristic of private industry generally as well as of government operations.

Another major program by the Navy resulted in the following accomplishments: 3,000 types of electron tubes were reduced to 800 of which procurement is focused on 195 types; 37,000 types of meters were reduced to 3,700; 1,400 vibrators were reduced to 18; 1,000 molded thermoplastic materials were reduced to 29; and 659 capacitors were reduced to 93.[16] The Army alone had six separate item numbers for an identical one-and-a-half-pound claw hammer of the usual type used around a home.[17] One Federal Specification was issued providing for 12 types of roasting pans which replace 26 types previously covered in 5 different agency specifications.[18]

These examples illustrate the simplification in procurement and supply resulting from standardization of demand. No precise overall estimates of the possibilities are available although the estimated 75 per cent reduction in items, from 12,000,000 to 3,000,000, which could be made through the development of a uniform commodity catalog for all government departments gives a rough measure of the minimum that might be accomplished.

Standardization of demand on the minimum number of items required to satisfy the needs of the government results in increased purchase quantities, but may not of itself be sufficient to increase quantities to the most economical point from the viewpoint of procurement. Other devices are needed to consolidate requirements to the point where desirable low prices and low administrative costs of bulk purchasing may be realized. These consist of various forms of centralized purchasing.

---

[16] Letter from M. E. Andrews, assistant secretary of the Navy in U.S. Congress, Senate, Committee on Expenditures in the Executive Departments, *Federal Property Act of 1948,* Hearings, 80th Cong., 2d sess. March 31–April 3, 1948 (Washington: 1948), p. 79.

[17] *Treasury Department Appropriation Bill for 1950,* Hearings, p. 359.

[18] *Task Force Report on the Federal Supply System* (Appendix B), p. 88.

Centralized Purchasing

As stated in Chapter II, the Federal Supply Service has the responsibility for conducting centralized purchasing operations, as well as for devising and putting into effect purchasing policies for all government agencies. In exercising this authority it has put into effect a number of programs which are designed to bring to the government the advantages of large-quantity procurement. The programs are: the federal supply schedules; the establishment of regional stores to supply the needs of agencies for commonly used goods; the consolidation of demand for specified articles of equipment and their central purchase by the Service for direct delivery to the requisitioning agency; and the purchase of the requirements of individual agencies at their request.

Table 10 gives an idea of the relative importance of these programs. The federal supply schedules are the most important, quantitatively, with the direct-delivery and stores programs following in that order. The three programs in total accounted for $443,000,000 of purchases in the fiscal year 1952.

The General Supply Fund.—The supply centers (stores) and purchase-for-direct-delivery programs require funds for financing purchases for the period between the time when the Federal Supply Service must make a payment to take advantage of cash discounts and the time, after the receipt of the requisitioned goods, when the using agency is able to make payment to the Service. The General Supply Fund was established[19] to provide the capital necessary for such financing. The original authorized capital of $300,000 has subsequently been periodically increased until in September, 1950, it stood at a little more than $44,000,000.[20] For long periods of time the size of this fund limited the amount of centralized procurement that was practically possible, but in 1953 it was considered to be sufficient to finance the programs in prospect.

At that time, therefore, the way appeared to be open for an expansion of the programs for centralization of purchasing. In the remainder of this chapter the working of the programs and the types of purchasing devices used to procure for each of them is described in some detail. The analysis of the operation of the devices is discussed in later chapters.

[19] Chap. ii, p. 13.

[20] In the fiscal year 1950 the appropriated capital in the Fund was a little over $10,000,000. In the fiscal year 1951 regular and supplemental appropriations increased this by $34,000,000.

Federal supply schedules.—The federal supply schedules represent an attempt to combine the advantages of centralized purchasing with those of decentralized procurement. They are indefinite-quantity time contracts providing for local ordering in small quantities by the using agency and for local delivery by the supplier directly to the agency.

There are about one hundred federal supply schedules in use, each of them covering either a whole or part of one class of the Federal Standard Stock Catalog. Each schedule is the subject of many contracts the total number of which is about 2,500. The contracts are let by the sealed-bids procedure and cover periods of various lengths—most frequently one year, but they may be as short as three months if market conditions warrant it. An attempt is made to stagger the expiration dates of the contracts so as to smooth out the work load for the buyers of the Federal Supply Service, but there have been instances of discontinuity of the contracts.

The total number of items included in all schedules was about 40,000.[21] In 1952 it was estimated that 500,000 orders were placed against the schedules and the total value of business they represented was about $300,000,000. The low amount during the 'thirties was $38,000,000 for 1935. Variations in the volume of the consistently heavily used schedules such as those for fuel and office equipment are shown in Table 9. Use of the schedules may be mandatory or voluntary, may apply to military as well as civilian agencies, and may extend over the nation or only designated regions. Thus several important schedules, such as those for drafting room and office supplies and for electric light globes, are mandatory for civilian and military agency orders delivered anywhere in the country. Many schedules are mandatory for civilian agency orders delivered in the Washington region, and optional for delivery elsewhere. Still others are prepared individually by each regional office for use in its region only, and some schedules are optional in their entirety.

The procedure for the use of the schedules is simple for the ordering agency. The schedules are much like catalogs giving item descriptions, sources of supply, and the prices at which the items may be procured. By reference to such schedules the purchasing

[21] Testimony of C. E. Mack in U.S. Congress, House, Committee on Appropriations, *Treasury Department Appropriation Bill for 1949, Part I*, Preliminary Hearings, 80th Cong., 2d sess. (Washington: 1947), p. 328.

officer simply places the agency's own order with the contract supplier without advertising for bids or negotiating prices, obtains delivery, and makes payment just as he would for any orders he places. Where use of the schedules is voluntary for the agency, the purchasing officer may buy from alternative sources if he is able to obtain better prices in this way. Normally, however, there is a price advantage to be obtained from the use of the contract sup-

TABLE 9

VARIATION IN PURCHASES UNDER FEDERAL SUPPLY SCHEDULES
(Selected schedules under which purchases are consistently large in volume)

Class	Variation in dollar volume from 1936 to 1946	1946
	(in millions of dollars)	
7 Fuel	10 to 50	20
8 Motor vehicle parts	4 to 60	6
18 Precision instruments	1 to 7	3
26 Furniture	3 to 35	4
51 Acids, chemicals, etc.	0.2 to 3	2
53 Stationery	1 to 8	3.5
54 Office equipment	7 to 77	41

SOURCE: *Detailed Report on the Federal Supply System*, submitted by the Federal Supply Project to the Hoover Commission, September 28, 1948, p. 41, mimeographed.

pliers listed in the schedules. Some idea of the magnitude of the administrative problem of maintaining these schedules is given by the fact that about 350,000 copies of them are distributed each month by the Federal Supply Service to government agencies in Washington and in the field, in order to keep the system up to date.[22]

The federal supply schedules are most appropriate for three groups of items: those not used in sufficient quantity or with sufficient regularity to make it profitable to buy in definite quantities and carry them in stock; perishables, and items such as fuel that cannot be economically carried in stock by the government at

[22] The information on the federal supply schedules was in part provided by the Federal Supply Service and in part taken from the *Detailed Report on the Federal Supply System* (as identified in chap. ii, n. 14), pp. 40–48.

many points about the country; and items which can be procured only from a single source and are therefore noncompetitive.

Federal supply centers.—The federal supply schedules represent one method of profiting in buying through the anticipation of demand. Another way, more effective where it is appropriate, is to order the goods in as large quantities as the anticipated demand justifies and store them until they are needed. For this purpose the Federal Supply Service operates 12 supply centers. They are located in Atlanta, Boston, Chicago, Cleveland, Dallas, Denver, Kansas City, Los Angeles, New York, San Francisco, Seattle, and Washington, D.C. They are in effect mail-order houses because they serve the territories adjacent to the cities in which they are established.

The stores are operated under the direction of the Purchase and Stores Division of the Federal Supply Service in Washington which prints and distributes a national stock catalog of the items carried by the stores. The goods stocked are limited to administrative and housekeeping items commonly used by various agencies. The total of items stocked by the stores averaged about 9,800 in 1953. Use of the stores for the procurement of all stocked items is mandatory for all civilian executive agencies with specified exceptions which include food, items procured under federal-supply-schedule contracts, and small purchases of items which are urgently or only occasionally needed in small quantities.[23]

The stores program is financed by use of the General Supply Fund. Turnover is comparable to private mail-order business with yearly sales running about four-and-a-half times the average investment in inventory. Prices are firm for six months, are based on the costs of the goods, and do not include any markup.

Purchases of the items stocked in the supply centers are made by use of the sealed-bids device on definite-quantity contracts and on term contracts when they yield favorable prices. Where savings can be made by consolidating requirements and purchasing in large quantities, contracts are let centrally from one of the regions, usually Washington, for direct delivery to the various supply centers. The majority of the items, however, are procured by the regional stores themselves, each for its own requirements.[24]

Central procurement for direct delivery.—Aside from requiring

[23] *Regulations of the General Services Administration,* 1–II–302.02 (1–22–53).

[24] The information on the stores program was obtained from records of the Federal Supply Service in Washington, D.C.

the use of federal supply schedules and stores as previously noted, the GSA requires that the requisitions for specified articles of equipment be consolidated and procured through centralized purchasing by one of its regional offices. In February, 1953, the principal items were automotive vehicles, electric water coolers, and domestic mechanical refrigerators.

These consolidated purchase programs are closely tied in with

TABLE 10

CENTRALIZED PURCHASE PROGRAMS; FEDERAL SUPPLY SERVICE
(Fiscal years 1946–1952;[a] volume in millions of dollars)

Fiscal year	Stores issues[b]	Direct delivery[b]			Federal supply schedules[c]	Total
		Consolidated requirements of agencies	Requirements of individual agencies	Total		
1946	19	..	..	11	95	125
1947	24	..	..	19	84	127
1948	24	..	..	36	89	149
1949	27	..	..	64	90	181
1950	26	27	24	51	100	177
1951	45	36	30	66	200	311
1952	64	35	44	79	300	443

[a] The figures for the years 1946 through 1949 are for the Federal Bureau of Supply of the Department of the Treasury.

[b] Figures for 1946 through 1949 from Subcommittee of the Committee on Appropriations, H.R. 81st Cong., 2d Sess., *Independent Offices Appropriations for 1951,* Part 5, p. 1716; for 1950 through 1952 from *Annual Reports of the Administration of General Services,* General Services Administration, Washington, D.C. The breakdown of direct-delivery purchases into those for consolidated and individual requirements of agencies is not available for the years before 1950.

[c] Figures for 1946 through 1949 from *Annual Reports of the Secretary of the Treasury;* for 1950 through 1952 from *Annual Reports of the Administration of General Services, op. cit.*

the stores programs and the utilization of excess stocks. In general the items are consolidated first by the regional offices, and where possible they are filled from excess equipment available in the stocks of various agencies. If this is not feasible and the items are stocked by the regional stores, they are provided from that source. Otherwise they are sent by the regional offices to the region responsible for centralized procurement of the item. There they are purchased by the sealed-bids procedure on contracts calling for definite quantities and delivery direct to the using agencies. Interim requirements may be purchased in small lots as ordered by the using agency after clearance through the Federal Supply Service. The volume of these programs amounted to $35,000,000 in the fiscal year 1952 (Table 10).

Some agencies have taken advantage of the provision of the law that the administrator of the GSA shall provide purchasing services to any agency which requests it. Upon request of the Department of the Interior the Federal Supply Service through its stores depot at Seattle makes all purchases required for the Alaska Native Service, the Alaska Railroad, and the Alaska Road Commission. It has also made large purchases of household furniture for the Departments of the Army and Air Force, and for other agencies which were faced with special procurement problems they felt they were not well equipped to handle. On occasion the Service has found it to be more economical to convert large orders from a single agency on the stores stock into direct-delivery orders. The sum of these direct-delivery purchases which are not the result of consolidating requirements amounted to more than $44,000,000 in the fiscal year 1952.

Influence of Internal Policy

The programs described in the foregoing pages represent the effort of the Federal Supply Service to increase the utility received by the government per dollar spent in purchasing and to minimize costly shortages by (1) reducing the administrative costs of purchasing, (2) prescribing the manner of conducting uncentralized procurement which is at once legal and best under the given circumstances, and (3) requiring the use of centralized procurement techniques where these are most economical. The effectiveness of these policies is assessed in Chapter X after the operation of the buying devices in various markets has been analyzed and a more adequate idea of purchase prices has been obtained. Internal purchasing policies are intended to set the stage for effective buying. They determine (1) the quantities to be procured under single contracts; and (2) the type of contract—either a federal-supply-schedule term contract or a definite-quantity–definite-delivery contract.

IV

Product Policy

Significance of Product Policy

According to a survey conducted by the National Association of Purchasing Agents, the "buying of proper quality" is generally considered by purchasing agents to be their most important function, taking precedence over other factors, such as price, service, and the financial responsibility of vendors.[1] What the purchasing agents really mean is that the most perplexing difficulties of their job are encountered in developing and applying effective definitions of the physical product rather than in developing and applying effective policies with regard to price, service, and the financial responsibility of vendors. Quality is no more important than price, because the utility per dollar, which purchasing agents attempt to maximize, is a ratio of the two and can be increased or lowered by variations in either one. Furthermore, at every stage in the development of the product policy, which provides the basis for bidding and award of contracts, the effect of the policy on price must be considered. The problem of defining the product to be purchased is perplexing, because utility is difficult to measure and the product policies of sellers serve to confuse rather than clarify the patterns of products and prices from which buyers must choose.

Product policies in purchasing come to a focus on the decisions of (1) what quantity to buy and (2) how to compare the utility of competitive products offered by bidders in order to relate utility to price and make the award of contracts. As with all purchasing policies, however, the product policies are inextricably related to the broader supply policies. These include the guides for choosing the product to be purchased from the first expression of the need through to the final agreement to buy, and the guides for decisions

[1] National Association of Purchasing Agents, *Handbook of Purchasing Policies and Procedures* (New York: 1939), I, 227.

regarding centralizing purchases and the time for which contracts shall run.

In the government the choice of the product is largely completed in the process of standardizing demands, which was described in the previous chapter. There the effect of standardization and of centralized contracting in the form of increased purchase quantities was considered. In the present chapter the effect of standardization on the quality rather than the quantity of the product is examined.

The process of choice.—When the process of commodity cataloging has reached the point where all obvious duplications and irrelevant varieties of products are eliminated, a certain number of kinds, grades, and qualities of products which are substitutes for a given use will remain. These can be further weeded out only after a careful study of the use requirements and the utility of the products in satisfying them has resulted in the development of a specification for the most suitable product. The promulgation of the specification at the same time completes the cataloging process of concentrating demand on the minimum necessary number of goods and provides the commodity definition for purchasing.

A number of items serving closely related uses may be listed in the catalog. Most of these have their prescribed uses, and individual preferences are not considered. Thus items of office furniture used by employees are assigned to them on the basis of their work and salary grade, and most office supplies, such as typewriter paper and carbon paper, are designated for specific uses. For some goods, however, such as typewriters and other business machines, substitute products are available from which the user may requisition the one he believes to be most efficient. For all goods, cataloging and the promulgation of a Federal Specification substantially complete the process of choosing the product for purchase.

This process of choosing the optimum quality of product and writing a specification for it involves (1) an analysis of the use requirements the good must fill, (2) a determination of the utility of the substitute products which are available in markets to satisfy the use requirements, and (3) an estimate of the utility-per-dollar ratios which the purchase of the commodities can be expected to yield considering their customary prices, their differences in cost, and the number of competitors who will be in a position to bid on contracts for the product.

The analyses of the use requirements—the needs goods must satisfy—are within the immediate control of the government officials and cause no great difficulties. Yet such analyses often require considerable skill and ingenuity.

When attempting to measure and compare the utility of competitive products in satisfying the use requirements, buyers find that markets provide many claims of superiority the accuracy of which must be assessed before they can be accepted as reliable guides for purchasing. The buyer must use the product and is interested in its utility. The seller, because he obtains his profit from the sale and not the use of the product, is interested in the product's salability; he is concerned with utility only to the extent that it increases salability.

In order to cope with the confusion which arises from the fact that the motivation of the buyer is different from that of the seller, the buyer must be able to distinguish from among the characteristics of the product which give it salability generally, and those which give it utility to him. The government is in an advantageous position to do this because of the nature of its needs and the resources at its disposal to test goods and to survey the products and the prices offered. To the government, utility is the sum of all those characteristics of a product which satisfy specific government needs. Salability may be defined as the sum of all those characteristics of a product which make buyers in general decide to buy it. Salability is derived both from the qualities of a product which in fact give it its utility and from qualities, either existent or claimed though nonexistent, which do not yield utility but are impressive to the buyer. The salability of a product is not important to the government. The utility of the product is paramount.

Utility can be determined only by reference to the specific needs it must fill. Of course, the judgments of a product's utility may differ among those empowered to make the decision on behalf of the government. For example, hospitals managed by the civilian agencies are authorized to buy drugs of different manufacturers as designated by their physicians even if the same drug is produced by many manufacturers to identical specifications. In general, however, the government undertakes to make purchases upon the basis of utility judged independently from the personal preferences of the immediate user.

If the government is persuaded by sales promotion that claimed product qualities—which may contribute to its general salability but do not contribute to its utility—are significant, it will fail to realize in consuming the product the full measure of utility it expected to receive at the time of purchase. The government may or may not be aware of this fact, but, so far as it purchases goods to fill needs for which objective criteria of measurement are available, it nevertheless will suffer a loss.

In many markets in which the government buys, sellers profitably pursue price policies backed by product policies built upon claims of product differences which are only partly significant. The success of these selling policies depends in part on the buyer's irrationality and lack of knowledge of the utility of products. Conversely, the success of buying policies, including the government's, depends in part on the rationality with which the buyers are able to sort out from among the claimed differences in competitive products those which are significant to them.

Significant qualities are not clearly revealed by the claims of manufacturers, manufacturers' names, brand names, price lines, or differences in the prices of competitive products. Those responsible for writing the specifications must rely in the final analysis on market information, the reliability of which they can check by their own investigation, or on information newly developed by test programs which they control directly.

Importance of objective product definition.—A few examples will serve to illustrate the inadequacy of data obtained from market sources and the magnitude of the effect the choice of specifications can have on the utility-per-dollar ratios of goods.

A large part of the products the government uses is available in "price lines" which presumably vary in utility directly with the price. Tests made by the government on standard-duty, reinforced-link, and heavy-duty tire chains illustrate the danger of relying on price lines as a measure either of quality or of utility-per-dollar ratios. The reinforced-link chain sells at 22 per cent higher than the standard-duty chain, while the heavy-duty chain is priced at 50 per cent higher than the standard-duty (Table 11). The tests revealed that the standard-duty and the heavy-duty chains of various manufacturers on the average give the same life in actual use, while the reinforced-link type lasts 250 per cent as long as either of the other two. In terms of utility per dollar the reinforced-link chain is twice as good a buy for the government as the standard-duty chain and three times as good a buy as the heavy-duty chain.

Before the tests were made, the manufacturers offered no information which could be considered reliable for writing the specifications for chains. It may be that they did not know themselves what the relative wearing qualities of the different types of chains were. It is interesting to note that the prices vary almost directly with the weight of the chains, which is a rough indicator of their costs.

Individual prices at which goods are offered for sale, as contrasted with price or quality lines, are obviously no indicators of quality. The experience of the government in contracting, which is discussed in later chapters, shows that price quotations for a contract to supply a specified product will vary anywhere from 20 to 100 per cent or more above the low bid.

TABLE 11

TIRE CHAINS: VARIATION BETWEEN TYPES OF THE SAME MAKE IN PRICE, WEIGHT, WEAR, AND WEAR PER DOLLAR

Type of chain	Net price to government per set		Weight per set		Wear index (per cent of standard-duty chain = 100)	Index of wear per dollar	
	Dollars	Variation (per cent)	Pounds	Variation (per cent)		Wear index ÷ net price	Variation (per cent)
Standard duty	4.88	100	15.75	100	100	0.20	143
Reinforced link	5.95	122	19.00	121	250	0.42	300
Heavy duty...	7.32	150	25.00	159	100	0.14	100

SOURCE: Computed from information in the files of the Federal Supply Service, Washington, D.C. The chains are all for 600 x 16 size tires; the exact date of the tests and prices was not shown, but was between 1940 and 1945.

Manufacturers' brand names are similarly unreliable as measures of product quality unless buyers know that the quality-control methods of the manufacturers are adequate and consistently applied. Because manufacturers are more interested in selling their products than in utility, control methods may be directed toward insuring the products' salability rather than their utility. The following objective studies made for two commodities illustrate the fact that buyers should not rely on brand names as measures of quality.

Tests under controlled conditions of use of the "first line" tires of eight tire manufacturers, including all major ones, were made for the Federal Supply Service by the National Bureau of Standards. The term "first line" tire identifies the highest-quality brand of tire of each manufacturer, all such brands being sold at competitive "price lines." The tests revealed that the longest wearing "first line" brand gave 56 per cent more miles in service than the shortest wearing "first line" brand (Table 12).

The same tests also showed that the serviceability of different sizes of tires of the same manufacturer and the same brand name varied significantly. The brand which gave the greatest wear in the passenger-car size ranked fourth in wear in the popular light-truck size, while the brand which ranked fifth in the passenger-car size ranked first in the truck size. These tests were of the nature of pilot tests to prepare the way for more comprehensive ones to be made later, but they confirmed previous tests conducted by the Post Office Department under different conditions of use.

TABLE 12

AUTOMOBILE TIRES: VARIATION IN WEAR BETWEEN MAKES AND BETWEEN SIZES OF THE SAME MAKE

Manufacturer	Average estimated tread wear of tires expressed in percentage of shortest-wearing make			
	6.00 x 16, 4-ply "first line" tires[a]		7.00 x 20, 10-ply "first line" tires[a]	
	Per cent	Rank	Per cent	Rank
A	156	1	138	4
B	140	2	150	3
C	123	3	158	2
D	122	4	105	7
E	114	5	191	1
F	114	6	110	6
G	112	7	100	8
H	100	8	130	5

SOURCE: Computed from information in the files of the Federal Supply Service, Washington, D.C., on tests in use, completed in 1949, of eight makes of tires. Tests were only for tread wear, but results were consistent with previous tests made by the Post Office Department, which covered both tread and carcass.

[a] The term "first line" tire originally identified the highest quality line tire of each manufacturer, not a level of quality common for all manufacturers. The "first line" tires of all manufacturers are roughly competitive in price, but are not of the same quality. At present some manufacturers make a higher quality line of tire than their "first line" tires.

Another test conducted by the National Bureau of Standards compared three sizes of dry batteries from 11 prominent manufacturers. (Table 13). The results were similar to those of the tire test.

The results of the Bureau of Standards tire tests are confirmed by tests conducted by a consumer goods rating agency, Consumers Union, which show the variation in quality among competitive brands of tires (not sizes). This investigation also included information on prices and, therefore, provides a basis for comparing the estimated tread wear per dollar offered by various brands of tires at retail (Table 14).

The examples indicate the magnitude of the effect which variations in quality can have on utility-per-dollar ratios. In the examples shown, the variation, if prices were constant, would be from 56 to 250 per cent. Furthermore, in the tire and battery tests only

TABLE 13

Dry Batteries: Variation in Life Between Makes and Between Sizes of the Same Make

Manufacturer	Average estimated life of battery expressed in percentage of minimum required by Federal Specification					
	Flashlight—D size Item no. 17-B-7210		No. 6 dry cells Item no. 17-B-7600		Radio B—N size Item no. 16-B-3340	
	Per cent	Rank	Per cent	Rank	Per cent	Rank
A	159	1	135	3	103	5
B	157	2	104	7	...	..
C	150	3	105	6	...	..
D	146	4	141	2	185	1
E	138	5	163	1	...	..
F	130	6	100	8	132	4
G	122	7	120	5	177	3
H	119	8	121	4	181	2
I	116	9	...	..	...	..
J	109	10	85	9	...	..
K	101	11	...	..	...	..

Source: Computed from information on qualification tests for batteries, made during 1949, in the files of the Federal Supply Service, Washington, D.C.

the "first line" qualities were compared. If the various kinds and quality lines are also considered, the pattern of variation is further complicated and the ranges in utility between substitute products further widened. If prices were included in the calculation the price–quality ratios for competitive products may be brought closer together or sent further apart in magnitude depending on whether the prices vary directly or inversely with quality. Because the selection of the commodity specification must be made well in advance of the purchase, the magnitude of the utility-per-dollar ratio is in substantial part determined from a month to years in advance of the purchase.

The decision to adopt a specification also affects the chance of maximizing the utility-per-dollar ratio by its effect in determining

TABLE 14

AUTOMOBILE TIRES: VARIATION IN PRICE, WEAR, AND WEAR PER DOLLAR BETWEEN MAKES IN THE $19–$24 RETAIL-PRICE RANGE
(Summer, 1950)

Make of tire[a]	Ret. list price, NYC (dollars)	Variation (per cent)	Rank	Est. total tread wear (miles)	Variation (per cent)	Rank	Est. miles tread wear per dollar	Variation (per cent)	Rank
Sears Roebuck and Co. "Allstate Premium Quality"	19.04	100	1	33,000	122	3	1,733	142	3
Montgomery Ward and Co. "Cat. No. 64 C 1713 M"	19.04	100	1	29,000	107	6	1,523	125	4
B. F. Goodrich Co. "Silvertown"	19.79	104	3	36,000	133	1	1,819	149	1
Goodyear Tire and Rubber Co. "De Luxe Rib"	19.79	104	3	36,000	133	1	1,819	149	1
Firestone Tire and Rubber Co. "De Luxe Champion"	19.79	104	3	28,000	104	7	1,415	116	6
U.S. Rubber Co. "U.S. Royal De Luxe"	19.79	104	3	27,000	100	8	1,364	112	7
General Tire Co. "Silent Grip"	21.89	115	7	31,000	115	4	1,416	116	5
Seiberling Rubber Co. "Seiberling Safety"	24.54	128	8	30,000	111	5	1,222	100	8

SOURCE: Based on test results and prices given in *Consumer Reports*, Vol. 15, No. 11, December, 1950.
[a] 6.00 x 16, standard 4-ply, blackwall, "first line."

the number of firms which will bid for contracts. The products of many or a few firms may qualify as acceptable depending on the quality specified and on the terms and method used for defining the quality of the products. The goal is to define the optimum quality of product considering both utility and costs and at the same time to write the specification so that the maximum number of firms will be able to bid in competition for contracts. How successfully this is done depends in large measure on the methods used in defining the product characteristics.

METHODS OF PRODUCT DEFINITION

Government purchasing officials have no objection to the legal requirement which restricts the government's product policy to the use of objective commodity specifications, except where these are impracticable and specification by the maker's name or brand name may be used, provided the words "or equal" are included.[2] They would in all probability adopt the technique if it were not required, because they believe the use of objective specifications is the soundest method of obtaining active competition, and the most effective basis for making awards of contracts.[3] The administrative decisions elaborating the details of the product policy have, therefore, encouraged the fullest use of commodity specifications and have permitted the use of alternative methods only where specifications have not been available or have not been practicable. There are two alternative methods: lists of qualified products and brand or manufacturer's names. Combinations of the three methods are also used, but whatever the method, the goal is to provide the most objective commodity definition possible in the circumstances.

Whatever their forms, commodity definitions are an integral element of every stage of the purchasing procedure—invitation to bid, offer of bids, award of contracts, and final determination of satisfactory performance of contracts. To serve these purposes effectively, commodity definitions must (1) define a product which will yield the greatest utility per dollar if the product is procured at the prices assumed at the time of the definition; (2) be so worded as to be suitable, when included in the invitation to bid, to enable potential bidders (a) to determine whether they can provide the desired product and (b) to calculate the price at which they are

[2] Chap. ii, p. 26.

[3] C. E. Mack, *Federal Procurement* (Washington: Government Printing Office, 1943), p. 12.

willing to offer the product; (3) permit all qualified and willing suppliers to submit bids; (4) provide a standard for measuring the quality of products offered in bids on the basis of which price offers can be considered and awards made; and (5) define the methods of test and inspection by which suppliers and the government can economically compare products with the requirements of the contract to determine whether or not it has been fulfilled.

Objective specifications.—A "specification" as used in purchasing is a definition, written in terms of objective measurements of those characteristics of a commodity or service which state its utility in its intended use. The measure of such characteristics and the methods for determining their magnitudes must be such that any qualified person with proper testing equipment is able to duplicate results when measuring identical commodities in different places or at different times.

The chief difficulties in drafting specifications which will satisfy the requirements of an adequate commodity definition, are to insure (1) that they in fact sufficiently define the product's utility; (2) that they do not exclude any product which will give the desired utility, nor restrict the use of efficient materials or methods of production; (3) that they are easily and inexpensively applied in measuring the product; and (4) that they define the grade and price line offering the prospect of the best buy.

The most obvious way to prevent specifications from being undesirably restrictive is to limit the characteristics to the minimum number necessary for adequate description. This is a generally accepted rule which permits many designs of products to meet a given specification provided they are equivalent in utility. The number of factors required as well as the restrictiveness of any particular factor depend upon how much is known about the relation of the utility of the commodity to its measurable characteristics.

The only completely reliable method of measuring the utility of a particular commodity is to use it. For purposes of buying, such performance tests must be made in advance of the purchase. Where they are practicable they offer the best available method both for measuring utility and for avoiding restrictive requirements.

The difficulties of applying tests in actual use, however, severely restrict their utility for arriving at a definition. The utility of different units of a maker's product varies, as do the conditions of use by different consumers. The sample tested must be sufficiently large to give results which are representative both of the product and the varying conditions of use. Such samples must be tested for each seller who wishes to bid on a contract. Therefore the costs of the tests may be high and the time taken to make them, long. If the contract covers a period of time with deliveries in small quantities, samples must be tested periodically to insure that the utility of the seller's product has not been lessened during the life of the contract.

Although it is not often practicable to apply tests in use, they still provide the basis for all methods of definition. The mentioned difficulties, however, modify the way in which the method is applied. Its widest application is as a control for the development of performance requirements of commodities which can be measured in laboratories by accelerated tests simulating conditions in use. By correlating the results of such performance tests with the results of using the products under carefully controlled conditions, the relationship of the laboratory-measured performance characteristics of the commodity to its utility can be discovered. Often the results of performance tests can be translated into quantitative measures of utility. At least they can serve to array products tested on a qualitative scale in order of their relative utility.

Specifications of such performance requirements have a number of important advantages and are used wherever they are available. They provide the most direct measure of utility short of actual use, they permit compliance to be determined by testing the final product, they are relatively inexpensive to perform, and they can be completed fairly quickly.

Where performance tests are not available, alternative and less desirable methods must be chosen. A method frequently used is to define the product by its chemical analysis or by description of its mechanical construction details. These are also based on correlations with the utility of products in actual use, but the relationship between measurements of these characteristics and actual performance is that of an indirect and a direct test. Performance requirements are equally suitable from the viewpoint of the ease with which tests for compliance may be performed on the final product. Products which are homogeneous in use, however, may well be produced by many different methods of compounding and mechanical construction, and specifying these details runs the danger of causing the specifications to be restrictive of innovation and of present competition. When properly devised and revised to keep abreast of new techniques, however, specifications of composition and mechanical details need not be restrictive.

In some goods, in which the identity of the ingredients cannot be adequately determined in the final product, neither of the methods just discussed is sufficient to define the product's utility, and it may be necessary to specify the ingredients used in manufacture or processing. This is likely to be even more restrictive than the specification of composition or construction, and has the additional disadvantage of limiting the possibility of testing for compliance in the final product. For these reasons specification of ingredients used in manufacture is avoided where possible, particularly since compliance can often be determined only by inspection of the goods in process, which is expensive to the buyer and also undesirable from the maker's viewpoint.

In extreme cases it may be necessary to prescribe the process of production to arrive at an objective specification. This has all disadvantages of other methods and is likely to be particularly distasteful to those makers who do not wish to make their processing techniques available to competitors.

In practice most specifications include combinations of the types of definition described. Where possible the government uses performance specifications and resorts to other, less desirable, methods only when lack of data makes their use necessary.[4]

Criticisms of Federal Specifications.—No criticism has been made of the policy of using objective specifications to define commodities purchased by the government, but only of particular specifications. Suppliers, buyers, users, Congress, and interested taxpayers accept the policy as the only one which will at the same time encourage competition among suppliers, give all suppliers equal opportunity to obtain government business, and protect the taxpayer against graft and fraud in buying.

In fact, the most sweeping criticism of Federal Specifications is that they are not sufficient in number to cover the purchasing needs of the government.[5] A variation of the same criticism is that specifications in some instances do not provide for alternative grades of a given kind of product. So long as the grades specified are required for government use, this is simply additional evidence of lack of coverage. The effect of this lack of coverage is that less desirable methods of commodity definition are used in purchasing commodities for which there are no Federal Specifications.

[4] Mack, *op. cit.*, p. 125.

[5] See chap. iii, "Federal Specifications program."

The other major criticisms of existing Federal Specifications are: (1) that they work to restrict competition, (2) that they fail to define commerically standard products, (3) that they are not consistent with the standards developed by nationally recognized bodies, such as the American Standards Association and the American Society for Testing Materials, and (4) that they define obsolete commercial practice. All these criticisms are variations of the charge that Federal Specifications do not define commodities which are standard according to current efficient industrial practice and do not, therefore, offer the government the greatest chance of maximizing the utility received for the dollars expended.

In most instances it is obviously desirable for specifications to define current practice; where they fail to do so, their use may have adverse effects both for the government as a buyer and user, and for the supplying industries. As a rule nonstandard products are more costly to produce than standard ones and consequently may well command higher prices for equivalent quality. Specification of nonstandard products tends to restrict competition because some potentially successful bidders may be expected to find it uneconomical to bid on goods, the manufacture of which would entail costly production adjustments.

It is clearly advantageous for Federal Specifications to incorporate specifications promulgated by nationally recognized agencies, such as the American Standards Association, when they are generally in use in the industry and define products required by the government. Federal purchasing is then focused on requirements that can be generally met by competing suppliers, and the cost of developing specifications is minimized. To the extent that the government fails to utilize such standards it fails to make these gains. It is the established policy of the government to use such standards, and many Federal Specifications are, in fact, replicas of nationally recognized standards. Sometimes, however, the standards of such bodies are not yet used generally by the industry, and, even if they are, may not define the particular quality of product that is most efficient for government use. For these situations the government, like any large-quantity purchaser, must develop its own specifications to meet its particular needs.

The same consideration holds for industry standards which have not been promulgated by nationally recognized agencies. Industry standards, however, are more likely to be developed with the needs of the manufacturer rather than the user in mind. They are less likely, for this reason, to meet the needs of the government and may well require revision before they can be incorporated into Federal Specifications.

On occasion specifications are consciously designed to force departures from established practice and are used to introduce desirable innovations. The most suitable product for a given use may not be offered among the standard competitive varieties in the market. In such circumstances, standards defining new and more efficient products may serve to force their adoption by competing suppliers. If the order quantities are sufficiently large to enable the government to purchase at a favorable price products with utility in addition to that otherwise available, the government gains immediately, and the industry may gain in the longer run if the innovation proves to be applicable to a wider segment of the market.

It is the basic function of the government's use of specifications to eliminate from consideration competitive products which are unsuitable or uneconomical. In this sense specifications must be restrictive to be effective. Complaints are often heard that specifications are restrictive, when an unsuccessful bidder's product falls slightly below the specification; such complaints, while understandable, are not justified from the government's point of view. If the complaints reflect the fact that desirable products are excluded by specifications which are unnecessarily restrictive, they work against the government's interest. Such restrictive specifications may be caused by the failure of the group of technicians, which developed them, to keep abreast of current developments in the industry. Where this is true, the remedy is consistent and effective enforcement of the established policy of the government to review and revise its specifications. Where the restrictive effect of specifications arises from lack of knowledge of commodity characteristics and the difficulties of choosing factors for defining products which are at once related to utility and unrestrictive with regard to competitive products providing that utility, some alternative method of commodity specification may be desirable.

Qualified-products lists.—Private purchasers often prefer qualified-products lists to objective specifications. The government's qualified-products lists, however, are simply the result of using specifications to preselect bidders whose product is acceptable. The specifications are similar to those described in the preceding section, but a paragraph is added requiring the product to be tested and qualified before the supplier's bid will be considered. Contracts for such products call for adequate check testing and inspection at intervals during the life of the contract; the contract may be canceled if the tests are unsatisfactory. Current contractors may qualify for bidding on ensuing contracts on the basis of the performance of their product as revealed by such check testing and inspection.

Purchasing experts have recommended that qualified-products lists be used only where (1) it is impossible to write a specification which will eliminate inferior articles, (2) long or expensive tests are required to determine conformity to specifications, (3) complicated testing apparatus not commonly available is required, and (4) determination of acceptability requires data which can be gained only through the use of the product.[6]

The Federal Supply Service has made very limited use of qualified-products lists. Only five Federal Specifications require that bidders qualify their products as a requisite for bidding. Two of these cover tungsten-filament electric lamp globes; one, batteries and dry cells; and two, accoustical materials and units.[7] In these specifications the products are purchased on federal-supply-schedule contracts, and although the yearly purchases are large, deliveries are made to many points in small quantities. Adequate inspection of the products requires long and expensive performance tests which are not only uneconomical but practically impossible to perform at the time of delivery in view of the small quantities and the desirability of prompt supply. Federal Supply Service officials consider it desirable to extend the use of qualified-products lists to other products, but this has not been possible in the past because of lack of funds for testing the products. The funds available must be provided by appropriations, and Congress has not been inclined to approve amounts adequate for the purpose. Even where suppliers pay for the testing, such payments go to the Treasury and cannot be used directly to pay the expenses incurred in testing. In 1953 it was expected that the provision of the law, which allowed such payments by manufacturers to be made into the General Supply Fund and corresponding transfers from the Fund directly to the accounts of the testing agencies, would help extend the use of qualified-products lists in the future.

[6] *Detailed Report on the Federal Supply System* (as identified in chap. ii, n. 14), p. 297.

[7] As of December, 1950. Information supplied by the Standards Division of the Federal Supply Service.

The principal disadvantage of the use of qualified-products lists is the time and expense required to qualify products and to test them during the life of the contract. Where products can be adequately defined in specifications and where inspection of the products at the time of delivery can be made adequately and economically, the normal use of specifications is preferable to qualified-products lists.

Seller's identification.—A second alternative to the use of objective specifications is the definition of the product by the maker's or seller's identification, such as a brand name or catalog number. This method relies on past experience and personal inspection, or, sometimes, on tests of samples for determining the utility of the product. It is used in the sealed-bids procedure only when specifications or qualified-products lists are not available or are not appropriate.

Purchase by maker's or seller's identification is considered an undesirable method because it fails to provide an adequate definition either for making awards or determining compliance with contracts. In the sealed-bids procedure it must be used with the term "or equal" following the seller's identification. As a result, bids may be received on products of unknown quality. If one of these bids is low, the buyer must either make the award to the low bidder and assume the risk that the product may be unsatisfactory, or reject the low bid on the grounds that the product offered is not equal to the product named. In either case he must be prepared to defend his decision.

For the most part the use of seller's identification is confined to small purchases where the use of specifications is uneconomical and the use of sealed bids is not required procedure, and to purchases of items for which there is a single source of supply.

Comparison of alternative methods.—Comparison of these alternative methods with the requirements of effective commodity definitions set forth at the outset of this section highlights their relative advantages and disadvantages. Controlled tests in actual use are the only adequate ultimate basis for determining which competitive product offered in the market will yield the greatest utility. All three methods described are based on the realization of this fact, and the product procured by any of the methods will be the one offering the government the greatest value.

Where it is possible to construct adequate objective specifications for products, all potentially successful bidders are automatically qualified to bid, and the probability of procuring the greatest value is maximized so far as this is determined by competition. Qualified-products lists are more likely to exclude potentially successful bidders, but are preferable to specifications which do not define products precisely, or which are too expensive to use.

Compared with other methods, specifications require somewhat more careful consideration by prospective bidders in deciding whether their products conform to the government's requirements. Manufacturers who qualify in other respects, however, normally have sufficient technical competence to reduce such comparisons to routine.

Specifications require tests to determine compliance, but where comparatively simple tests are available and order quantities are large the unit costs of inspection are nominal. Where these factors result in high unit costs of inspection, then the other methods prove to be best.

At the time of award objective specifications provide a simple method of determining that the bidder qualifies so far as his product is concerned. The fact that he bids on the specified product is usually sufficient—determination of ultimate compliance with the terms of the contract must in any event await inspection of the delivered product. Qualified-products lists are equally simple to use in making the award. The same is true for seller's identification if the low bidder's product is known to be "equal" to the brand of product specified. If it is a product of unknown quality, then the process of award is complicated by the necessity of deciding whether the product offered can be considered to be "equal."

None of the three methods is perfectly applicable to all purchases, but the government's policy of applying them seems to offer a constructive solution to the problem of choosing the most effective commodity to purchase.

Additional conditions of the purchase.—The methods of definition described so far are confined to the physical attributes of the product. These do not, however, embody all utilities sought in the purchase of many commodities. "Utility" in the wider sense applies also to conditions accompanying the sale, such as service agreements, installation of the product, prompt delivery, and convenience of location. The government's product policy includes definition of any such conditions which are considered important. If such utilities are not specified, the contractor is neither required nor expected to provide them.

PROCEDURES FOR DEVELOPING DEFINITIONS

When maker's or seller's identification is used as the product definition, no formal development procedure is needed. All that is necessary is sufficient knowledge of the sources of supply to insure that that brand name or seller's catalog number is selected for use which will best facilitate the comparisons required to judge if other products qualify as equal under the "or equal" clause.

Similarly, writing definitions for the nonphysical attributes of the product, such as service, installation, and delivery, requires no formal procedure. These characteristics vary with individual purchase transactions, and are normally defined by special provisions inserted by buyers in the invitations to bid.

Where Federal Specifications are not available, individual agencies often develop their own specifications, called "agency specifications" in government parlance. The procedures by which agency specifications are developed are determined by each agency and are usually informal.

Development of Federal Specifications.—The great majority of specifications used by the civilian agencies in government purchasing are Federal Specifications which are required for general use by all such agencies. They are widely used by the Department of Defense, by state and local government buyers, and by many private buyers as well. These, therefore, have wide influence, and considerable care is taken to insure, so far as procedures can do so, that the specifications take into account the needs of all agencies and the production and marketing problems of suppliers.

Until the end of 1952 Federal Specifications were developed by the technical committees of the Federal Specifications Board. The work was done by the part-time effort of more than 700 technical experts who were members of the committees, with the aid of the technical staff of the Federal Supply Service. Final review and approval of the specifications so prepared was the responsibility of the Standards Division of the Federal Supply Service, and all Federal Specifications were officially promulgated by the administrator of the General Services Administration. This procedure required, on the average, more than two years to complete a new Federal Specification and it seldom took less than one year.[8]

The formal use of committees for developing specifications was

[8] *Detailed Report on the Federal Supply System,* p. 287.

in accord with practices which had proved effective by private standards development agencies and private industrial companies. The Federal Supply Service, however, came to the conclusion that the procedure was too rigid and too slow to meet the needs of the government. Standardizing agencies, such as the American Standards Association, find it essential to sacrifice speed of development where time-consuming committee action is required to obtain assurance that the views of all interested parties have been properly considered. Private business firms have close enough control over their employees to speed up committee action where a specification is urgently required for its purchasing operations. The government, like private business, requires specifications for use in its purchasing, but unlike private business does not have close enough control of committee members to force quick action where this is necessary. Furthermore, in contrast with private standardizing agencies which do not use the specifications themselves, it is costly for the government to wait for committees to complete their work. In view of these considerations it was decided to abandon the use of the committee procedure, to discontinue the Federal Specifications Board, and to revise the development procedure in order to speed the work.

The present procedure adopted in the fall of 1952 relies on the assignment of the responsibility for developing a standard to some one agency in the government which is most interested and well qualified to complete the work ably and expeditiously (Figure 2). As under the committee procedure, all interested agencies and industries are consulted, but a time limit is placed on the submission of comments. If the assigned agency is convinced it has considered all important viewpoints, it may proceed with the development even though it has not heard from all agencies or industrial firms from which it has solicited comments. The procedure in Figure 2 is shown in the simplest and most direct form. If it is advisable, agencies and industries may be solicited for information several times, and meetings may be called of interested parties to resolve disputed points. The procedure shown for promulgating Interim Federal Specifications makes such specifications available to all agencies for optional use during the period regular Federal Specifications are being developed. This saves the agencies the time and expense of developing their own specifications. It is expected that the time required to develop Federal Specifications will be cut at least in half by these new procedures.

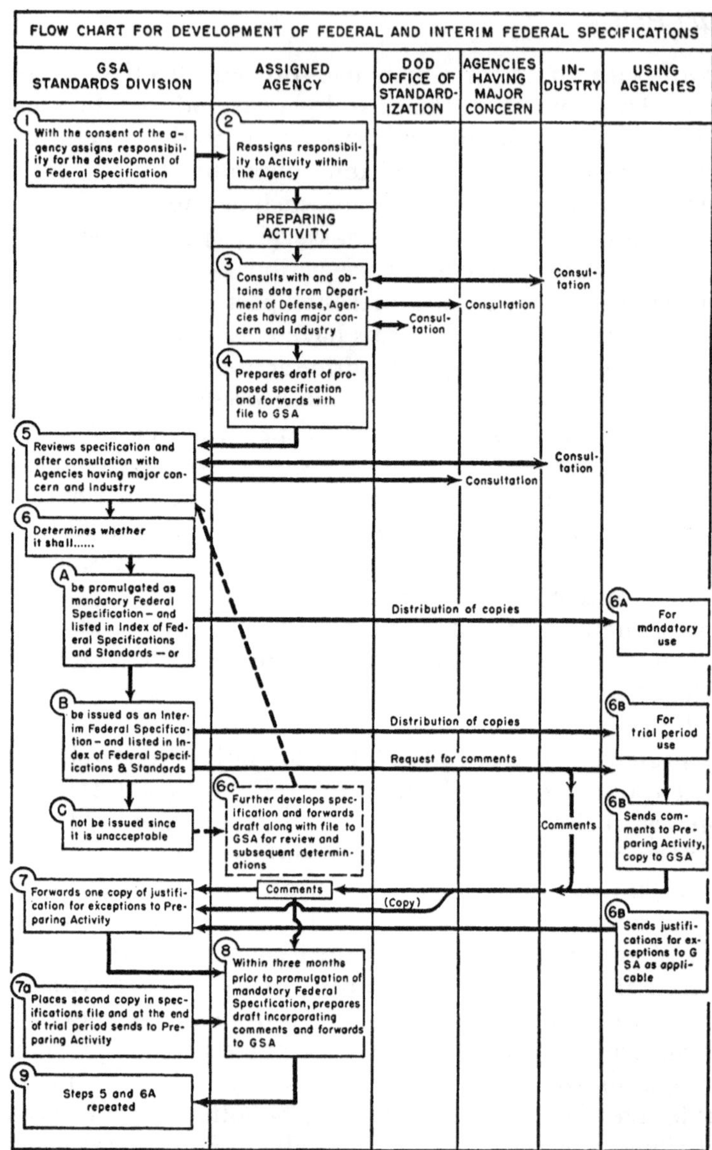

Fig. 2. Procedure for the Development and Promulgation of Federal Specifications. The procedures shown include the minimum number of steps which must be taken. In operation the procedure is flexible and often includes repeated consultation with agencies and industry either by mail or by informal meetings of interested parties. Source: Draft (November, 1953) GSA, *Reg.* 1–VI–202.04, exhibit 13, appendix C.

Methods of Using Specifications

Basically, objective specifications, as used in buying, provide a defined quality level against which the utility of competitive products may be compared. The standard so provided can be used in three principal ways which vary substantially in their effects.

The government usually divides all competitive offers into those which fail to meet the requirements and are, therefore, rejected, and those which meet or exceed them and are, therefore, acceptable. This can be called "the policy of product homogeneity" because all products meeting the specification are considered to be equally acceptable. This method is generally used in sealed-bids procedure where there are no low-tie bidders.

The second method is to use the specification (1) to reject all products failing to meet the requirements, and (2) as the basis for comparing the utility of products which equal or exceed them. This is used in government practice when low bids are tied and award may be made to the low bidder offering the highest quality product, or in the few instances where quality above the minimum is evaluated when awarding contracts.

The third method is to use the specifications to compare all competitive products offered regardless of whether they fall short of or exceed the requirements. This method is used where it is permissible to negotiate contracts and to make the award not necessarily to the low bidder, but to the bidder whose price and product offer the greatest utility per dollar to the government.

At the time specifications are developed it must be assumed that they will be used in the sealed-bids procedure and, therefore, will define the quality level above which all products will be considered homogeneous for government use.

V

The Nature of Government Contracting

When the government invites bids, the contracting procedure is largely determined by law, by the results of programs which concentrate demands and centralize requirements, and by the product definitions available. However, significant variations in contracting are open to the government buyer, affecting his chances of concluding a successful purchase.

Provisions of Contracts and Invitations to Bid

An invitation to bid is the basic document of the sealed-bids procedure. It is a quotation form which provides all information necessary for the bidder to calculate prices and which, when filled in, signed, and returned to the government agency, becomes his bid. In addition it includes all applicable contract provisions and is so written that it becomes an enforceable contract upon acceptance by signature of a responsible government officer.[1]

Standard conditions.—The standard form of government contract contains two provisions which rank with the legally required features of the sealed-bids device in their effect on the decisions of sellers as to the price to quote. One provides for price reductions and the other penalties for default.

Government term contracts have been called a "one-way street" for the reason that one standard provision requires contractors to extend to the government price reductions proportional to those extended to other customers after the date of the bid, while no provision is made for escalator clauses which raise the price to the government.[2] In effect this gains for the government an advantage

[1] See Appendix, for a copy of the standard contract form.

[2] This applies to "normal" times. Escalator clauses are used, on occasion, in periods of rapid general price advances.

corresponding to any reductions in published prices of standard items of suppliers. If the item is made to a government specification and is not standard with the supplier, the provision has no effect—and it probably has no effect in practice if the supplier makes unpublished price concessions to customers other than the government on standard items.

All contracts provide that if suppliers default on contracts, the government may terminate them by written notice, procure similar goods elsewhere, and collect from the original contractor any excess costs which may be incurred. This provision is used most frequently when the supplier delivers goods which fail to meet specifications. When this happens attempts are made to obtain prompt replacement of the substandard goods from the contractor, or, if the goods are needed badly and are useable, to negotiate a price adjustment with him which will compensate the government for the difference from contract specifications. If the contractor refuses to make a reasonably prompt adjustment, the contract is terminated and bids are invited on a contract to replace the defective goods. After the award is made, the original contractor is charged with any difference in the price if it is higher. If the goods are procured at a lower price, no charge is made against the original contractor, but repeated instances of default would provide reason for debarring him from bidding for government contracts.

The importance of strict observance of the terms of the contract, particularly those relating to commodity specifications, is accentuated by this default provision. Contractors who are well established, and who have sufficient technical competence and quality control over their production to work to specifications, experience no difficulty because of this provision. It does serve, however, to discourage firms which do not have such competence or quality control from bidding on government contracts because default on a sizable contract by a small firm may well result in financial failure. This provision is a logical and necessary counterpart of the policy of awarding contracts to any low bidder who is considered responsible by the necessarily broad standards of responsibility.

Special conditions.—The special conditions appended to the standard contracts can be grouped into (1) those serving to define the commodity and its utility, (2) those directly affecting the price to be quoted, and (3) those requiring information to facilitate future contracting and the placing of orders under term contracts.

The conditions which concern the commodity, in addition to

the requirement that it be according to specification, may include any of the following: (1) the submission of samples with the bid, (2) the submission of certified test reports showing the quality of the material to be shipped, (3) special inspection requirements, (4) the requirement to name the manufacturer if wholesalers or jobbers are expected to bid, and (5) any labeling necessary to identify the goods with the shipper or the production batch. These provisions are to insure that the government receives bids on and delivery of goods of the quality it has decided to buy.

Provisions directly affecting the prices quoted include the requirement that prices cover delivery to specified points. This may require submission of a number of prices for a single item to cover deliveries f.o.b. various destinations. On term contracts maximum quantities on individual orders are specified. This protects both the government and the supplier. At times when prices are stable or declining, this provision offers the government the alternative of purchasing large quantities on definite-quantity-definite-delivery contracts. At all times it protects the supplier from possible default when very large orders would make it difficult or impossible for him to meet the delivery requirements of the contract; and in times of rising prices it permits him to avoid delivering large quantities at low contract prices.

Invitations to bid on term contracts require information necessary for future contracting and for placing orders under the contracts for which bids are invited, such as periodic reports by contractors on the value of purchases by the ordering agencies. When multiple awards are made on groups of items contractors are required to provide the government with sufficient copies, usually 2,000, of their price lists for distribution to the agencies which will place orders under the contracts.

Other provisions of invitations to bid.—If special considerations are to enter the determination of awards, they are explicitly stated in the invitation. This is a matter of policy adopted to place all bidders on an equal footing and to avoid public criticism, rather than a requirement of law, because the law empowers the government to make award to the bidder whose offer is "most advantageous to the Government."

These provisions regarding awards may reserve the right to make dual or multiple awards where alternative sources are desirable to assure adequate supply or to reduce shipping costs; they may provide for awards on the aggregate price for a group of items rather than on prices for individual items; they may provide for qualification testing in advance of submitting bids and, in a very few instances, for evaluation of the utility of the product above that specified.

Contracting Procedure

Sealed bids.—Action on a purchase contract begins with the receipt by the buyer of an approved purchase authority. Using the information supplied on the purchase authority the buyer selects the appropriate commodity specification, normally a Federal Specification or, if there is none, an agency specification, and prepares the invitation to bid. Copies of the invitation are mailed to prospective bidders, posted in the offices of the Federal Supply Service, and sent to the Department of Commerce where an abstract is teletyped to the Department's regional offices and made available there to prospective bidders.

Normally invitations are sent and bids received by mail. The interval between mailing and the official opening of bids may be any reasonable length of time, usually from ten days to two months, depending on the nature of the trade, the location of prospective bidders, the complexity of the product, and whether or not subcontractors are used by contractors. Where delivery requirements or market conditions for the product do not allow sufficient time for use of the mails, bids may be telegraphed. Invitations and the bids must, however, be written; they cannot be made orally.

Bids are kept sealed as they are received, in a locked compartment until the specified hour and date of opening. Then they are publicly opened, read, and recorded. Any interested person may attend the opening and copy any information from the bids. The bids are then tabulated and evaluated. The award is recommended, approved, and the bid becomes a contract upon acceptance by signature of a qualified government official. Copies of the tabulations and the considerations affecting the awards are preserved and made available to anyone. The successful bidder is notified of the award, perhaps simply by the issuance of the purchase order. He then delivers the specified material and sends his invoice for payment. The invoice is held until the goods are received, inspected, and officially accepted by the agency for which the purchase was made, and is then paid.

The two crucial points in the procedure are advertising for bids and the award of contracts.

Advertising for Bids

Advertising for bids is of crucial importance because it is a principal determinant of the number of bidders who compete for contracts. The bidders' lists, which are the basis for advertising, are compilations of names accumulated during decades of purchasing experience from which, repeatedly, the names of sources holding no promise of developing into successful bidders have been eliminated. Inclusive lists provide the essential means of obtaining effective competition, but they do result in considerable administrative expense in duplicating and mailing invitations to bid.

The general rule is that any seller may have his name placed on the bidders' list simply by request and that the government may remove the name of any bidder who fails to respond to three successive invitations. The government buyers may, of course, and often do, add the names of any promising sources they may discover in the course of their work.

The number of suppliers who are invited to bid varies from 15 to 1,000 depending on how many lists are necessary to cover all items.

When advertising is by telegraph, three or more—usually more—names of suppliers from whom favorable quotations can be expected are selected from bidders' lists, and invitations are sent only to them.

The problem of insuring that all favorable prospective bidders are notified of the issuance of invitations to bid has always been difficult for government officials. It is politically not feasible and perhaps economically risky to limit bidders' lists to half a dozen or a dozen suppliers as is done in private purchasing. All those who desire to receive invitations to bid and who respond to them must be kept on the lists. On the other hand the mere existence of lists does not insure that the maximum potential competition is obtained. Certainty that the lists are adequate could come only from intimate knowledge of the industry and channels of distribution from primary producers to the various points at which the government might buy, and a constant revision of lists in the light of such knowledge. Attempts have been made periodically to provide market-research programs which, among other results, would increase the effectiveness of the invitation procedure, but Congress has repeatedly reduced the funds for such work in appropriation bills.

Awards.—An invitation to bid may be for one or thousands of items and may result in the award of one or more than one hundred contracts. For example, the invitation to bid for Class 51, Part 1, Drugs, Medicinal, Laboratory and Industrial Chemicals, includes not only many items for which prices are quoted directly, but also complete lines of laboratory, industrial, medicinal and special chemicals, pharmaceutical preparations, and biological products which are listed in the contractors' catalogs and for which prices are quoted on the basis of discounts to the government for all items listed in the catalogs. For this class of items there are 132 contractors.

Contracts may be let not only for each item, if different bidders are low for different items, but for different delivery points for a single item, if bids are invited for prices in that fashion. This is illustrated in Table 15 which presents bids offered in response to such an invitation. In the case shown bids were invited on one item for delivery in various quantities to eight supply centers scattered throughout the country. Of the 14 bidders who responded to the invitation the bids of 6 were rejected because the samples submitted failed to meet specifications or because the bids were not responsive to other requirements of the invitation. Contracts were awarded to 3 of the remaining 8 bidders whose bids were low for one or more different destinations.

Usually the award of contracts to successful bidders is an automatic process that offers few, if any, complications. The bids are first tabulated. If the low bids are not responsive to the invitation, notes are made on the tabulation explaining the reasons. The responsibility of the bidders is either known from past experience or, if not, can be checked through information readily available. Award is then made to the lowest responsible bidder whose bid meets all requirements of the invitation. Problems arise where (1) the responsibility of the low bidder is open to question, (2) there are duplicate low bids, and (3) prices are judged to be unreasonable.

When the responsibility of the low bidder is open to question, the judgment of the contracting officer is heavily influenced by legal and political considerations. On the one hand he is charged with making a sound economic decision to protect the interest of the government, and on the other hand he must be prepared to defend his decision to the General Accounting Office and possibly to the rejected bidder's congressman. He is, therefore, not free, as a private buyer is, simply to reject the bid if he is convinced that accepting it involves some risk of subsequent difficulties of slow delivery, receipt of substandard goods, or even default on the contract by the supplier. The situation might be summed up by saying that in government contracting the low bidder is considered to be responsible unless the buyer proves beyond doubt that he is not. The test is often whether or not the bidder can buy a performance bond. The effect of this policy is consistent with the underlying theory of sealed bids. Contracting is kept open to the maximum number of sources of supply even at the cost of some additional risk of subsequent difficulties in fulfillment of the contract conditions by suppliers.

If the lowest prices of responsive and responsible bidders are tied, the award is made to the bidder whose bid offers the government extra value over the minimum specified in the invitation to bid. This may be quicker delivery, a longer period within which time discounts can be taken, better maintenance or servicing agreements, installation service, or better product quality. If the low bids are identical in all these respects and one bidder employs fewer than 500 persons, award is made to him in order to encourage small business concerns.[3] If all tied bidders employ either fewer or more than 500 persons, the award is made by lot. If in the opinion of the administrator of the General Services Administration tie bids reflect collusive bidding, he may reject them and refer the matter to the Department of Justice for possible action under the antitrust laws. In fact, however, the evidence rarely leads the administrator to take such action.

If all prices quoted on an invitation are judged to be unreasonable, several courses are open to the purchasing official. It may be that the using agency is able to postpone its purchase until a more favorable market develops. The government's demand for almost all the goods it requires, however, is not postponable without considerable loss of efficiency and is inelastic over wide price ranges. For this reason the term "unreasonable" does not normally mean that the price is so high that the government will forego purchasing

[3] This policy was adopted in response to various inquiries from congressional committees interested in the problems of small business. Occasionally it is possible to make awards on the basis of the size of the firm. For example, in response to the invitation for bids on stencil paper (item no. 53-P-20836-b-2) term contracts for December 1, 1950—November 30, 1951, the bids of A. B. Dick and Co. and the Frankel Carbon and Ribbon Co. were tied for delivery to zones 2 and 3 at $1.82 per package of 2 quires in quantities of 50 to 249 packages. Award was made to the Frankel Carbon and Ribbon Co. because they employed fewer than 500 persons while A. B. Dick and Co. employed more than 500.

TABLE 15

TOILET TISSUE[a]: BIDDERS' PRICES AND CONTRACTS AWARDED ON A TYPICAL INVITATION TO BID

(Net prices per carton, f.o.b. destination. Definite-quantity contracts for delivery to various federal supply centers, awarded May 27, 1948. Prices of successful bidders in bold face.)

Bidders	Destination and quantity							
	Washington 3800 cartons	Cleveland 300 cartons	Chicago 610 cartons	Atlanta 650 cartons	Fort Worth 450 cartons	Kansas City 650 cartons	San Francisco 300 cartons	Seattle 650 cartons
Park Tissue Mills, Inc.[b]	7.21	7.29	7.37	7.36	7.69	7.53	7.97	7.97
Raycarr Sales Co.[c]	9.19	9.34	9.47	9.44	10.01	9.74	10.86	10.19
White Washburne Co., Inc.[d]	9.80	10.03	9.93	9.97	10.43	10.19	11.80	10.78
Paper Service Co., Inc.[e]	9.85	9.85	9.85	9.85	9.85	9.85	9.85	9.85
Walker Goulard Plehn Co., Inc.	**9.89**	**9.64**	10.07	**10.17**	10.92	10.43	11.52	**11.00**
Inlander Steindler Paper Co.[f]	10.15	10.15	10.15	10.15	10.15	10.15	10.15	10.15
Winchester Paper Co.	10.20	10.20	10.20	10.20	10.20	10.20	10.20	10.20
International Cellucotton Products Co.[g]	11.23	11.23	11.23	11.23	11.23	11.23	11.23	11.23
Marcallus Falls Paper Mills, Inc.	11.28	11.56	11.45	11.48	12.05	11.76	13.72	12.51
S. Freedman and Sons	11.38	.....	.....	.....	.....	.....	.....	.....
Hanover Paper Corp.	10.91	.....	.....	.....	.....	.....	.....	.....
Howard Paper Co.	.....	.....	.....	10.39	.....	.....	.....	.....
Wexler Paper Products	.....	.....	**10.05**	.....	**10.58**	.....	**11.49**	.....
Wertgame Paper Co.	.....	.....	.....	.....	.....	**7.37**	.....	.....

SOURCE: Based on data in the contract files of the Federal Supply Service, Washington, D.C.

[a] In 1000-sheet rolls, 100 rolls to the carton, in accordance with Federal Specification no. UU-P-556b and Amendment 1, Type i.

[b] Bid rejected; quotation based on 650-sheet roll, no sample submitted.

[c] Bid rejected; sample failed to meet specification requirements. Weight basis of sample: 10 pounds (specification: 11.5 pounds minimum), absorbency: 145 seconds (specification: 120 seconds maximum), sample contained many small holes (specification requires paper reasonably free from holes).

[d] Bid rejected; sample failed to meet specification requirements. Absorbency of sample tested: 137 seconds (specification: 120 seconds maximum).

[e] Bid rejected; prices quoted f.o.b. mill, location of mill not given.

[f] Bid rejected; prices quoted f.o.b. mill, Lititz, Pa.

[g] Bid rejected; quotation based on 850-sheet roll, sample failed to meet specification requirements. Weight basis of sample tested: 10.4 pounds (specification: 11.5 pounds minimum).

the item, but that it is high as compared with prices which can be expected by alternative methods of purchasing.

One alternative is to reject all bids and re-advertise. This serves notice on bidders that the previous prices were considered unreasonable by the government and at times induces new bidders to quote more favorable prices. It also provides the government an opportunity to vary the quantities, commodity specifications, or other requirements of the invitation to suit current market conditions and thus obtain better quotations.

If the contract is for consolidated requirements of a number of agencies, the bids may be rejected and local purchases authorized. In times of rapidly rising prices local suppliers may quote lower prices than primary sources.

In times of extremely severe shortages of raw materials the administrator may determine that conditions are so stringent that in order to get supplies it is necessary to negotiate contracts with individual suppliers based on new specifications and terms which fit individual circumstances. In such situations he may decide to make use of the exception to the law for "supplies or services for which it is impracticable to secure competition" and reject all bids in favor of negotiated contracts.

Negotiation.—As in sealed bids, the contracting procedure in negotiation is initiated by the receipt of an approved purchase authority or a stock replenishment request. From that point until the award and signing of the contract, however, the buyer is free to use whatever procedure he believes will result in the most favorable contract for the government. Once the contract is signed, the steps for completing the contract procedure are the same as when sealed bids are used.

Importance of sealed bids and negotiation.—In federal-government purchasing during normal times when demand does not exceed capacity, negotiation is used principally for special military equipment, supplies, and services, and for critical materials—items which have been excluded from consideration in this study. It is also used for small purchases and for buying urgently needed goods, both of these being instances where the law exempts the transactions from the requirement that sealed bids be used. In these instances, however, buyers typically use an impersonal, competitive bidding procedure which differs from the sealed-bids procedure only in that fewer bids are solicited, and the bids may be made orally. Negotiation by conference, with a view to arriving at a settlement of differences, is used by civilian agencies principally where the nature of the product or the magnitude of the government's demand requires awards of contracts to the single available source or to all sources of supply.

In the following chapters emphasis is placed on the operation of the sealed-bids device because of its dominant importance in purchasing by civilian agencies. Negotiation is discussed only in those instances where it is the method chosen in the purchase of important items.

In order to analyze the effectiveness of the sealed-bids device, as we shall in the following chapters, it is necessary to compare it with some alternative device, or devices. These can be found in the practices of large-quantity private buyers.

Alternative Contracting Devices

The sealed-bids device which is characteristic of government buying and the various devices used in private purchasing are, from the economic viewpoint, alternative methods which could be used either by private or public buyers. The distinctive differences which cause them to operate with different effects are, however, largely the result of differences in the nature of public and private purchasing.

Comparison of governmental and private contracting.—The government buyer is responsible ultimately to the public for the legality and administrative wisdom of his decisions. The General Accounting Office and Congress attempt constantly to insure that the letter of the law and its interpretations are observed by purchasing officials. In consequence, every transaction is reviewed to insure that it cannot be subjected to criticism by any citizen who is a competitor for government contracts. The executive head of the purchasing agency, and more remotely the president through the Bureau of the Budget, supervise the administrative decisions. In fact, Congress, through its appropriation powers, exercises as strong a control over such decisions as the executive branch. This occurs not only when appropriation bills are acted upon, but throughout the year. Hardly a week passes during which there is not some inquiry from congressmen regarding contracts and awards.

The past history of recurrent scandals in government contracting and the ever-present possibility of pressure from disgruntled bidders applied through congressmen has led purchasing officials to be very conservative in making administrative decisions. Government buyers have developed the maxim that "a contract must not only be right, it must look right." The net result of these forces has been the development of the strict legal controls over contracting described in Chapter II and the impersonal, objective, and relatively inflexible administrative procedures operative within the legal limits which have been described above.

In contrast, the private buyer is legally free to employ any procedure he chooses. Administratively he is responsible through the officials and directors of the company to a relatively few stockholders, all of whom are principally concerned that the firm make a profit. His decisions regarding such matters as numbers of bidders, methods of award, and disclosure of bid and contract prices can be based simply on economic considerations. The result has been the development of buying devices, described below, which in general are less objective, more personal, and more flexible than the sealed-bids device.

Private contracting policies.—Private buyers usually limit the number of sellers who are invited to bid on contracts. All vendors who are not considered to be acceptable as suppliers are excluded even though their bids, if solicited, might be low. In addition, bids are requested only from those acceptable vendors who are expected to bid favorably. According to a survey conducted by the National Association of Purchasing Agents, private buyers believe that sufficient competition is secured if bidding is limited to six or eight potentially satisfactory suppliers.[4] Only about 20 per cent of the companies responding to the N.A.P.A. survey stated that they require competitive bidding on all purchases, the remaining 80 per cent reporting a flexible policy.

A large number of firms use competitive bidding when an item is first procured, for purposes of exploring the market. After their experience with a number of contracts has satisfied them that they have developed acceptable sources, they shift to the policy of purchasing without competition from these sources until they find some reason to suspect that further recourse to competitive bidding

[4] N.A.P.A., *Handbook of Purchasing Policies and Procedures* (New York: 1942), II. The N.A.P.A. sent a comprehensive questionnaire which contained questions regarding all facets of purchasing policy to its more than 500 member purchasing agents. The largest number of these were industrial buyers, although a few were institutional and government buyers. All sizes of firms were included as were most, if not all, of the important industries. The *Handbook* was composed largely of summaries of the answers to this questionnaire with discussions of their significance. No statements were used unless they were based on replies of at least 200 purchasing agents.

will result in lower prices from equally acceptable sources. In view of these practices, it appears that heavy reliance is placed on the skill of purchasing agents in selecting sources that will offer the best prices and products. These practices are also a reflection of the often-repeated opinion of private buyers that price is not the most important factor in awarding contracts.[5]

Seventy-seven per cent of the respondents to the N.A.P.A. questionnaire stated that they require quotations to be final as submitted by bidders. These answers, however, were accompanied by important qualifications. Generally speaking, changes prompted by reasons other than simple price revisions are permitted. These include price changes made possible by the bidders' suggestions to adjust specifications to allow cost savings, and revisions considered reasonable because of any significant changes in cost occurring during the time between the submission of bids and the making of awards.[6] Thus significant negotiations are possible in private contracting after bids are submitted. It is generally felt, however, that if the buyer has a reputation of allowing quotations to be revised at the seller's option after they are submitted, the result will be higher bids in prospect of subsequent bargaining which would serve only to increase the complexity and expense of contracting without bringing any lower price at the completion of the process.

Specific information on the extent to which different methods of product definition are used in private purchasing is not available, but it is clear that two policies, or variations of them, are widely used.

One policy of product definition is the use of objective specifications. Many companies prepare their own specifications, and also use nationally accepted specifications when they are available. According to the same N.A.P.A. survey, 31 per cent of the companies reporting used Federal Specifications to some extent; 44 per cent used specifications of the American Society for Testing Materials; 41 per cent, those of the American Society of Mechanical Engineers; 49 per cent, those of the Society of Automotive Engineers; 44 per cent, those of the Underwriters Laboratories, and 24 per cent, those of the National Safety Council.[7] The survey did not reveal the extent to which any one company used these or

[5] *Ibid.* (1939), I, 227.
[6] *Ibid.*, p. 369.
[7] *Ibid.*, p. 261.

other specifications, so it really discloses little except that a substantial number of companies use national specifications to some extent in their purchasing.

The other method of product definition common in private purchasing is the use of "approved products lists." There is a variety of methods of approving products included in such lists, but essentially it means purchasing, by brand names, products which have been examined by the purchasing agents and other interested officials of the firm and found to be acceptable. The examination may be visual or by tests in laboratories or in production processes, and the inspection upon receipt of the goods may similarly vary. The important point is that principal reliance is placed on the brand name rather than objective specification for judging the quality of the product.

Private purchasers generally reserve the right to make awards on any basis that appears to be most profitable for the firm. In addition to price, quality differences of various offers, reciprocity, continuity of supply, and the avoidance of troublesome adjustments may be considered. At times, factors other than price are given heavy weight in making awards.[8] Characteristically purchases are made from more than one firm to help insure continuity of supply in case of work stoppages or shortages of materials.

Private buyers generally treat all quotations and contract prices as confidential and withhold such information from bidders and the public generally. Ninety-six per cent of the purchasing agents queried by the N.A.P.A. reported that quotations were considered to be "entirely confidential,"[9] and half of them reported that the price is even omitted from one or more copies of invoices for the same reason.[10] The principal reason for this practice is well stated in the *N.A.P.A. Handbook:* "When vendors generally recognize that a buyer deals confidentially with their quotations they are much more apt to give him the benefit of their best price treatment. Conversely, if they have reason to believe their quotations are likely to become public property, they are bound to withhold certain concessions that might otherwise be extended."[11] Another reason is that if awards are not made on a previously announced

[8] Cf. Howard T. Lewis, *Procurement* (Chicago: Richard D. Irwin, Inc., 1948), p. 534 and Stuart F. Heinritz, *Purchasing* (New York: Prentice-Hall, 1947), p. 235.

[9] *N.A.P.A. Handbook,* I, 370.

[10] *Ibid.,* II, 26–27.

[11] *Ibid.,* I, 370.

Elements of the buying devices	Federal-government device sealed bids	Large-scale private buyers' devices	
		Limited competitive bids based on objective specifications	Limited competitive bids based on approved products lists
Number of suppliers invited to bid	Bidding open to all responsible sellers	Bidding limited to a few—about six—preselected prospectively favorable sources of supply	Same
Permitted negotiation after bids are submitted	Bids retained sealed until public opening, no negotiation permitted	Bids considered to be final as submitted, but negotiation permitted except for price cutting	Same
Method of product definition	Objective commodity specifications wherever possible	Objective commodity specifications	Lists of approved products defined by brand names
Award of contracts	Single award to the responsible bidder offering lowest price for product meeting requirements of Federal Specifications	Often multiple or rotating awards to encourage continuity of supply	Same
Public accessibility to bid and contract information	Public accessibility to all bidders' prices and to basis for making awards	All bid and contract information held in strict confidence	Same
Contract enforcement policy	Rigorous enforcement of contract provisions, including those providing penalties for default	Reasonably strict enforcement of contracts, but adjustments allowed where they are deemed conducive to long-run profit interests	Same

Fig. 3. Comparison of Sealed Bids With Contracting Devices Commonly Used by Large-Scale Private Buyers.

and generally known basis, bidders may question why they were not awarded contracts and the explanations might involve considerable expense and trouble.

Sealed Bids and Alternative Devices

The next four chapters will assess the effectiveness of government contracting in bringing low prices by competition. For this purpose it is necessary to compare the operation of the sealed-bids device with alternative devices which reasonably might be employed by the government. Two such devices have been selected because they typify the methods most widely used by private large-quantity buyers who often purchase in the same markets as the government. For purposes of convenience they are both labeled "limited competitive bids." The difference between the two devices lies in the product policy, the price policy being the same; one is based on objective specifications while the other is based on approved products lists.

The essential differences between the elements of the three devices, (1) sealed bids, (2) limited competitive bids based on objective specifications, and (3) limited competitive bids based on approved products lists are shown in Figure 3. In general, the sealed-bids device is more rigorously designed to evoke competition, but is less flexible than the other devices. When the sealed-bids device is used all prospective responsible suppliers are permitted to bid, no negotiation is permitted after bids are submitted, awards are made to single low bidders, the public is permitted access to bid and contract information, and contracts are rigorously enforced. In contrast, if the limited-competitive-bids devices are used, bidding is severely restricted, negotiation may be permitted after bids are received, specifications are not used in many instances, the basis for award is more flexible and multiple awards are often made, all bid and contract information is kept confidential, and, while enforcement is usually strict, adjustments in quantities, prices, and delivery terms may be made when they are considered to be reasonable.

VI

Buying Homogeneous Products in Competitive Markets

Classification of Markets

The government's buying policy operates with varying effects in different markets depending on the price and product policies of the sellers and the persistence with which they adhere to them. This and the following three chapters will present evidence on the operation of government purchasing policies.

The markets from which the evidence is taken are divided into two broad categories: (1) markets in which the price offers of sellers reflect competitive bidding for government contracts and (2) markets in which the price offers of sellers reflect adherence to their established stable or uniform prices rather than the results of direct price competition. The criteria used to place markets for particular commodities in one class or the other are: (1) whether or not price offers of all bidders for each contract and of particular bidders for successive contracts present a range of different prices, and (2) whether or not the prices quoted to the government reflect decisions made in apparent independence of any established policies of sellers to quote stable or uniform prices. The first criterion is insufficient by itself because differences in bids for government contracts may simply reflect different stable prices and not competitive bidding.

In all markets in which sellers bid competitively, the government assumes that all products meeting the commodity specification are homogeneous. In order to help disclose the effectiveness of this policy, these markets have been further classified according to the characteristics of the products as they are viewed by sellers and buyers other than the government. These subclasses are: (1) markets for homogeneous products, discussed in the present chapter,

(2) markets for differentiated products, discussed in Chapter VII, and (3) markets for government specification products, discussed in Chapter VIII. The markets for differentiated products are subdivided into those in which, according to the judgment of the government, the products are differentiated in a measure of significance to the government and those which are not.

The common characteristic of the markets, where the price offers for government contracts reflect adherence to established stable or uniform prices, is that the sealed-bids device is ineffective. These markets are subclassified according to the cause of this ineffectiveness—either the firmness with which sellers adhere to their established price policies alone, or firmness supported by successful policies of product differentiation. Both types of markets are discussed in Chapter IX. In the markets of the first type, the government regards the products as homogeneous and attempts to obtain price competition by use of the sealed-bids method. In the markets of the second type, substitute products are sufficiently different in the government's opinion to make the policy of assuming product homogeneity in purchasing inappropriate, with the consequence that contracts are awarded, without direct price competition, at prevalent prices to the sole manufacturer of the differentiated product. In both types of markets the government must supplement the simple application of the sealed-bids device with other measures to increase its chances of buying at the most favorable price.

The classification outlined above groups the markets in the order of their competitiveness as viewed by private buyers and sellers. From this viewpoint the most competitive markets are those for homogeneous products where sellers bid competitively to the government; the number of buyers and sellers is relatively large, buyers generally consider the products of rival sellers to be homogeneous and are, therefore, able to make precise comparisons of competitive offers, and the emphasis in bidding to private buyers as well as to the government is on price competition rather than product differentiation. The markets where products are differentiated, but where the government policy evokes price competition, are less competitive from the viewpoint of most private buyers; stable and in some cases uniform prices prevail, most private buyers do not make precise product comparisons, and sellers ordinarily find it unnecessary to resort to direct price competition. The markets of the final group, in which the sealed-bids device evokes no price competition, are also the least competitive from the viewpoint of all buyers. In some markets suppliers are numerous and the products essentially homogeneous, and yet price competition is avoided because all sellers effectively adhere to uniform price policies. In many other markets direct competition is avoided by successful product differentiation. Patents, heavy investment in tools, heavy investment in distribution organization and facilities, or investment in sales and advertising promotion effectively retard entry of competitors who might evoke price competition.

Actual markets are often difficult to fit into any classification because their characteristics vary in gradual progression from one to the other, and also because they are constantly changing. Some markets fit quite clearly into a particular class, others could logically be fitted into more than one classification.

Characteristics of Markets for Homogeneous Products

Competitive products are "homogeneous" if the buyer believes they are equally useful in filling his needs. The products discussed below are homogeneous in the sense that the government and some other buyers consider the competitive offerings of sellers to be substantially equal in utility with respect to substantially the same needs. Sellers in these markets do pursue policies aimed at differentiating their products, largely stressing the nonphysical attributes of the product, such as delivery and, sometimes, service in the form of technical advice, but in the main they must underbid their competitors to obtain business.

The government often buys in primary markets, but sometimes in intermediate wholesale markets. At all times, however, manufacturers, intermediate wholesalers, jobbers, agents, or retailers may bid for contracts. Typically, either manufacturers or wholesalers are successful bidders. It is at these stages in the channel of distribution that the products are homogeneous; almost all of them are differentiated by brand names and advertised claims of distinction at later stages, and particularly at retail.

The products purchased in these markets are quantitatively important in government procurement. They include many processed foods, paper products, and construction and maintenance materials.

The relevant and more detailed characteristics of markets, such as the types of products, number of sellers, and related markets for each illustrative product will be discussed along with the evidence on prices and bidding.[1]

Paint

Characteristics of markets and government contracting.—There are in the paint industry many small-scale manufacturers of products which can be formulated to given specifications economically in quantities typically purchased by the government. The efficient technological unit is within the resources of small as well as large

TABLE 16

Paint Industry: Distribution by Size of Establishment, of the Number of Establishments, Employees, and Value Added by Manufacture

Size of establishments (number of employees)	Number of establishments	Per cent of total	Total number of employees	Per cent of total	Value added by manufacture (thousands of dollars)	Per cent of total
1-19.........	779	60	5,403	10	43,972	10
20-499........	501	39	39,426	74	348,957	74
500-2,499......	11	1	8,583	16	76,655	16
Total......	1,291	100	53,412	100	469,584	100

Source: Adapted from data given in *Paint, Varnish, and Lacquer Handbook*, 1950 edition, National Paint, Varnish, and Lacquer Association, Washington, D.C.

establishments. For the most part small as well as larger companies use the same types of mills for grinding and mixing the ingredients of paint.

The 1947 figures in Table 16 from the Bureau of the Census show that 1,280 of the 1,291 establishments in the industry had fewer than 500 employees and contributed 84 per cent of the value added by manufacture. Additional data from the same source show that production is scattered throughout the country with heavy concentration in the New York and northeastern New Jersey, Chicago, San Francisco, Philadelphia, and Los Angeles metropolitan areas.

From the viewpoint of distribution, output is classified as (1) trade sales and (2) industrial sales. Trade sales comprise all kinds of packaged paints sold through various wholesale and retail channels. These paints are standard items for each company and are

[1] The evidence presented in chaps. vi–ix was obtained from the files of the Federal Supply Service, Washington, D.C., and from buyers and suppliers of each commodity except where stated otherwise.

sold under brand names backed, with various degrees of effectiveness, by the usual techniques of product differentiation, such as periodical and newspaper advertising, dealers' display aids, and direct-mail promotion. A few of the largest companies, such as Sherwin Williams and Glidden, distribute and advertise their products nationally through company-owned stores and authorized wholesale and dealer channels. Others distribute regionally through wholesalers and dealers, while the majority rely on local distribution, and upon relatively few outlets.

Industrial sales include all paints which are made either to buyers' specifications or to formulae developed by the company to meet specific and typical coating problems. Most of these paints are used as finishes for manufactured products. Usually they differ in quality from the standard packaged paints sold as trade sales, but some are the same as the branded products. All are typically sold on quantity contracts directly to users by paint manufacturers. Many producers specialize in industrial sales. Government requirements for civilian agencies are for paints which are similar in formulae to those sold as trade sales, but are classified as industrial sales because they are made to meet Federal Specifications and are sold by manufacturers directly to the government.

The government buys paint at its 12 supply centers on definite-quantity-definite-delivery contracts for the commonly used items and on federal-supply-schedule term contracts for less frequently used items.[2] The following discussion of the purchase of white enamel paint illustrates the operation of government buying of paints.

Price comparisons.—The prices paid by the government for interior white enamel paint on definite-quantity contracts for delivery in Washington, D.C., are shown in Figure 4 for the period from April 1, 1948 through May 4, 1950. The Bureau of Labor Statistics mill prices for the nearest comparable commodity are also shown.

Contract prices varied during the period from $1.59 per gallon in April, 1948, to $2.17 in May of the same year and then settled to a level close to $1.50 from October, 1949, through May, 1950. These prices are considerably lower than the average wholesale prices collected by the Bureau of Labor Statistics which varied from about $4.00 to $4.50 during the same period. A part of the

[2] In the fall of 1950 term contracts for paint were discontinued because sellers were uncertain about future costs and their ability to deliver paints.

difference in prices may be accounted for by the fact that the Bureau of Labor Statistics figures included tinted as well as white enamels and were for paint delivered in one-gallon instead of five-gallon containers, but the resulting higher costs would be at least in part offset by the fact that the government prices included freight.

The quality of the paint priced by the Bureau of Labor Statistics is also said to be higher, but it is considered by the government to

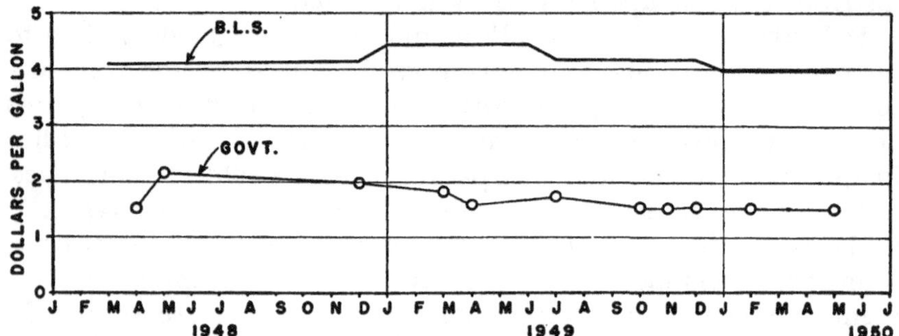

Fig. 4. Interior Enamel Paint: Government-Contract Prices and Mill Wholesale Prices.

Source: For government-contract prices, Table A, Appendix; for mill wholesale prices, *Average Wholesale Prices and Index Numbers of Individual Commodities*, Bureau of Labor Statistics. The government-contract prices are for white enamel only, f.o.b. Washington, D.C., in five-gallon containers. The Bureau figures are mill prices, f.o.b. plant for white and tinted enamel in one-gallon containers.

be no more suitable for its purposes than that of the paint it buys. As the government buys in no larger amounts than batch or run quantities usual in the industry, the largest part of the difference in these prices is attributable to the different price policies applied by paint companies when selling to the government and when selling to wholesalers, retailers, and industrial users. This is consistent with the opinion of informed sources that the government buys paint at lower prices than any other large-quantity purchaser.

Costs.—No specific information is available to compare these prices with costs, but obviously manufacturers' costs vary. Federal Specifications are performance specifications and different combinations of raw materials may be used to obtain paints which meet the specific requirements. Thus, the cost of raw materials per gallon of paint may be different for different manufacturers, but the cost of particular ingredients should be relatively constant for all makers, except for ordinary price fluctuations. Labor costs vary with locality and also, to some extent, with the particular method of organizing production. Some firms, for example, may reduce unit labor costs by running mills all night with no one but the watchman to check their operation. On the whole, costs of materials and direct labor should be reasonably uniform for all manufacturers. The effects of different calculations of overhead costs are discussed later.

Analysis of bidding.—The prices offered by bidders for the 11 contracts let in the three-year period, 1948–1950, are summarized in the frequency distribution shown in Figure 5. Only those firms which bid in response to more than two invitations are included in the distribution, because those which bid once or twice quoted high prices and were not active competitors. The figure shows the number of bids in each ten-cent price class, from that in which the successful bidder's price fell, up to that in which the highest price fell.

Two facts revealed by this frequency distribution are of outstanding interest. First, for any one contract, there is an extremely wide range of prices quoted and an absence of any pronounced central tendency for prices to cluster at any particular position. Second, there is a tendency for a number of prices offered in response to many of the invitations to cluster around the prices at which the immediately previous contract was awarded, with one or more quotations dropping below the previous contract price.

The wide range of quoted prices is partly explained by the fact that each contract is awarded independently. Neither past experience, nor prospect of satisfactory supply by a bidder in the future can be given consideration by the government in making current awards. Thus, firms do not prejudice their supply relationship with the government either by failing to bid or by bidding high prices.

A study of the quotations of individual bidders shows that many firms bid for contracts. Almost all of them bid sporadically, but the successful bidders are among those which show some continued interest in bidding. Thus, the number of bidders for each contract (including the one- and two-time bidders who were excluded from the frequency distribution) varied from 23 to 63, and over the three-year period, during which the 11 contracts were awarded, 125 different firms bid on this item. The consistency with which firms bid is shown below. More than half of the firms bid for only 1 or 2 contracts and only one-third bid for 6 or more of the 11 contracts. All awards were to firms which bid 6 or more times, and 7 of the 11 contracts were awarded to firms which bid for only 6 or 7 of the contracts. Although most of these firms bid sporadically, they showed a continual interest in bidding (Table 17).

No one firm was consistently the successful bidder. The 11 contracts examined were awarded to 7 different firms, 4 of which received 2 contracts each and 3 one contract each. The prices bid

TABLE 17

RELATION BETWEEN SUCCESS IN BIDDING AND FREQUENCY OF BIDDING FOR WHITE ENAMEL-PAINT CONTRACTS
(April, 1948–May, 1950)

Number of firms (A total of 125 firms bid on 11 invitations.)	Number of contracts for which bids were submitted by each firm in first column	Number of contracts awarded to the group of firms in first column
47	1	0
21	2	0
10	3	0
8	4	0
2	5	0
13	6	3
9	7	4
6	8	1
3	9	1
5	10	0
1	11	2

SOURCE: Compiled from information in the files of the Federal Supply Service, Washington, D.C.

by these 7 firms were consistently lower than the prices bid by most of the firms which received no awards (Table A, Appendix). Still they varied considerably in comparison with the low bids. Many firms pursue consistently the policy of bidding on all contracts during periods when they need the business, with the expectation of occasionally receiving an award. The cost of bidding is negligible, and there is always a chance that an otherwise low bidder will not bid on the current contract. An analysis of awards made on all paint contracts let by the government which totaled $10,000 or more, shows a similar wide distribution of awards among bidders as that for the 11 white enamel paint contracts; 388 contracts were awarded to 122 contractors.[3]

[3] *Summary of Awards Subject to the Walsh-Healey Public Contracts Act, July 1948—July 1949* (Washington: National Paint, Varnish and Lacquer Association), mimeographed.

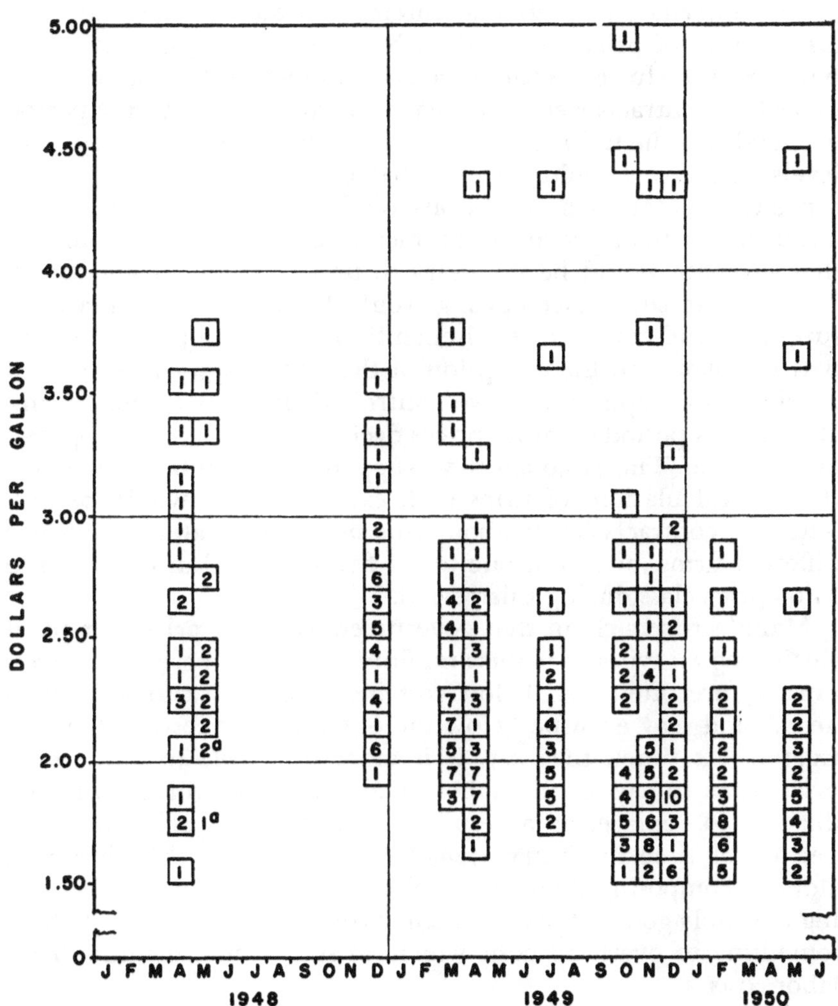

Fig. 5. Distribution of Prices Bid for 11 White Enamel-Paint Contracts, April, 1948–March, 1949.

The number of bids in each 10-cent price interval is noted in each square. Prices are dollars per gallon, f.o.b. Washington, D.C.

Source: Table A, Appendix.

[a]Bids were rejected because they were based on furnishing a product not meeting specifications.

The other fact of particular interest revealed by the frequency distribution of prices bid is that, beginning in 1949, numbers of bids begin to cluster in the price classes in which the immediately preceding contracts were awarded. This coincided with the period when sales in the industry were declining somewhat from past high levels, and firms could be expected occasionally to have excess capacity.[4] Under such conditions bidders would be expected to quote lower than previous contract prices by whatever amount they estimate would be necessary to underbid their competitors. The limit to such price cutting would be their marginal costs of supplying the contract requirements. During 1949 and the first part of 1950, with the exception of the July, 1949, contract, such considerations appear to have controlled the bids of most firms. During this period contract prices declined from $2.17 to approximately $1.50. The $1.50 figure was apparently the minimum which the cost calculations of firms with excess capacity would permit. The five contracts let at about this figure were awarded to five different firms, but from one to six firms bid within the $1.50 to $1.60 price class during this period.

Manufacturers claim that government-contract prices for paint (including all types of paints and finishes) during periods of excess capacity are often well below cost including a "reasonable overhead," and may even be below the out-of-pocket costs of the contractors. At times, they say, it is more profitable to quote such prices than to pay for idle labor or to risk losing workers who are difficult to replace, as a result of temporary layoffs. For short periods of time firms may consider material and shipping costs alone as composing their marginal costs for the order and be willing to supply goods at prices which cover these costs and contribute something to overhead costs which, at such times, include direct labor costs.

Firms may pursue such a policy with impunity for two reasons: first, because the government is looked upon as a special buyer, whose contracts do not establish precedents for the prices which other buyers consider to be "fair"; and, second, because a low bid for one contract followed by a higher price for another does not

[4] Sales of paint, varnish, and lacquer totaled $1,050,000,000 in 1948 which was an all-time high, and $942,000,000 in 1949. After the first months of 1950, which were comparable to 1949 in sales levels, sales again rose to new heights. See Bureau of the Census figures shown in *Paint, Varnish and Lacquer Statistical Handbook, 1950 edition* (Washington: National Paint, Varnish and Lacquer Association).

prejudice the supplier's relations with the government. The bids of individual firms, therefore, tend to vary considerably from contract to contract depending, apparently, on the shifting relation of their current sales to the capacity of their plant, and the resulting intensity of their desire to obtain contracts.

Another factor in quoting prices is the relatively low cost of doing business with the government, which involves a minimum of sales, advertising, and engineering expense and no risk of credit losses. Invitations are received without the solicitation of salesmen; advertising cannot possibly have any influence on the award; no expense is incurred for a chemist's time as a part of the sales effort because the Federal Specification provides the requirements beforehand.

The successful bidders for the white enamel paint contracts were, without exception, relatively small firms which rely for their volume on industrial and local or regional trade sales. Only two large firms which sell in nation-wide markets, the Glidden Company and the Sherwin Williams Company, bid consistently, but their prices were just as consistently high. The contracts ranged in value from about $2,000 to $12,000 and are typical of most paint contracts let by government agencies.

Purchasing officials report that the large companies are seldom successful in obtaining contracts for standard paint items. They do, however, obtain their share of government business. Of the 388 contracts exceeding $10,000 in value, which were mentioned above, 38 were awarded to four national companies—the Sherwin Williams Company, the Glidden Company, the Pittsburgh Plate Glass Company, and the American Marietta Company. It appears that large companies have no cost advantage over smaller ones. Besides, the value of one government contract is a small percentage of their total sales in any one period. The opposite is, of course, true for a small company. Furthermore, in periods of high sales volume, such as those studied here, national firms may quote on the basis of average rather than marginal costs. These could be expected to be higher than marginal costs of some small firms which happen to need the business badly at the time of bidding. Some national companies, such as the E. I. Dupont de Nemours Company, the Devoe and Raynolds Company, and the National Lead Company quote infrequently, or not at all, for government contracts for paint.

TOILET TISSUE

Characteristics of market and government contracting.—There are more than a hundred mills which produce toilet tissue.[5] Most of these produce the finished product from pulp. Others are converters—companies which buy tissue paper and cut, perforate, wrap and package it. The tissue from which toilet paper is made may also be used to make other products, principally wrapping tissue. The machines which make the tissue may be specialized for that purpose alone, but more often they can be adapted to make a range of papers of which tissue is one kind. The production facilities and the raw material for toilet tissue can thus be shifted to the production of other commodities with comparative ease.

Almost all mills manufacture a product for general sale that meets the requirements of the Federal Specification. If a mill does not, the government buys in sufficiently large order quantities, from 500 to 3,000 cartons of 100 rolls each, to make it economical to adjust machines to produce a paper to meet the requirements of the specification.

The demand for toilet tissue is considered to be inelastic over the wide price ranges at which it has sold during the past few years, and is fairly stable over time increasing with the growth of the population. Sales of toilet tissue, however, may fluctuate considerably over short periods because of changes in stocks held by dealers and by large users, such as the armed forces.

Sales of toilet tissue are classified by the industry as (1) industrial and (2) resale. Industrial sales, which include those to the federal, state, and city governments, are frequently transacted on a specification basis with price, as a rule, the dominant factor in award of contracts. In contrast, brand names count heavily in resale sales which modifies to some degree the influence of price.

A few large companies, such as the Scott Paper Company which dominates the field, produce and sell nationally advertised brands, but the brand-name advertising of most mills, which are relatively small, is limited and directed more toward wholesalers and retailers than the consumer. Both industrial and resale sales may be made either directly by the mills or by the mills through jobbers to the industrial firm or retail store. Of the approximately 60 firms which

[5] *Lockwood's Directory of the Paper and Allied Trades, 1950,* pp. 802–804, lists 101 firms under Toilet Paper in the classified list of products of paper mills and converters. While this is accepted as the most comprehensive list, it is thought to be incomplete.

have bid on General Services Administration contracts during the past two years, half were jobbers and half producing mills (Table B, Appendix). Small mills may rely almost completely upon jobbers for the distribution of their products.

Toilet tissue is supplied to the civilian agencies of the government through the 12 regional supply centers of the General

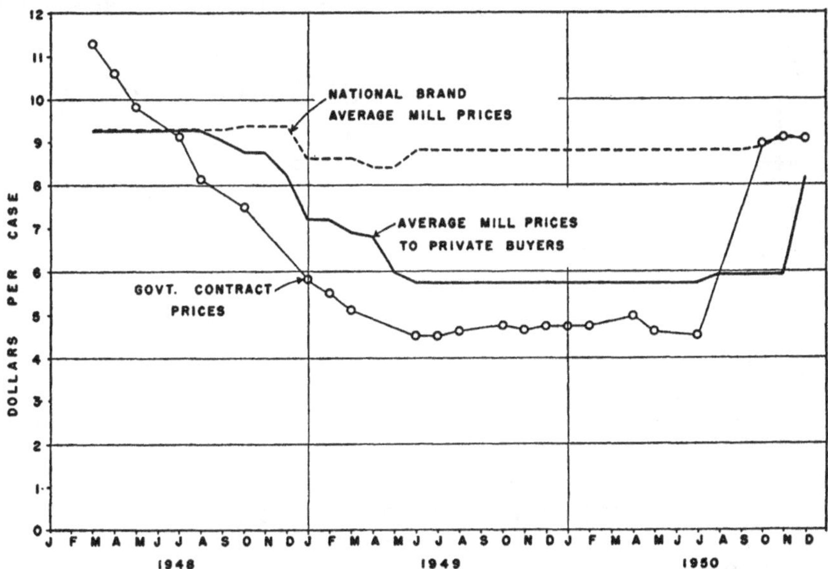

Fig. 6. Toilet Tissue: Government-Contract Prices and Mill Wholesale Prices for Nationally Advertised Brands and Brands Sold to Industrial and Jobber Buyers.

Source: Government-contract prices are from Table B, Appendix. Mill prices are averages of the weekly prices published in the *Paper Trade Journal,* New York.

Services Administration. The requirements of these stores are centralized periodically by the Washington region and invitations are issued to bid for contracts to supply definite quantities for delivery to each of the supply centers. Awards are made separately on the requirements for each delivery point but, of course, one firm may bid and receive contracts for all requirements. A tabulation of a typical set of bids on an invitation is shown in Table 15, Chapter V. It is required that samples be submitted with the bids; these are analyzed before awards are made. Shipments on contracts are again sampled and the samples analyzed to determine fulfillment of contract provisions.

Price comparisons.—The prices at which the government has purchased toilet tissue have varied from more than $11 a carton in

March, 1948, to about $4.50 in June, 1949, and up again to more than $9 in December, 1950 (Figure 6).

These prices were 25 per cent higher than the average prices at which mills sold to private industrial and wholesale buyers in March, 1948, but were about 20 per cent lower, than prices to the same buyers during the two-year period from July, 1948, to July, 1950. From the fall of 1950 the prices to the government rose

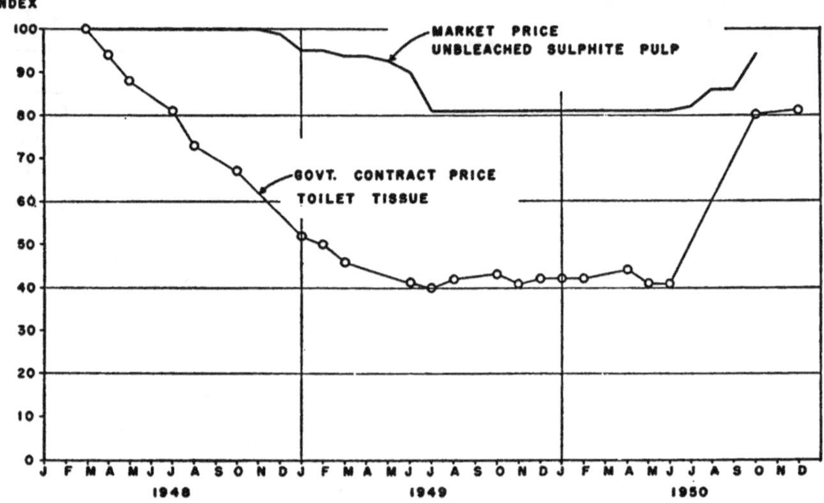

Fig. 7. Indexes of Government-Contract Prices for Toilet Tissue and Bureau of Labor Statistics Average Wholesale Prices for Unbleached Sulphite Pulp (March, 1948 = 100).

Source: The index for government-contract prices was calculated from the prices shown in Table B, Appendix; that for unbleached sulphite pulp from the figures obtained from *Average Wholesale Prices and Index Numbers of Individual Commodities,* Bureau of Labor Statistics.

sharply and were again substantially higher than prices to private buyers.

Costs.—Costs declined only moderately during the period from March, 1948, to October, 1950, compared with the movement of the contract prices to the government and the mill prices to private buyers. The principal cost element in toilet tissue is domestic unbleached sulphite pulp. From March, 1948, to July, 1949, pulp prices decreased 19 per cent while the contract prices to the federal government on toilet tissue decreased 60 per cent (Figure 7). Between June and October, 1950, the price of pulp moved the index up from the low of 81 to 94, an increase of about 15 per cent, while the contract prices to the government for toilet tissue doubled between the same dates. The other major element of direct costs is wages, and these, according to those familiar with the industry, did not vary significantly during this period.

Analysis of bidding.—It seems to be clear that the sharp movements in prices for toilet tissue cannot be explained by changes in unit variable costs. One logical explanation is that the changes were occasioned by the shortage of pulp following World War II relative to the demand for paper products and profit possibilities offered by the inelastic demand for toilet tissue. When output is limited by the amount of pulp available, firms would be expected to maintain their production of the items for which inelastic demand would permit sales volume to be maintained at highly profitable prices. This is said to account for the high prices of toilet tissue in early 1948. By the latter part of 1948 supplies of pulp were adequate, and additional firms could have been expected to enter production, attracted by the opportunity to make large profits at the high prevailing prices. Adequate statistics on the entry of new firms are not readily available, but it is reported that there are "opportunistic" firms which produce toilet tissue during periods when prices are high and cease production during periods of low prices. Other adjustments through additional installations of equipment and conversion of general-purpose machines to the production of toilet tissue would be similarly expected.

With adequate supplies of pulp and an increase in the production capacity of the industry, competition would be expected to force prices toward costs. The price to the government fell rapidly, and this downward movement was followed, after a lag of seven months, by mill prices to jobbers. Prices in both markets leveled off in June, 1949, with prices to the government varying from $4.50 to $5 and mill prices to jobbers holding at about $5.75, and remained at those levels until the late summer of 1950, after the outbreak of war in Korea.

In contrast with this movement of prices of government and nationally not advertised brands, the prices for nationally advertised brands to jobbers remained stable at a level close to the 1948 high during this entire period (also shown in Figure 6). These national brands are higher in quality than the tissue sold to the government and to jobbers. Furthermore, the product is apparently successfully differentiated from substitutes by national advertising directed at the users. The products, which these prices

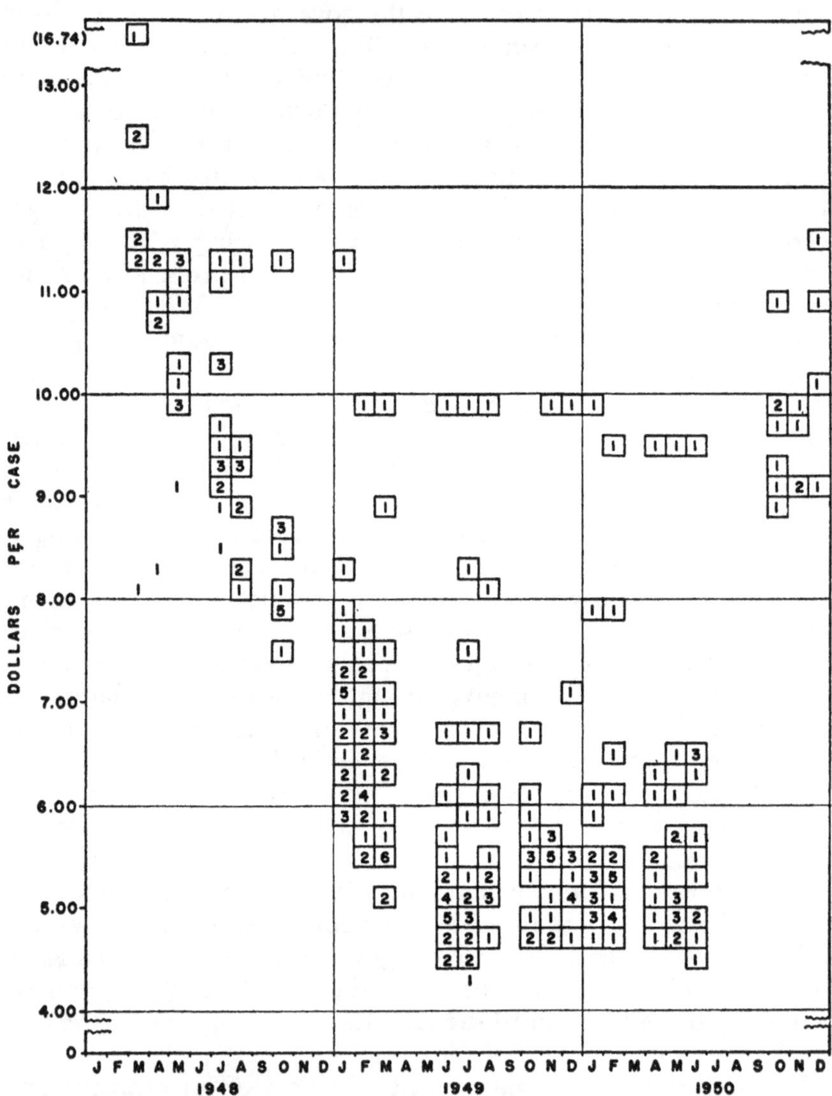

Fig. 8. Distribution of Prices Bid for 23 Toilet-Tissue Contracts, March, 1948–December, 1950.

The number of bids in each 20-cent price interval is noted in each square. Numbers not in squares represent bids which were rejected because they were based on furnishing a product not meeting specifications. Prices are dollars per case of 100 1,000-sheet rolls, f.o.b. Washington, D.C.

Source: Compiled from information on individual bids in Table B, Appendix.

represent, account for a substantial segment of the total sales of toilet tissue, and the stability of the prices at a high level, compared with the prices of substitute products, indicates that the policy of product differentiation has in large part eliminated the necessity for these products to compete on price with substitute products in mill-jobber markets.

An analysis of the bids and prices quoted by individual bidders helps to reveal the effects of the sealed-bids procedure on these prices. The distribution of the bids on each of the 23 invitations to bid by twenty-cent price classes reveals that most bids ranged from the low bid to prices from 30 to 50 per cent higher than the low bid (Figure 8). The highest bids may be disregarded as they represent bids made for the purpose of remaining on the bidders' list,[6] or bids of infrequent bidders who apparently were not in a position to compete for government contracts. It is worthy of note that during 1949 and the first six months of 1950 most bidders quoted prices which range from the mill prices to other large-quantity buyers down to the prices quoted by low bidders. Apparently those who bid on government contracts when supplies are adequate expect sufficient price competition to induce them to bid substantially below their prices to private buyers.

As is true for many markets in which the government purchases, sellers of toilet tissue consider government business to be "undesirable." By this they apparently mean that since the government buys on specifications and awards contracts to the low bidder, the contract prices are usually lower than the prices at which they sell to other buyers. Nonprice factors of product differentiation and continuity of supply have no influence. Although a few firms quote consistently, most of them bid on government contracts only when they "need the business," that is, when they have excess capacity and business at low prices appears to them to be profitable. The same is true for jobbers who have contract relations with mills and obtain special quotations from them in order to bid for government business; only when the supplying mills are in need of the business are they willing to give the jobber an especially low price to use when quoting for a government contract.

Table 18 indicates that, as was shown in paint contracts, most firms bid in a sporadic fashion. Of the 57 producers and jobbers

[6] The names of bidders who do not respond to three successive invitations may be removed from the lists. Bidders may keep their names on the lists either by bidding or by explaining their reason for not bidding and requesting that their names be retained.

who bid for the 23 contracts studied, 25 bid for only one or two contracts. It is apparent from a study of the complete tabulations of bids that these firms found after one or two experiences that government business held little prospect of profit for them, and, therefore, discontinued bidding. They were not active competitive factors in the government market. Four firms bid on 20 or more

TABLE 18

RELATION BETWEEN SUCCESS IN BIDDING AND FREQUENCY OF BIDDING FOR TOILET-TISSUE CONTRACTS (March, 1948–December, 1950)

Number of firms (A total of 57 firms bid on 23 invitations.)	Number of contracts for which bids were submitted by each firm in first column	Number of contracts awarded to the group of firms in first column
20	1	0
5	2	0
7	3	0
4	4	1
4	5	1
2	6	1
3	7	1
1	8	0
2	9	0
1	11	2
1	13	1
3	14	1
3	20	8
1	23	8

SOURCE: Compiled from information in the files of the Federal Supply Service, Washington, D.C.

of the 23 invitations and two of these received 15 of the 24 contracts (on one invitation 2 contracts were awarded; the awards are shown in Table B, Appendix). The third company bid competitively, but received only one contract while the fourth company bid consistently very high, apparently only to be kept on the mailing list. The remaining 8 contracts were awarded to 8 different companies all of which bid on 4 or more invitations. Altogether 11 companies were awarded the 24 contracts.

Of the 24 contracts let, 22 were awarded to mills and only 2 to jobbers (Table B, Appendix). Although half of the firms which quoted on this series of invitations were jobbers, it is apparent that they were seldom able to quote competitively. They often, however, obtain local contracts from government agencies. When prices bid by mills are so high as to be considered excessive, as in the first part of 1948, the government may make no award and authorize the supply centers to purchase their requirements locally.[7] When that happens jobbers who have stocks acquired at previously lower prices can offer better prices than the mills which are bidding on the basis of a more accurate estimate of the current profit possibilities.

As happened in the bids for white enamel paint contracts, competitive bidding for toilet-tissue contracts drove prices down to levels where they were apparently close to the marginal costs of the contractors. The rapid rise of prices of toilet tissue in late 1950 is explained by increased purchases by many jobbers, wholesalers, retailers, and other buyers to build up stocks. As a result each bidder quoted higher than past contract prices with the expectation that his competitors would do likewise.

Interestingly, when the government was paying high prices the number of bidders was small and when it was paying low prices the number of bidders was large. The number varied from 8 in March, 1948, to about 20 in the first part of 1949, then settled to about 12 to 17 during the period of low prices and fell off to 4 at the end of 1950 when prices rose again. This is consistent with the opinion that government business is "undesirable" and that many firms bid for it only when the pressure of overhead costs during periods of some excess capacity makes the business particularly profitable.

The question remains, however, as to why more bidders do not bid for government contracts when prices are higher than mill prices in other markets. The answer given is that many firms prefer to supply customers who will continue to buy from them during periods when they have excess capacity in their plants. For example, companies which rely mainly on sales of their own nationally advertised brands, and many substantial but smaller concerns, do not quote for government contracts. They state as their reason that when business is slack they cannot make a profit at the prices at which the government buys, and when sales are high they prefer to supply their regular customers. The implication is that they are willing to forego the chance of making extra present profits

[7] For example, in response to an invitation issued March 22, 1948, the only bids received on 100 cartons of toilet tissue for San Francisco delivery and 100 cartons for Denver delivery were $15 to $16 a carton, which was higher than reported prices of jobbers to industrial and other users. No awards were made and the requirements were cleared for local purchase by the supply centers.

on government contracts in favor of building customer loyalty, which will repay them with continued business in the future when sales volume is low. Some firms, however, do bid on government contracts but at higher prices than they quote to other customers.

Canned and Dried Foods

The basic characteristic of the canned- and dried-food industry is its seasonal nature. A large part of the output of processors is contracted for by the chain stores and wholesalers either before or during the packing season and is stored until it is sold during the year. A basic problem, therefore, of a buyer, such as the government, is whether he can organize his requirements so as to enter the primary market during the period when contracts are made. The alternative is to buy in the intermediate wholesale market during the course of the year and to pay higher prices as a consequence.

In primary markets by far the largest part of canned and dried foods is purchased on the basis of objective grades. In later stages in the channel of distribution the product becomes differentiated by brand names and advertising, but foods sold under different brand names and at widely varying wholesale and retail prices are often processed on the production line of a single canner who labels the goods with the different brands of his customers. A large part of the intermediate wholesale-market transactions is also conducted on the basis of objective grades, while grades for a few canned foods are shown on the cans through detail channels to the consumer.

The food demanded by the civilian agencies of the government is largely for use in various government-supported institutions, such as hospitals and prisons. The quantities of a single item demanded by any one institution or group of institutions within reasonably convenient delivery areas are not large enough to permit contracting with the packers once a year. A further barrier to this type of contracting is interposed by the difficulties of consolidating requirements and of obtaining appropriations needed to finance such purchases. For these reasons the government procures processed foods for the requirements of civilian agencies on periodic definite-quantity-definite-delivery contracts in each Federal Supply Service region. Bids are invited for quotations by grades defined by Federal Specifications which are the same as the grades by which the products are normally identified in the market.

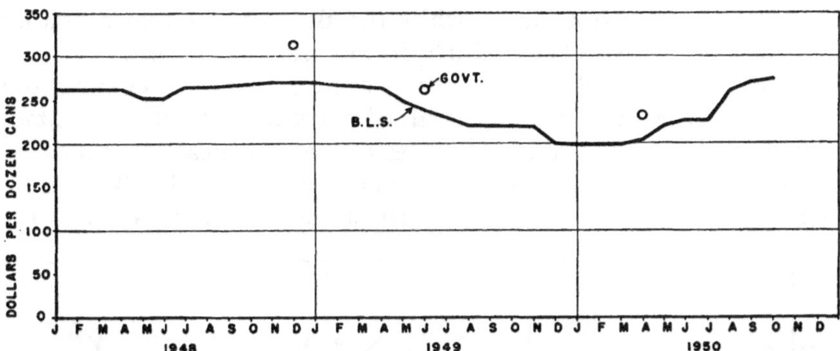

Fig. 9. Canned Peaches: Government-Contract Prices and Bureau of Labor Statistics Average Canners' Prices.

Source: For government-contract prices, files of the Federal Supply Service; for average canners' prices, *Average Wholesale Prices and Index Numbers of Individual Commodities,* Bureau of Labor Statistics. The Bureau figures are cannery prices per dozen cans, Grade-B cling peaches, no. 2½ can, f.o.b. cannery (usually in California); the government-contract prices are for the same commodity, grade, and quantity, but f.o.b. Washington, D.C.

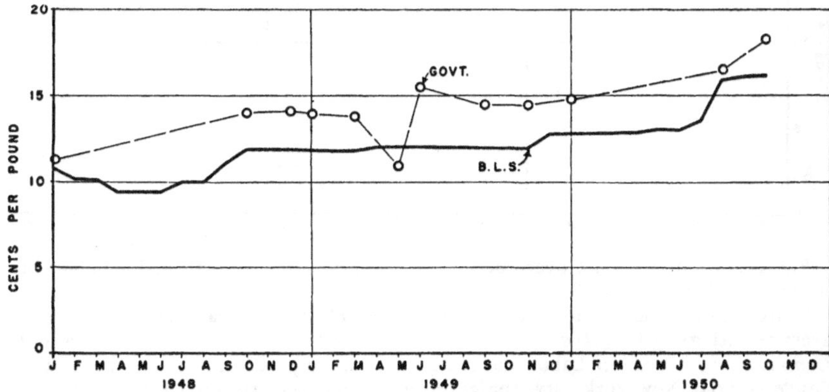

Fig. 10. Dried Prunes: Government-Contract Prices and Bureau of Labor Statistics Average Packers' Prices.

Source: For government-contract prices, files of the Federal Supply Service; for average packers' prices, *Average Wholesale Prices and Index Numbers of Individual Commodities,* Bureau of Labor Statistics. The Bureau prices are per pound of California prunes, 50/60 size, f.o.b. packer; the government-contract prices are for the same commodity, size, and weight unit, but are f.o.b. Washington, D.C.

The only statistical comparisons available for canned and dried foods are with Bureau of Labor Statistics wholesale price averages for a few commodities. The government and Bureau of Labor Statistics prices for canned peaches and dried prunes which are given in Figures 9 and 10 are related to the same grades, but the government prices are those of intermediate wholesalers and include freight to Washington, D.C., while the Bureau of Labor Statistics lists the prices of packers, which do not include freight.

Most peaches and prunes are packed in California, and the freight together with the wholesalers' markup account for the fact that the government contract prices for canned peaches and dried prunes range from 10 to 20-odd per cent above the Bureau of Labor Statistics prices. The Bureau of Labor Statistics prices for

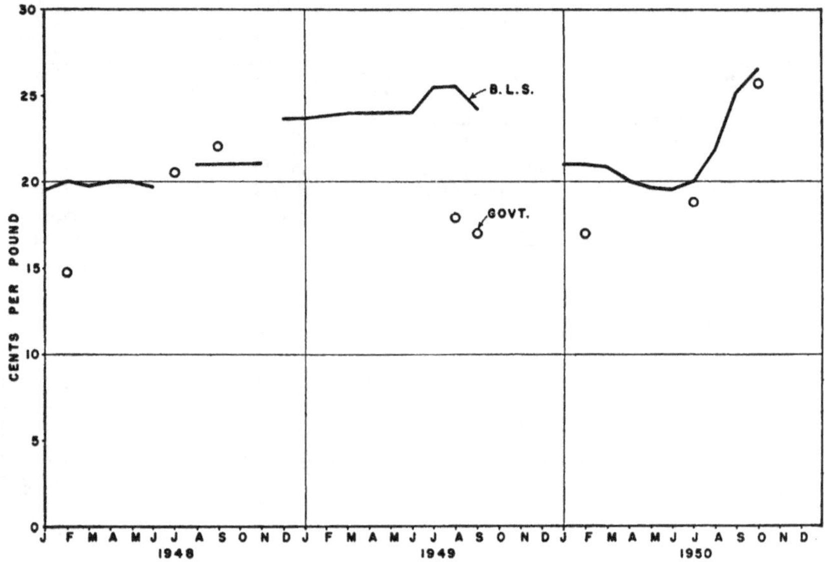

Fig. 11. Dried Apples: Government-Contract Prices and Bureau of Labor Statistics Average Packers' Prices.

Source: For government-contract prices, files of the Federal Supply Service; for average packers' prices, *Average Wholesale Prices and Index Numbers for Individual Commodities,* Bureau of Labor Statistics. The Bureau prices are per pound of apples, Grade B, f.o.b. New York City; the government-contract prices are for the same commodity, grade, and weight unit, but f.o.b. Washington, D.C.

dried apples are compared below with government contract prices (Figure 11). The former are f.o.b. New York City and are comparable with the government prices which are for the same grade of commodity, f.o.b. Washington, D.C. In spite of the fact that the figures of the government represent the prices paid to wholesalers while the Bureau of Labor Statistics lists packers' prices, the government-contract prices were substantially lower than the Bureau's averages.

In view of the fact that the government prices include both margins for the wholesalers and freight to Washington, D.C., the evidence given above, although not conclusive, partly supports the opinion of the buyers that the government contract prices are favorable compared with those at which other large-quantity buyers purchase these items.

An examination of the bids for these and similar food items shows that from six to twelve food wholesalers in the area between Philadelphia and Richmond, Virginia, respond to each invitation to bid. Figures range from the low bids receiving awards to prices 20 to 30 per cent higher.

Many firms have received awards during the periods for which data are available. For example, the 14 contracts for dried prunes awarded between October, 1947, and October, 1950, went to 10 different firms, 2 of which received 3 contracts each. Prices of bidders on successive contracts vary and, as in other commodities in competitive markets for homogeneous products, few firms bid consistently for all contracts. They appear to bid only when they have ample stocks which they cannot expect to sell in less competitive markets at more favorable prices.

When there were requisitions to fill for substantial quantities of processed foods, the government has, on several occasions, sent invitations to canners in an attempt to induce them to bid, but they did not respond. One reason for this was, FSS officials believed, that many canners sell their entire pack before or during the canning season, and another that many canners have a policy of not selling direct, but only through jobbers. The government apparently cannot enter the primary market unless it arranges to contract for large parts of a canner's output during the normal period for such contracts.

Method of Contracting for Flour

A discussion of the method of purchasing flour is included here to illustrate the necessity for a flexible purchasing device when prices fluctuate daily and raw-material costs are a large part of total unit costs.

Bids for flour contracts are invited by telegraph, and telegraphic replies are required. Bids are binding for 24 hours only, so bidders need not allow in their bids for variations in the price of wheat that may occur over periods longer than one market day. Millers calculate their prices and wire their bids after the wheat market closes on the day the bids are to be opened. Awards are telegraphed either late the same afternoon or the following morning so that contractors may immediately cover their requirements by purchasing wheat. Buyers report that telegraphic bids made in this manner result in lower prices and greater competition than bids solicited and submitted by mail.

The prices and bids for flour are not shown here, but they follow the Bureau of Labor Statistics averages very closely with the differences largely attributable to the freight included in the government prices. Six to eight bids are received from about a dozen mills which are invited to bid; no one mill is consistently the low bidder and the bids show a small but significant variation in prices quoted.

VII

Buying Differentiated Products in Competitive Markets

Characteristics of the Markets

In contrast with the markets discussed in the preceding chapter, those discussed here are characterized by products which are differentiated as they are sold to most large-quantity buyers. The difference between the two types of markets, however, is one of degree rather than kind because the government and a few other large-quantity buyers consider these products to be homogeneous.[1] For the most part private buyers purchase the products on the basis of approved products lists rather than objective specifications and evaluate differences in brands in making awards of contracts. Sellers in these markets rely on product differentiation in selling and generally quote prices as list prices less discounts which are stable over comparatively long periods of time.

The significance of the distinction between the markets for homogeneous and differentiated products is seen in the effect of the government's product policy. In competitive markets for homogeneous products the government's use of specifications fits its buying into the existing market practice. In competitive markets for differentiated products the government's use of specifications is contrary to the usual market practice and forces sellers to adjust their price and product policies when bidding for government contracts. The markets in which the government buys are, therefore, somewhat different from those in which most other large-quantity buyers purchase, but the products and the sellers are the same.

The markets for differentiated products are classified into two

[1] They do so with the exception that the government, in awarding contracts for dry batteries, evaluates quality beyond that specified.

groups: (1) those for products which are differentiated through seller effort but which the government judges to be essentially homogeneous, and (2) those for products which are differentiated by characteristics which the government judges reflect real utility differences. This distinction is based on the government's judgment of the importance of the differences claimed by sellers and of the differences which are measurable in the product.

Both types of markets are quantitatively significant in government procurement. The products in the first group include large numbers of items of office supplies, so-called housekeeping items, such as soaps, maintenance supplies, and certain fuels. The products in the second group include passenger automobiles and trucks, many items of office, maintenance, and transportation equipment, and household and office furnishings.

The products used as illustrations of the operation of the government's purchasing policy have been chosen largely because the evidence available for them demonstrates more clearly the effects of the buying policy than the evidence for other commodities which sometimes are quantitatively more important. In particular, some products have been chosen for which evidence of product characteristics and prices is available before and after the promulgation and use of Federal Specifications. For most commodities the government's policy of buying on specification has been in operation for so long that such evidence has been destroyed.

Products Judged by the Government to be Homogeneous

Resin-emulsion paint.—Resin-emulsion paint is of interest because it affords a clear comparison of buying on specification with buying on the basis of brand name "or equal." At the same time it is the largest-volume item purchased on federal-supply-schedule term contracts for paint.

This type of paint is sold as a paste which can be thinned with water and is particularly convenient for home use because it is easily applied, relatively inexpensive, and has some of the advantages of more expensive oil paints. Therefore, it has strong promotional possibilities for sale to retail customers. It is not protected by patents and was first offered by companies which did not exploit its full retail possibilities. The Sherwin Williams Company recognized the opportunity of selling it widely at retail and advertised its version of the product on a national scale as "Kemtone." The promotion campaign was conducted with considerable success, with the result that other companies developed similar products and marketed them under their own brand names.[2]

In the early 1940's the government bought resin-emulsion paint on a brand name "or equal" basis with each agency buying its own requirements. The retail price at that time was $2.98 per gallon and the government was paying $1.76 per gallon.

Subsequently, a Federal Specification was developed for the item and invitations were issued for federal-supply-schedule six-month term contracts to supply the government's requirements for orders placed by the several agencies. The number of bidders was substantially increased and the price was reduced from $1.76 to $1.03 per gallon during a period when the retail price did not change. The lower price was doubtless the result of three factors: (1) bidders were given an objective specification which enabled them to quote on the lowest-cost product which would be acceptable, (2) the number of bidders was greater and the chance of obtaining a low price was, therefore, increased, and (3) the prospect of a succession of small orders totaling a large volume in place of the uncertain volume of individual orders gave sellers an inducement to quote favorable prices to the government. All these factors were dependent on the use of specifications. For items such as paint the use of brand names in buying would require the submission of samples against which shipments could be checked; this would clearly be impracticable for shipments under term contracts to widely scattered points.

No commitment was made by the government to buy any definite quantity of the item under term contracts, but the volume of orders placed under previous contracts was reported in the invitations for the information of bidders. The contracts for resin-emulsion paint were mandatory for use by all executive government agencies in Washington, D.C., and contiguous areas; the sales reported by previous contractors for the year November 1, 1948, through October 31, 1949, totaled about $76,000 for the tinted paint and $30,000 for the white—$27,000 of the latter being for the paint in five-gallon containers. Awards were made separately for each size of container shown, so bidders could expect to receive

[2] During the early promotional period resin-emulsion-base paint was successfully differentiated in primary as well as retail markets. At the present time specifications are generally available for the paint, and it is sold on specifications in primary markets to many large-quantity buyers just as other paints are. It is included here rather than in chapter vi because it illustrates the effect of specification buying on the market structure.

the full amount of the prospective business only if their quotations for all sizes were low.

The tabulations of bidders on white and tinted resin-emulsion paint contracts (Tables 19 and 20) show that the number of bidders is smaller, and the range of prices bid, while wide, is not so wide as in the definite-quantity-definite-delivery contracts for paint.[3]

TABLE 19

WHITE RESIN-BASE PAINT: BIDDERS' PRICES AND CONTRACTS AWARDED
(Net prices per gallon, f.o.b. Washington, for term contracts May 15–November 14, 1950. Prices of successful bidders in bold face.)

Bidders	Prices				
	1-gallon containers			5-gallon containers	
	1 to 5 containers	6 to 11 containers	12 or more containers	1 container	2 or more containers
Color Craft Corp.	**1.44**	1.39	1.29	**1.34**	1.34
Lasting Products Co.	1.58	**1.38**	**1.28**	1.37	1.26
Long Island Paint and Chemical Co.	1.62	1.39	1.30	1.39	**1.25**
Midwest Interiors, Inc.	1.73	1.73	1.39	1.39	1.39
Kleen Kote Co.	1.50	1.50	1.45	1.43	1.42
Atlantic Calsomine Co.	1.50	1.50	1.50	1.44	1.44
Hoboken White Lead & Color Works, Inc.	1.53	1.48	1.43	1.48	1.42
Pur-All Paint Products Co.	1.60	1.50	1.48	1.50	1.45
The Glidden Co.	1.65	1.45	1.40	1.55	1.32
Casein and Oil Products Co.	1.73	1.73	1.73	1.73	1.73
Tamms Industries, Inc.	2.10	2.10	2.10	2.00	1.91
M. Ewing Fox, Inc.	....	....	2.08	2.03	2.01
The Synkaloid Co.	2.19	2.13	2.08	2.13	2.08
Sinclair Paint Co.	2.60	2.60	2.60	2.55	2.55
Jack Citrin	....	....	1.98	....	1.86

SOURCE: Based on data in the contract files of the Federal Supply Service, Washington, D.C., for paint, resin base, emulsion, paste (for thinning with cold water), interior, in accordance with Federal specification no. TT-P-88a. Item no. 52-P-9180.

When bidding, firms would be expected to take into account the savings in sales expense and credit losses resulting from doing business with the government, but they would also need to consider the expense of packing, shipping, invoicing in small-order quantities, and of storing batch quantities of finished paint until they are ordered for shipment. Calculations of bidders would be based on the profit they could expect from the indefinite business in prospect at costs which they estimate will be incurred at various

[3] Cf. evidence on interior white enamel paint, chap. vi, fig. 5.

intervals over the life of the contract. Decisions would not be based on current marginal costs but still an assured, even though indefinite, amount of business might be welcomed to allow batches to be produced during dull periods and stored until shipment. If bidders anticipated continued excess capacity during the life of the contract, they might quote prices based on their estimates of future

TABLE 20

TINTED RESIN-BASE PAINT: BIDDERS' PRICES AND CONTRACTS AWARDED
(Net prices per gallon in 1-gallon containers, f.o.b. Washington for term contract May 15–November 14, 1950. Prices of successful bidder in bold face.)

Bidders	Prices		
	1 to 5 containers	6 to 11 containers	12 or more containers
Color Craft Corp.	**1.34**	**1.29**	**1.24**
Atlantic Calsomine Co., Inc.	1.50	1.50	1.50
Kleen Kote Co.	1.50	1.50	1.45
Hoboken White Lead & Color Works, Inc.	1.53	1.48	1.43
Lasting Products Co.	1.58	1.38	1.28
Pur-All Products Co., Inc.	1.60	1.50	1.48
The Glidden Co.	1.65	1.45	1.40
Long Island Paint and Chemical Co.	1.68	1.52	1.42
Casein and Oil Products Co.	1.73	1.73	1.73
Midwest Interiors, Inc.	1.73	1.73	1.40
Tamms Industries, Inc.	2.15	2.06	2.06
The Synkaloid Co.	2.19	2.13	2.08
R. S. Carlisle Chemical and Mfg. Co., Inc.	2.18	2.08	1.98
Sinclair Paint Co.	2.65	2.65	2.65
Jack Citrin	....	....	1.96
M. Ewing Fox Co.	....	....	2.13

SOURCE: Based on data in the contract files of the Federal Supply Service, Washington, D.C., for paint, resin base, emulsion, paste (for thinning with cold water), interior, in accordance with Federal Specification no. TT-P-88a. Item no. 52-P-9172.

low marginal costs. If they anticipated that sales would press production up to and exceeding optimum capacity they would quote prices high enough to cover future high marginal costs plus their profit. If they expected very rapidly increasing and relatively unpredictable costs, they might either refuse to quote or quote prices so high as to discourage the government from awarding contracts.

In late April, 1950, when bidders were preparing their quotations shown in Tables 19 and 20, sales in the paint industry had been below the 1948 high for more than a year; and the prospects were that the then current situation would continue for some time.

The contracts were let at a fortunate time from the government's point of view because bid prices on paint, as well as on most other commodities, rose sharply after the outbreak of war in Korea. In October when invitations for new contracts normally would have been issued, a survey of suppliers revealed that the continued supply of materials and the probable course of costs were so unpredictable that it would be useless to invite bids for term contracts, but that better prices could be secured by individual agencies buying in the market in small quantities. The use of term contracts for this commodity was, therefore, abandoned for the time being.

Liquid type cleaner.—Liquid type cleaners for typewriters are typically the same simple chemical compound differentiated only by brand names, packaging, advertising "secret ingredients," and a bit of perfume to give each a pleasant odor. Manufacturing costs consist largely of expenditures for bottles, daubers for applying the cleaner, and packaging. Sales, advertising, and other distribution costs weigh heavily in the determination of retail prices. It is a low-value item demanded infrequently and in small quantities by any one user. Although liquid cleaners represent the most adequate means of cleaning type yet devised, they are not completely effective, with the result that users would welcome some simpler and more effective cleaning substance. For these reasons type cleaner is susceptible to immaterial product differentiation. Sellers frequently offer new brands claiming that they contain some magically effective but unspecified ingredient; upon test, however, the government has found their composition identical with existing brands.

Type cleaner is purchased under a six-month term contract for delivery to the federal supply centers. Government agencies procure their requirements from the centers. The contract prices for the fall of 1950 for four-ounce bottles with daubers delivered in any quantity to Washington, D.C., are compared with retail prices of an equivalent product of the same manufacturer in Table 21. The retail list price was about 16 cents an ounce and the price to dealers (assuming a 50 per cent discount off the list price) was about 8 cents an ounce compared with less than 2.5 cents an ounce paid by the government. The retail prices of other brands were about the same. The government buys in no larger order quantities than dealers. Most buyers purchase type cleaner by brand name from dealers.

Seven companies bid for the type-cleaner contracts covering the period from August 16, 1950, through February 15, 1951 (Table 22). The bids of six firms were responsive to the invitation while the bid of one was not and was, therefore, rejected. Three of the six companies bid competitively with methods of figuring delivery costs obviously playing a decisive role in determining the low prices. Three bidders were awarded contracts, each being low in his bid for the federal supply center located in the same town as

TABLE 21

LIQUID TYPE CLEANER: GOVERNMENT-CONTRACT AND RETAIL PRICES (December, 1950)

Source of supply	Prices in dollars			
	1 bottle		12 bottles	
	Per bottle	Per ounce	Per bottle	Per ounce
Walter G. Gies product:				
Contract prices delivered to Federal Supply Service stores, 4-ounce bottle..	.094	.0235	.094	.0235
Stores-issue price to agencies...........	.11	.0275	.11	.0275
Walter G. Gies' "Nutype", as sold by Stockett and Fiske, Washington, D.C.:				
2-ounce bottle, retail price...........	.50	.25	.36	.18
6-ounce bottle, retail price...........	1.00	.167	.70	.117

SOURCE: Government contract and stores issue prices from files of the Federal Supply Service, Washington, D.C.; retail prices from personal shopping.

his factory, with two of the three also receiving awards for other delivery points. For the Seattle contract, the successful bidder was low by only two-hundreds of one cent per bottle. The three bidders who were high were apparently bidding on the basis of discounts off list prices rather than costs, and their quotations were in one bid double and in the other about four times the low bids.

The low prices to the government are a reflection of the force of competitive bidding and of savings in sales and advertising costs rather than reduced delivery or production costs as the contracts call for delivery in any quantities in packages in all ways like the usual packages in which the commodity is sold at retail. The government uses about 100,000 bottles or 400,000 ounces each year.

Carbon paper.—Carbon paper is another example of a differentiated product sold through wholesale and retail channels. Any well-established firm produces brands of carbon paper which meet

Federal Specifications, and the brands furnished to the government are normally sold widely in other markets. Like type cleaner, carbon paper is purchased on six-month term contracts for delivery on orders of any quantity to the 12 supply centers. The contract covers about 40 items with prices varying according to weight, finish, and size. The most popular item is light weight, medium finish, 8- by 11-inch paper for which the contract price for the period February 1, 1950, through July 3, 1950, was $.675 for a box of 100 sheets delivered to any supply center. This compares with retail prices which vary from $3 to $4.50 and manufacturers' prices to retailers upward of about $1.40 per box.

Carbon paper is distributed through the 12 supply centers, and all civilian agencies of the government are required to obtain their supplies from the centers. The issues from the supply centers for the fiscal year 1949 totaled approximately $185,000. The prices the government pays result in a substantial saving to the agencies which would otherwise pay a little more than the wholesale price. This appears also to be a market in which the sealed-bids device is effective because the price is less than half the usual wholesale price to dealers many of whom order in quantities comparable to those ordered by the federal supply centers. Again the low prices are apparently the result of price competition and lower costs which exclude those attributable to sales and advertising.

Stencil paper.—In some markets product differentiation is successfully maintained by patented processes or designs, and no method of bidding is successful in obtaining price competition simply because there are no competitive suppliers. Stencil paper affords an example of the manner in which this type of differentiation obstructs the government's efforts to evoke price competition and thus to maximize the utility per dollar of its purchases.

The A. B. Dick Company owned the patents covering the production of cellulose-base stencil paper. Substitutes made by other processes were available but were substantially inferior for most purposes. The government and most other users considered it profitable to use cellulose-base stencils and purchased them on the basis of a description which cited a standard sample of the A. B. Dick Company paper "or equal."

About 1940 when the company's patents expired, additional firms began to produce cellulose-base paper, and the government prepared an objective specification for use in buying. The specification called for a sheet designed to give 2,500 satisfactory copies

TABLE 22

Liquid Type Cleaner[a]: Bidders' Prices and Contracts Awarded

(Net prices for any quantity per 4-ounce bottle with dauber, f.o.b. federal supply centers for term contracts August 16, 1950–February 15, 1951. Prices of successful bidders in bold face.)

Bidders	Destination											
	Atlanta	Boston	Chicago	Cleveland	Denver	Fort Worth	Kansas City	Los Angeles	New York	San Francisco	Seattle	Washington
American Writing Ink Co., Inc.	**.103**	**.096**	**.103**	.103	**.118**	**.117**	**.110**	.145	.096	.146	.145	.096
Dicol Chemical Co.	.104	.098	.104	.104	.120	.119	.111	.146	**.094**	.146	.146	.094
Walter G. Gies Co.	.108	.108	.108	**.102**	.127	.118	.118	**.1448**	.098	**.145**	**.1448**	**.092**
Underwood Corp.	.42	.42	.42	.42	.42	.42	.42	.42	.42	.42	.42	.42
Winn Products Corp.	.200	.201	.199	.203	.236	.223	.219	.262	.190	.266	.263	.244
Webbers	....	....	....	....	....	....	....	.211	....	.206	.211	....
Imperial Products Corp.[b]	.099	.099	.099	.099	.099	.099	.099	.099	.099	.099	.099	.099

Source: Computed from information in the contract files of the Federal Supply Service, Washington, D.C.

[a] Type cleaner, liquid, in accordance with federal supply specification no. 797. Item no. 53-T-3510.

[b] Bid rejected because bidder failed to submit sample, and quotations were f.o.b. factory.

TABLE 23

STENCIL PAPER[a]: BIDDERS' PRICES AND CONTRACTS AWARDED

(Net prices per quire, f.o.b. Washington and contiguous areas for term contracts covering two periods: December 1, 1949–November 30, 1950 and December 1, 1950–November 30, 1951. Prices of successful bidders in bold face.)

Bidders	20 to 99 quires		100 to 499 quires		500 to 999 quires		1,000 to 5,000 quires		5,000 quires or more	
	12-1-1949 through 11-30-1950	12-1-1950 through 11-30-1951	12-1-1949 through 11-30-1950	12-1-1950 through 11-30-1951	12-1-1949 through 11-30-1950	12-1-1950 through 11-30-1951	12-1-1949 through 11-30-1950	12-1-1950 through 11-30-1951	12-1-1949 through 11-30-1950	12-1-1950 through 11-30-1951
Frankel Carbon & Ribbon Co.	1.20	1.02	1.10	**0.92**	1.05	0.92	1.00	0.92	0.96	0.92
A. B. Dick Co.	1.00	1.10	**0.92**	0.95	0.92	0.93	0.90	0.90	0.90	0.89
Marr Duplicator Co., Inc.	1.04	**0.94**	0.921	0.921	**0.91**	**0.89**	**0.88**	**0.87**	**0.87**	**0.86**
Niagara Duplicator Co.	1.19	1.17	1.09	1.16	1.09	1.15	1.09	1.14	1.09	1.13
Polychrome Co.	**0.94**	....	0.94	....	0.93	....	0.92	....	0.92	....
Remington Rand, Inc.	1.50	1.21	1.40	1.20	1.30	1.19	1.25	1.17	1.20	1.16

SOURCE: Compiled from data in the files of the Federal Supply Service, Washington, D.C.

[a] Item no. 53-P-20836. 8½ x 18 inches.

while the sheet sold by the A. B. Dick Company previously was capable of giving 5,000. For most government uses the 2,500-copy sheet is as satisfactory as the 5,000-copy sheet. The effect on prices of this combination of events is shown in Figure 12.

Following the expiration of the A. B. Dick Company's patents and before the specification was used, limited competition lowered the term contract price from $2.21 a quire (24 sheets)—which had been the contract price for at least five years—first to $1.93 on an interim contract and then to $1.73 on the 1941 contract. After the specification was included in the invitation to bid the

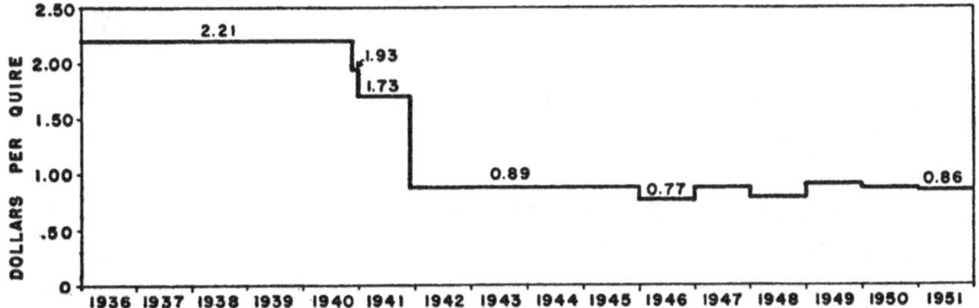

Fig. 12. Stencil Paper: Government Term-Contract Prices.
Item no. 53-P-20836; 8½ × 18 inches.
Source: Contract files of the Federal Supply Service.

price immediately dropped to $.89 and remained near that level through 1951. The price for the contract covering the period from December 1, 1950, through June 30, 1951, was about $.86 a quire in large quantities.

The bidding for the two yearly contracts let in 1949 and 1950 reveals that six companies compete for the business with every appearance of active price competition (Table 23). The high bids range up to 40 per cent above the contract prices, the prices of bidders vary from year to year, and during the two years four companies have been awarded contracts. The A. B. Dick Company bids competitive prices but is only occasionally low. As in carbon paper the prices are substantially below wholesale prices to dealers and apparently for the same reasons.

Antifreeze compound.—If the production of a firm is limited, the total amount of business offered by the government may be unattractive to it in view of the greater profit possibilities offered by sales of a differentiated product through its regularly established sales outlets. A part of the requirements, however, may offer an attractive profit possibly even at low prices. This is illustrated by the 1949 contracts for antifreeze compound.

Antifreeze compounds are differentiated by brand names and advertising in all sales except those to a few large-quantity users such as the government. The demand is seasonal with the heavy production period extending from fall to early winter. As a result, contracts calling for delivery during the summer months are attractive. To take advantage of this fact the government buys the item on definite-quantity contracts calling for delivery to the federal supply centers during July, August, and September. There the material is stored until it is requisitioned by the using agencies.

In 1949 the raw materials required for antifreeze compound were in short supply, and the low bidder at $1.61 per gallon limited his offer to 54,000 gallons. It was, therefore, necessary to make a dual award with the second low bidder receiving a contract for 180,000 gallons at $1.75 per gallon. During that year the retail price was $3.50 per gallon and the lowest price to jobbers was $2.34. The jobbers' price was considered by suppliers to be the lowest necessary to quote to obtain the business of users such as fleet owners who purchase by brand names in large quantities. The low price to the government is attributed in part to the off-season purchase, in part to the large quantity for definite delivery, and in part to the increased competition resulting from buying on objective specifications.

Ready-to-eat breakfast cereals.—Ready-to-eat cereals constitute an interesting example of highly differentiated products for which advertising and distribution costs bulk large in total unit costs. For some consumers the product is significantly differentiated by taste preferences. To the government as an institutional buyer the material differences lie in the types and varieties of breakfast foods, with differences between brands considered to be immaterial.

The government buys breakfast cereals on federal-supply-schedule term contracts at prices which cover delivery in any quantities to any point in the United States. All civilian agencies are required to procure any cereals they need under the contracts. The purchases under term contracts in 1949 totaled approximately $210,000 shared by nine contractors, all of whom were nationally known manufacturers. Invitations to bid are based on objective specifications for all types of cereals, and most brands of each type meet the specification just as they are processed and packaged for other markets. The low bidder for each type receives a contract for the entire requirement of that type.

The contract prices for the three-month period from October 1, through December 31, 1949, averaged 52 per cent below the manufacturers' prices to wholesale dealers for the individual package size and 30 per cent below the prices to wholesale dealers for the 8-ounce family size. When it is considered that these prices include delivery in any quantity to any point in the United States and that large-quantity users, such as institutions, typically must buy from wholesale dealers, it is apparent that the price is favorable.

Staples for staple fasteners.—Occasionally a manufacturer is able to differentiate his product by making it unique in form so that otherwise competitive products cannot be used interchangeably with it. This occurs particularly where a machine of some sort is required to use the product, and both are sold by one manufacturer. An illustration is paper-fastening machines using wire staples. Every manufacturer makes a machine that will accept a standard staple. Most manufacturers also make machines of unique designs which will accept only staples of a particular design which is, where possible, protected by patents from being copied. Manufacturers actively promote the sale of the specially designed machines, sometimes at low prices, in order to create an assured demand for the unique staples.

Tests have shown that the specially designed staples have no advantages over the standard wire staples for ordinary paper fastening required by the government. Many agencies in the past have purchased special machines with the result that the government must buy various types of specially designed staples as well as standard ones. A measure is thus available of the cost of immaterial differentiation to the ill-informed user-buyer. The cost of standard staples to the government is 25 cents a box of 5,000 compared with 35 to 70 cents a box for the nonstandard ones which can be used only with the machines of particular manufacturers. Immaterial differentiation for this product raises the price from 40 to 180 per cent.

Products Judged by the Government to Reflect Real Utility Differences

Dry batteries.—There are two commodities where the government, in applying the sealed-bids procedure, evaluates utility offered above the minimum required by Federal Specifications. One is dry batteries, the other electric fans. The latter is discussed in the next chapter.

The life of various brands of batteries varies substantially under standard-test conditions which reproduce typical conditions of use. They are thus materially differentiated.[4] In addition, they are differentiated by brand names and advertising claiming that each brand is the best buy. The buyer, as usual, is left with the problem of sorting out the differences which are significant from those which are unimportant to him in making his choice of which brand to buy. The government with the testing facilities at its disposal is in a particularly favorable position to make a rational judgment regarding the quality of batteries.

Batteries are purchased on federal-supply-schedule one-year term contracts at prices which cover delivery of orders for no less than specified minimum quantities to Washington, D.C. When shipments are made outside of Washington, any extra freight is added to the contract prices.

Bids for dry batteries are considered only for brands that have previously been submitted to the National Bureau of Standards for qualification tests. Bidders quoting the lowest prices are not necessarily awarded contracts even though their product has met the minimum requirements of the specification. The results of the qualification tests are summarized for each brand in terms of percentages which show the actual test life of the battery in comparison with the minimum test life required by the Federal Specification. The price quoted by each bidder is then divided by this percentage to give an evaluation factor, and the contract is awarded to the firm whose price and test results give the lowest evaluation factor. The evaluation factor expresses the cost to the government of the equivalent of the minimum acceptable quality battery. Contracts for the year beginning June 20, 1950, were let to General Dry Batteries, Incorporated, whose price and evaluation factor were low for D-size flashlight batteries; to the Union Carbide and Carbon Corporation whose price was second low, but for whose battery the evaluation factor was low for general-purpose dry cells; and to the Union Carbide and Carbon Corporation whose bid was third low, but was the only bid completely responsive to the invitation for radio-B batteries (Table 24).

The prices paid by the government for batteries appear to reflect effective price competition. The retail list price for D-size flashlight batteries in 1950 was 10 cents and the net price to dealers

---

[4] Results of tests showing the importance of this differentiation are given in chap. iv, table 13.

in standard packages of 250 varied for different manufacturers from 6.25 to 6.5 cents. These prices are comparable with the government's contract price of 4.25 cents delivered to Washington, D.C., in minimum-order quantities of 50 batteries. The retail list price for radio-B batteries, N-size, was $2.45 in 1950 and the net price to dealers in standard packages of 24 was $1.71 compared with the government contract price of $1.116 in minimum-order quantities of six. The net price to distributors was not available but the government contract prices are probably lower.

Sales to the government under the contracts for the year preceding the letting of the contracts noted above were reported to total about $33,000 for the flashlight battery and $13,000 for the radio-B battery. Costs of packing and shipping to the government would be no less and might be greater than to distributors and dealers, if agencies ordered in small quantities, and little sales expense and no advertising expense is necessary for sales to the government. In view of the moderate volume of sales under the contracts and the stable price policies practised in related markets, the low prices appear to be the result of the price competition between sellers who know that product differentiation stemming from sales effort is not a factor in the product's salability to the government.

It is interesting to note that two manufacturers maintain their customary policy of quoting only through their authorized distributors when bidding for government contracts, and two find it unprofitable to quote on the basis of small-quantity shipments specified in the invitations. Four of the six bidders were manufacturers, and four were willing to quote on the basis of delivering the specified small quantities. Successful bidders are usually manufacturers (Table 24).

Carpets and rugs.—Brands of carpets and rugs are differentiated both in their wearing qualities and their usefulness as decoration. The utility of any one pattern of rugs as decoration varies greatly for different individuals with the result that a rather large selection of kinds, patterns, and colors is required to satisfy the wants of any sizable group of users. In addition, there are grades within each kind of rug or carpet that offer different wearing qualities. The wearing qualities, of course, are wanted by all users.

In view of the varied demand the government finds it impracticable to stock rugs or to centralize requirements for direct-delivery contracts. Federal-supply-schedule term contracts, usually for one-

TABLE 24

DRY BATTERIES: BIDDERS' PRICES AND CONTRACTS AWARDED SHOWING METHOD OF EVALUATING UTILITY
(Prices for term contracts June 20, 1950—June 19, 1951. Prices of successful bidders in bold face.)

Bidders	Minimum order	(P) Net price each f.o.b. destination (dollars)	(A)[a] Average performance in per cent of minimum specified	(E) Evaluation of bid price $E = \frac{P}{A}$
	Flashlight battery, D-size cells, Item no. 17-B-7210			
General Dry Batteries, Inc.	50 units	**.04165**	157	.0265
U.S. Electric Mfg. Co.	50 units	.0436	150	.0291
Union Carbide and Carbon Corp.	50 units	.045	145	.0310
Bright Star Battery Co.	200 lbs.	.05[b]	138	.0362
Graybar Electric Co. (Ray-O-Vac)	50 units	.054	147	.0367
General Electric Supply Corp. (Burgess)	200 lbs.	.054[b]	130	.0415

	General-purpose no.-6 dry cells, Item no. 17-B-7600			
General Dry Batteries, Inc.	12 units	.3234	104	.3110
Union Carbide and Carbon Corp.	12 units	**.324**[c]	141	.2298
Union Carbide and Carbon Corp.	12 units	**.351**[d]	141	.2489
U.S. Electric Mfg. Co.	12 units	.3381	105	.3220
Bright Star Battery Co.	200 lbs.	.36[b]	163	.2209
Graybar Electric Co. (Ray-O-Vac)	12 units	.392	135	.2904
	Radio-B batteries, N-size cells, Item no. 16-B-3340			
General Dry Batteries, Inc.	6 units	1.078[d]	...	.....
U,S. Electric Mfg. Co.	6 units	1.10[d]	...	.....
Union Carbide and Carbon Corp.	6 units	**1.116**	185	.603
Bright Star Battery Co.	200 lbs.	1.240[b]	...	.....
General Electric Supply Corp. (Burgess)	200 lbs.	1.337[b]	132	1.013

SOURCE: Calculated from information in the files of the Federal Supply Service, Washington, D.C.
[a] From qualification tests conducted by the National Bureau of Standards.
[b] Bids rejected because delivered prices apply only to orders of 200 pounds or more.
[c] The price of $.324 is for East Coast delivery; the price of $.351 is for West Coast delivery.
[d] Bids rejected because bidders failed to submit samples for qualification test.

year periods, are let covering the required kinds and grades of rugs and carpets. Contractors are required to submit swatches of the selections of colors and designs they will agree to make available, and these compare with their regular selections offered to other customers. Sets of these swatches are available to ordering agencies. The wearing qualities of the rugs are defined by Federal Specifications which call for grades of medium quality that offer the most wear per dollar. For some kinds more than one grade is covered by the specifications and contracts. All kinds, grades, patterns, and colors specified are standard items in the regular production of the manufacturers.

Manufacturers sell directly to retail stores, interior decorators, wholesalers, and large-quantity users, such as hotels. Some mills quote to the government directly and others follow the policy of quoting only through their wholesale representatives. There is price competition, and awards are made for the entire requirement of the government to the low bidders for each item. Both manufacturers and wholesale representatives are successful bidders. Contract prices cover delivery in any quantity to any point in the United States so that the contracts afford a service to the users similar to that provided by retail stores with the exception that selections must be made from swatches rather than by viewing the rugs themselves.

Contract prices effective during 1949 and 1950 for the largest-volume item used by the government—plain-pile velvet rug—are shown below in comparison with prices collected by the Bureau of Labor Statistics for the same commodity which represent average prices at which the mills sold. During the year ending February 28, 1950, contractors reported that more than $444,000 worth of this item was purchased by government agencies under the term contract. Prices for 1949 were from 15 to 20 per cent above the mill prices reported by the Bureau of Labor Statistics while the 1950 contract prices varied from slightly below the mill prices to about 25 per cent less in October after the price rise following the outbreak of war in Korea (Figure 13). The commodity to which these prices are related is the same, but the government prices include delivery costs in any quantity anywhere in the United States, while the Bureau of Labor Statistics prices are f.o.b. mill. Comparative shopping in the Washington area revealed that the 1949 contract prices were from 40 to 45 per cent below those at which the rugs were offered to retail customers. The low 1950 contract prices to the government appear to reflect the increased incentive to bid competitively in the fall of 1949 when mills were able to obtain ample supplies of raw materials and were concerned about the appearance of excess capacity in their plants.

Contractors seriously erred in their estimates of the future course of costs and demand when bidding for the 1950 contracts. Supplies of carpet wools from China and India were cut off; costs, demand,

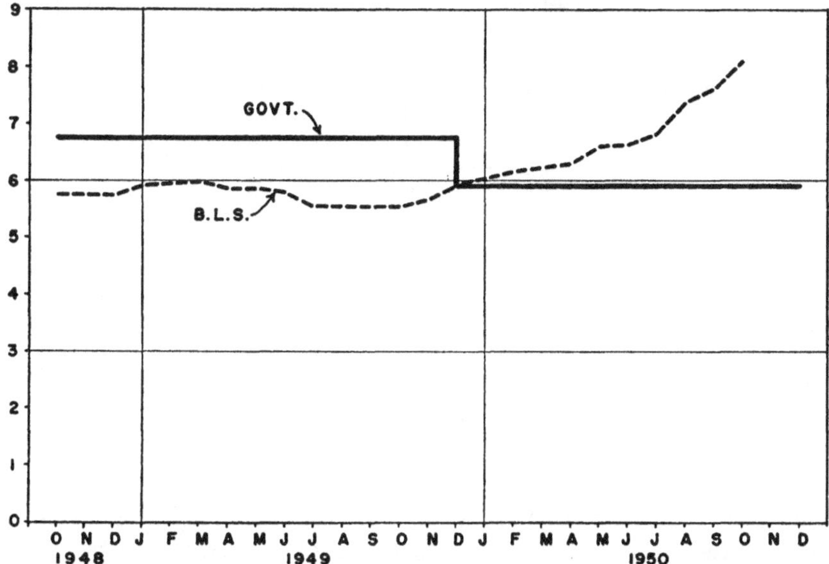

Fig. 13. Rugs; Velvet, Plain Pile: Government-Contract Prices and Bureau of Labor Statistics Average Mill Prices.

Source: For government-contract prices, files of the Federal Supply Service; for average mill prices, *Average Wholesale Prices and Index Numbers of Individual Commodities,* Bureau of Labor Statistics.

and mill prices moved upward rapidly from the time when the bids were figured in October, 1949, until October, 1950.

By the time invitations were issued for contracts for the year 1951, the supply situation was even more uncertain. As a result the prices bid on many items were considered excessive; on some items no bids were forthcoming. Awards were made on items for which prices were considered reasonable, but it was necessary to reject many bids on the ground that they were not reasonable. Contracts were then negotiated for these items individually with suppliers under a provision of the law which exempts the agency in such cases from the requirement to use the sealed-bids procedure.

This makes it possible to obtain satisfactory contracts because negotiation permits adjustments in the commodity specification and the duration of contracts to bring them in line with each contractor's estimate of his ability to supply the commodity.

The method used in awarding contracts for carpets and rugs offers an interesting contrast with that used in awarding dry-battery contracts. Both are commodities for which material differences exist among brands competing at the same general price

TABLE 25

TWISTED-PILE VELVET CARPET: BIDDERS' PRICES AND CONTRACT AWARDED SHOWING METHOD OF EVALUATING UTILITY

(Prices net f.o.b. any point in U.S. for a term contract awarded in 1948. Price of successful bidder in bold face.)

Brand name	(P) Price per square yard (dollars)	(W) Wear index	Evaluation factor $E = \frac{W}{P}$
Assembly	**4.40**	191	43.4
Caracul	5.12	192	37.5
Pinehill	4.57	110	24.0

SOURCE: Files of the Federal Supply Service, Washington, D.C.

lines, but the procedure for awarding contracts for batteries takes these differences into account while that of awarding rug contracts assumes that all brands meeting the minimum requirements of the specification are of equal durability.

An illustration of the possible loss through failure to consider quality above the minimum specified is afforded by a problem of award that arose in 1948. Bids were received on three different brands of twisted-pile velvet carpet none of which met the requirements of the specifications. It was, therefore, found necessary to make the award on some other basis. Samples of the carpets were obtained and tested, and awards were made on a quality–price basis. The prices and test results are shown in Table 25. The award was made to the company offering the "Assembly" brand, the bid for which was lowest in dollar price and also represented the most economical brand in terms of the wear per dollar. Patterns, colors, and other characteristics were equivalent for the lines offered.

This time the procedure was found necessary because no carpet offered met the specification requirements. Differences in wear are found in brands, all of which meet the minimum requirements of Federal Specifications. By failing to evaluate these differences in the usual process of purchasing where the low bidder whose product meets the specification receives the award, the government fails to maximize utility per dollar.

Automobiles.—The demand for automotive vehicles by any one civilian agency of the government is small during any year or shorter period. In the past, agencies have purchased their requirements through dealers on the same basis as any business firm at prices which varied from list according to the policies of particular dealers regarding trade-in allowances. By requiring all civilian agencies to submit their requisitions for vehicles every month to Washington for procurement, the Federal Supply Service was able to issue invitations to bid for the consolidated demand for vehicles and thus induce manufacturers to bid directly for government contracts. The consolidated requirements total from 15,000 to 20,000 vehicles of all descriptions per year, and invitations to bid usually list upward of a thousand vehicles. Most of these are passenger cars which are discussed below.

Detailed quality specifications are inappropriate for passenger cars because of the generally prohibitive expense of adjusting production facilities to design variations which might be required; and because of the reliability of the quality control applied by manufacturers. Government specifications for passenger cars, therefore, are used to define the general price class of the car to be purchased, to insure that only reliable manufacturers bid, and to insure delivery of the car that is normally provided to retail customers (that is, to prevent stripping cars of accessories when delivering them to the government). Manufacturers or their dealers provide the same guarantees and initial servicing on cars delivered to other customers. There were, in the 1950 specification, five classes of cars defined by length of wheel base and the minimum weight of the car. All approved makes and models are grouped into one or another of the five classes, and all makes grouped in each class are considered to be equally acceptable for purchase. Special colors, radiators, tires, and accessories may be specified in addition to the general requirements in order to meet the needs of particular users. A safeguard against the purchase of poor-quality cars is provided by the requirement that only well-established manufacturers who have been making automobiles for two years or more and who are equipped to give prompt repair service can qualify as contractors.

Awards are made on each item of the invitation which may be one or more cars for delivery to a specified location. All manufacturers and dealers are potential suppliers, although dealers ordinarily cannot compete. From the close of World War II until 1952 the General Motors Corporation and the Ford Motor Company were consistent bidders. Other manufacturers did not bid for government contracts.

TABLE 26

AUTOMOBILES: GOVERNMENT-CONTRACT AND RETAIL PRICES (July, 1948–October, 1949)

Date	Retail price (dollars)	Government contract price (dollars)	Percentage by which government contract price is less than retail
July–September, 1948	1,535	1,225	20
October–December, 1948	1,545	1,260	18
April–June, 1949	1,560	1,290	17
July–September, 1949	1,560	1,235	21
October, 1949	1,560	1,220	22

SOURCE: Files of the Federal Supply Service. Retail and government-contract figures are average delivered prices for all kinds of vehicles purchased—predominantly Fords and Chevrolets.

The prices paid by the government were close to dealers' prices which vary from 18 to 24 per cent off list prices depending on the make of car and the manufacturers' policies. The weighted averages of the contract prices and the retail list prices for all makes of standard four-door sedans in the latter part of 1948 and during 1949 are shown in Table 26. During the first half of 1950 contract prices were more favorable to the government than in 1949. However, the prices are not uniformly any exact percentage off list prices, but vary from time to time and from item to item on each individual invitation.

The evidence in the bids shows that the manufacturers appear to quote independently for government contracts. Two examples will serve to illustrate the nature of the bidding. On the invitation issued June 21, 1950, awards were made on 137 passenger cars, with 69 to Pontiac Motor Division, 32 to Chevrolet Motor Division, 1 to Buick Motor Division, all of General Motors Corporation; and 35 to the Ford Motor Company. Item 20 of this invitation, a standard black four-door car, was awarded to Chevrolet at $1,171.48, f.o.b. Indianapolis. Deducting the cost of heater, defroster, freight, and the cash discount brings the net price f.o.b. Flint, Michigan, to $1,035.18 which compares with the dealers' net price for the same model of $1,087.50 (Chevrolet Styleline Special 1500 HJ Sed. 4D-6 ADP $1450; *N.A.D.A. Western Edition Official Used Car Guide,* Vol. 17, No. 5, May 1950, p. 189). A dealers' discount of 25 per cent—a figure probably in excess of the actual—was assumed in figuring the comparable price. Ford bid $1,153.07 f.o.b. Dearborn, Michigan, on the same item which is equivalent to $1231.87 f.o.b. Indianapolis compared with the Chevrolet price of $1171.48. If the cost of heater, defroster, and cash discount is considered, the Ford price came to $1093.57 compared with a dealers' net of $1103.25.

On item 30 of the same invitation Ford was the low bidder on a car with the same specifications, but for delivery in Dearborn, Michigan. The company quoted $1187.97 less $25 for cash in 30 days. Less the accessories and the discount this comes to $1122.47 compared with the dealers' price of $1103.25.

Freight apparently plays an important part in determining whose price is low. If a company has other vehicles to deliver to a location specified in one of the items in the invitation, it may be able to combine the shipments and deduct the resulting saving in freight or some part of it from the delivered price quoted to the government.

Ford and General Motors during 1946, 1947, and 1948, when they were not producing enough cars to supply the demands of their dealers, bid for government contracts and supplied the needs of the government. This may have been in part because it was considered good policy to supply the government, in part for advertising purposes, and, of course, in part because the companies made about the same profit on government business as they did on cars supplied to their dealers.

State governments buy directly from manufacturers except when they pursue policies of buying through resident sources, but other large fleet owners buy through dealers. At times such buyers receive a special discount for quantity purchases. FSS officials believe the government is able to buy at least as favorably as any other user-buyer.

All cars in each price class are considered equivalent for government use, and agencies are limited to the use of cars costing less than $1,500 by law which requires special congressional approval for purchases of higher-priced automobiles. In fact, automobiles within price classes are materially differentiated in both durability and economy of operation. Thus a possibility of loss is introduced by applying the policy of product homogeneity to passenger vehicles.

Performance and construction specifications are used for purchasing trucks. These are considered necessary because the service requirements and performance characteristics of trucks vary widely. The specifications define the performance required to satisfy the service requirements and to sort the varieties of trucks offered into those which can meet the requirements satisfactorily and those which cannot. As with passenger vehicles, no evaluation is made of differences in quality offered beyond the specified minimum.

VIII

Buying Government-Specification Products in Competitive Markets

Characteristics of the Markets

The products in many markets discussed in previous chapters, for example paint and various kinds of paper, may be tailored specially for the government in the sense that their formulae or designs are adjusted in manufacture to meet the requirements of Federal Specifications. Such products, however, lie within the pattern of substitutes existing in the market. The adjustments made by manufacturers are made either to raise the quality of their products to the specified level to make them eligible for contracts, or to lower the quality to the specified level in order to reduce costs of manufacture. In contrast, the government-specification products discussed in this chapter were designed specially for the government because no product existed in the pattern of substitute products offered by manufacturers which adequately met the needs of the government.

The products thus specially designed were specified because existing products either were not sufficiently durable, were too costly to operate and maintain in good repair, or because as produced by different suppliers they were not dimensionally or functionally interchangeable in use. They provide the government with substantial savings in utility per dollar.

Some of these commodities have been offered by manufacturers to buyers other than the government. Generally speaking, however, the products are not considered to be sufficiently salable to make it profitable for manufacturers to promote them as vigorously as their own designs serving the same uses. As a result the markets are limited to those buyers who buy in large quantities and are aware of, and use, the government specifications. Sellers are few, largely because the products are not attractive for profitable promotion and also because the typical investment in tooling is high.

Government-Specification Products

Electric fans.—Heavy-duty fans sold to private buyers for office use are made by comparatively few firms. The dominant companies are the General Electric Company, the Westinghouse Electric and Manufacturing Corporation, the Emerson Electric Manufacturing Company, and Robbins and Myers, Incorporated. Streamlined appearance, quietness of operation, reasonable air-circulating effectiveness, and features permitting production-cost savings have been important in designing the product, with less attention focused on durability, cost of maintenance, and cost of operation. The products of different firms are materially differentiated with respect to all these features, but the stress in sales promotion is on features such as streamlining which are of no consequence to many users.

Tooling expense is heavy, and any substantial changes in design are economical only if production quantities are large. Most buyers purchase in quantities far less than those necessary to justify design changes and must choose from the alternative products offered them in the market.

Fans are sold to authorized distributors who resell them to dealers, industrial firms, and other users. If fans were purchased locally by government agencies they would have to buy from dealers, like most firms, although sometimes agencies might be able to buy directly from distributors. The prices at which individual manufacturers offer fans are stable and substantially uniform. They are quoted as list prices less discounts to established classes of trade.

The Federal Supply Service consolidates the requirements of all agencies for fans and invites bids for definite-quantity-definite-delivery contracts, usually one each year. Bids include prices f.o.b. shipping point, f.o.b. federal supply centers in carload lots, and f.o.b. any point in the United States in less than carload lots so that the government may specify shipment in the most economical manner.

Comparison of the prices paid by the government for Federal-Specification fans with those paid by other buyers are difficult to make because most companies do not list them for general sale, and few buyers—aside from the federal government—purchase them. One company does list them, and the prices at which it offers the 16-inch fan compared with the price paid by the government, under the contract let for 19,192 fans in April, 1950, are presented in Table 27. This company bid $23.79 per fan f.o.b. any point in the United States for the government contract. This was about 20 per cent lower than its price to distributors for the same fan. Only three bidders offered fans meeting the specification. The Emerson Electric Manufacturing Company was awarded the contract at the price of $22.24 f.o.b. shipping point; the Hunter Fan and Ventilating Company whose delivered price bid of $23.79 was discussed

TABLE 27

ELECTRIC FANS: GOVERNMENT-CONTRACT AND TRADE PRICES

Retail price	$ 52.95
Suggested net price to industrial users	40.39
Suggested net price to dealers (small quantities)	36.36
Suggested net price to dealers (large quantities)	34.86
Distributors' price	29.58
Price bid for the government contract	23.79
Price at which the government contract was awarded	22.94

SOURCE: The prices shown are all for the Federal Specification fan of the Hunter Fan and Ventilating Company, the only firm for which comparative prices are available, with the exception of the contract price which is that of the Emerson Electric Manufacturing Company, the successful bidder. Prices were calculated from the catalog information of the Hunter Fan and Ventilating Company or obtained from the files of the Federal Supply Service, Washington, D.C. All prices are f.o.b. any point in the United States, l.c.l.

above, was next to the lowest bidder, quoting $23.05; and the third low bidder was Robbins and Myers, Incorporated at $24.40 (Table 28). The General Electric Company and the Westinghouse Electric and Manufacturing Corporation bid through their distributing companies on their fans which failed to meet the specifications. The only other bidder was the A. C. Gilbert Company whose fan also failed to meet the specifications.

Contracts for electric fans are awarded to the bidder whose offer results in the lowest evaluation factor rather than the lowest price. For fans, the evaluation factor is the net price of the fan plus its cost of operation for 5,000 hours (about ten years of operation in service) less the part of the cost of operation attributable to the amount of air delivered above the minimum specified.[1] Bidders are required to furnish the technical information necessary to calculate the evaluation factor; this information is also available

[1] For a more complete explanation of the formula for calculation of the evaluation factor for fans see table 28, footnote a.

from the tests which are made on the samples submitted with the bids.

The calculations for the evaluation of the bids received in response to the invitation of May, 1950, revealed that the Emerson Electric Company's fan was not only the lowest in price but was also the most efficient of all fans offered for sale to the government. While the use of the evaluation factor in this case resulted in award to the bidder offering the lowest price as well, at times it results in awards to bidders whose offers are not the lowest in price but are the lowest in cost to the government when operating costs are added to the purchase cost of the fan.

For commodities such as fans, which require years to be used up, not only the efficiency of operation but the costs of repair and maintenance and the serviceable life are important in determining utility. These factors are not evaluated for fans when making awards, but they are taken into account in the minimum requirements of the specification. Durability, low maintenance costs, and efficiency of operation are the principal differences between the government-specification fans and those which are offered generally in markets.

Venetian blinds.—Hundreds of firms which typically sell in local or regional markets manufacture venetian blinds. Most firms buy the slats, tape, cords, and hardware from parts manufacturers and confine their production to assembly and installation of the blinds. Designs of different manufacturers differ widely in durability and often vary for one manufacturer at different times depending on his source of supply for the parts.

Installations are priced individually, tailor-made for each job, and sold by the manufacturers either directly to the user or billed through contractors, retail stores, or interior decorators. The products of competitive firms are highly differentiated both in durability and service.

Until the early 1940's the government, like any other buyer, found it necessary to buy venetian blinds from local suppliers. Difficulties in insuring the purchase of adequately durable blinds and of repair and maintenance led to the development of a Federal Specification and the use of federal-supply-schedule term contracts through which the requirements of all agencies of the government could be supplied.

The specification was developed with the aid of reputable firms in the industry and defines blinds which are not identical to those

TABLE 28

ELECTRIC FANS: BIDDERS' PRICES AND CONTRACT AWARDED SHOWING METHOD OF EVALUATING UTILITY
(Prices for contract for 19,192 fans[a], awarded April 4, 1950. Price of successful bidder in bold face.)

Bidders	Performance characteristics		(A)	Evaluation of utility above specified requirements[c]		
	Watts input (specification .80 maximum)	(PT) Pounds thrust (specification .90 minimum = RPT)	Net price each f.o.b. shipping point (dollars)	(C) Cost of operation for 5,000 hours at 2c per KWH (dollars)	$C\left(1-\frac{RPT}{PT}\right)$ Credit for ability to deliver air above specified minimum	(E) Evaluation factor $E=A+C-C\left(1-\frac{RPT}{PT}\right)$
A. C. Gilbert Co.[b]	...	.....	19.98	.....	.....	.....
Emerson Electric Mfg. Co.	55	1.12	**22.24**	5.50	1.08	26.66
Hunter Fan and Ventilating Co.	62	0.93	23.05	6.20	0.20	29.00
Robbins and Myers, Inc.	60	1.05	24.40	6.00	0.89	29.51
Westinghouse Electric and Mfg. Co.[b]	77	0.99	22.25	7.70	0.70	29.00
General Electric Supply Corp.[b]	110	1.12	25.43	11.00	2.16	34.27

SOURCE: Computed from information in the contract files of the Federal Supply Service, Washington, D.C.

[a] Fans, electric, 16-inch, 115 volt, 60-cycle A.C., oscillating, 3-speed, in accordance with Federal Specification no. W-F-101a and Amendment 2, except that either rip or nonrip type of cord will be permitted under paragraph E-11, and under Table I the minimum pounds thrust for the 16-inch fans shall be .90. Item no. 17-F-750.

[b] Bids rejected because fans offered failed to meet specifications. Performance characteristics for Westinghouse and General Electric fans are included for purposes of illustration only.

[c] The evaluation factor is used to evaulate only the performance of fans in excess of that specified. The specification requirements define a minimum quality that fans must meet for bids to be considered.

The formula for calculating the evaluation factor is $E = A + \left(.10\ MWI \times \frac{WI}{MWI} \times \frac{RPT}{PT}\right)$ in which E = evaluation factor; A = net price of fan; .10 = constant, equivalent to the cost per watt over a period of 5,000 hours at 2c per kilowatt hour; MWI = maximum watts input permitted by the specification; WI = watts input of the fan as measured by the National Bureau of Standards; RPT = minimum pounds thrust required by the specification; and PT = pounds thrust of fan as measured by the National Bureau of Standards.

For purposes of showing separately the two factors—(a) cost of operation for 5,000 hours, and (b) the credit for ability of the fan to deliver air above the specified minimum (pounds thrust)—the formula has been rewritten in this form: $E = A + C - C\left(1 - \frac{RPT}{PT}\right)$ where C = cost of operation for 5,000 hours at 2c per KWH (in the original form $C = .10\ MWI \times - \frac{WI}{MWI}$ as shown in the formula above) and $C\left(1 - \frac{RPT}{PT}\right)$ credit for ability of fan to deliver air above the specified minimum.

offered by any firm in the industry, but can be made by any firm because the parts, although of high quality, are standard and available from the manufacturers supplying parts to the assemblers. In addition to barring the use of inferior parts, the specification limits the types, classes, and sizes of blinds to the minimum number which would adequately serve the needs in order to increase quantities of each item purchased. The result is a better product, the receipt of bids from the better-established primary sources, increased competition, lower prices, and cheaper and more adequate maintenance.

A rough idea of the relative importance of the government contract to a supplier is provided by the fact that the government spent about $80,000 for venetian blinds in the year ending June 30, 1947. The figure is substantial, but would not amount to a major part of the yearly business of a well-established firm. Individual orders vary in size according to each installation and are placed under the term contract by the using agencies at whatever time they have requirements to fill, and budgeted funds to cover the purchase. They compare in size with the usual orders received by the suppliers from other buyers.

The price paid by agencies ordering locally before the specification was promulgated averaged 36.7 cents a square foot, which was considered to be in line with prices paid by comparable purchasers. The price, immediately after purchases were shifted to the term contract based on the new specification calling for a substantially improved product, was 20 cents a square foot or about 45 per cent lower than the previous price.

More than 250 firms are invited to submit bids, and usually more than 20 bids are received. Many bids are rejected because samples fail to meet the specification in some significant respect. A half dozen or more bids are responsive, however, and these reflect independent attempts of firms to obtain the awards by quoting favorable prices.

Steel filing cabinets.—Filing cabinets are given hard use in government offices, and as the government fully expects to be in business during the foreseeable future it finds it economical to buy long-lasting equipment. Although most users feel the same way, manufacturers have found that the salability of filing cabinets does not require maximum utility per dollar. Principally for this reason, but also because cabinets of various manufacturers differed in color and dimensions, the government developed a Federal Specification calling for a special design of cabinet which is more durable than the highest quality cabinets regularly sold and termed by the industry "Grade A" cabinets.

Government-specification cabinets are now purchased, not only by the government, but by large-quantity users such as insurance companies and railroads. The market originated for government purchases has thus broadened to include additional buyers. A number of the large-scale producers of steel office furniture are tooled to make the government specification cabinets. While it is at times possible for small-quantity purchasers to buy government-specification cabinets through usual retail outlets, manufacturers and retailers prefer to promote the sale of other grades of cabinets.

Before World War II the government was able to buy filing cabinets on term contracts at prices considered to be favorable. During the war, however, steel cabinets were not produced, and even wooden ones were difficult to procure. As a result, government agencies were encouraged to buy locally. By 1947 steel equipment was again available. Prices were high and the agencies were seldom able to procure government-specification cabinets but were forced to buy the lower-quality commercial Grade A cabinets. In 1947 when the government decided again to centralize its requirements, manufacturers were reluctant to bid. They were having difficulty in procuring the amount of steel required to fill the orders from their dealers, and also they preferred to sell to the government through their regular channels which gave them larger profits than they could expect from competitive bidding for the government's centralized requirements.

Faced with this situation the government took advantage of the fact that its requirements for high-quality filing cabinets are a sufficient part of the total demand to enable it to influence sellers' policies. A regulation was issued requiring that all requisitions for cabinets be submitted to the Federal Supply Service in Washington for procurement. A survey of manufacturers showed that one company was willing to allocate a part of its production to fill government orders, although this was not enough to meet all requirements. Bids were invited, and the contract was awarded to this firm which was the only manufacturer to bid and the only bidder who offered a Federal-Specification cabinet.

Later, when government agencies stopped buying from dealers, the latter were unable to use their full allocations from manufacturers. As a result, a number of manufacturers became willing to quote directly to the Federal Supply Service. By "drying up" the demand on dealers the government was able to use its buying power to make it profitable for manufacturers to open up primary markets for its purchases. This is, of course, possible only where the government requirements are a significant part of the production in the industry and where the type of good and the demand for it are of such a character that its purchase can be postponed for the time required to make the manufacturers feel the loss of sales.

The government is able to buy filing cabinets at prices below

TABLE 29

Filing Cabinets: Government-Contract and Dealers' Prices
(Prices net per cabinet, l.c.l., f.o.b. destination, fall, 1949)

Shipment zone	Dealers' list price (dollars)	Dealers' net price assuming 36 per cent dealers' discount (dollars)	Government contract price
Eastern	69.75	44.64	38.60
Central	76.75	49.12	40.02
Western	83.75	53.60	41.85

Source: Dealers' list prices were obtained from manufacturers' price lists. Exact dealers' discounts are not known but are believed by Federal Supply Service officials to be 36 per cent. Government contract prices are from contract files of the Federal Supply Service, Washington, D.C., for item no. 26-S-16030, sections: steel, 4-drawers high, 1-drawer wide, letter size, without lock, olive-green finish, in accordance with Federal Specification no. AA-F-791b.

those at which manufacturers sell to dealers. Table 29 compares the prices paid by the government during the fall of 1949 with dealers' list prices. It shows that the government was able to buy at 40–45 per cent off list prices compared with net prices to dealers assumed to have been 36 per cent off list. Direct comparisons with prices paid by other large-quantity buyers are not available, but these prices are probably the lowest offered by manufacturers to any buyer. The advantage to the user agencies is obviously great because they would otherwise pay net prices which experience has shown average about 15 per cent off dealers' list prices.

An examination of the bids received in response to five invitations issued from August, 1947, through July, 1950, shows that in 1947 the only manufacturer to submit a bid for cabinets which met the Federal Specification was the Art Metal Construction Company (Table 30). Five bids of dealers were rejected because the products offered failed to meet specifications. In 1949 and after, a dozen additional manufacturers bid but many of them were unable to offer a cabinet which met the requirements of the

TABLE 30

FILING CABINETS:[a] BIDDERS' PRICES AND CONTRACTS AWARDED
(Prices net per cabinet, f.o.b. shipping point. Prices of successful bidders in bold face.)

Bidders	Term of contract				
	8-8-1947 through 2-8-1948	3-19-1949 through 6-30-1949	9-23-1949 through 1-31-1950	1-31-1950 through 6-30-1950	7-1-1950 through 1-31-1951
Art Metal Construction Co.	**39.85**	**43.00**	**37.50**	**38.30**	**38.30**
Arnot and Co.	52.00[b]	.....	.....	.....	.....
The Albert Manlon Co.	44.85[b]	.....	.....	.....	.....
Griffith-Koch and Co., Inc.	45.60[b]	.....	.....	.....	.....
The Walcott Taylor Co., Inc.	49.35[b]	.....	.....	.....	.....
The Walten M. Ballard and Co.	45.68[b]	.....	.....	.....	.....
The Bentson Mfg. Co.	.....	40.74[b]	38.24	**37.40**	**38.20**
Columbia Steel Equipment Co.	.....	50.02	41.30[b]	39.30[b]	41.20[b]
Harrison Sheet Steel Co.	.....	41.00[b c]	.....	37.75[b]	38.75[b]
Hillside Metal Products, Inc.	.....	38.85	**36.22**	**36.22**	39.12
Security Steel Equipment Corp.	.....	**42.90**	**38.10**	**39.00**	**39.00**
All-Steel Equipment Co., Inc.	.....	38.40[b]	.....	.....	.....
Capitol Office Supply Co.	.....	38.00[b c]	.....	.....	.....
The Globe Wernicke Co.	.....	46.80	.....	.....	.....
Brown Morse Co.	.....	.....	40.00[b]	.....	.....
Miller Desk and Safe Co.	.....	.....	40.00[b c]	.....	.....
Steel Furniture Mfg. Co.	.....	.....	53.37[b]	.....	.....
Genessee Office Equipment Co.	.....	.....	45.00[b c]	.....	.....
Lyon Metal Products Inc.	.....	.....	.....	35.85[b]	.....
The General Fireproofing Co.	.....	.....	.....	.....	42.12

SOURCE: Based on data in the contract files of the Federal Supply Service, Washington, D.C.
[a] Sections: steel, 4-drawers high, one-drawer wide, letter size, without lock, olive-green finish, in accordance with Federal Specification no. AA-F-791b. Item no. 26-S-16030.
[b] Bids rejected or not considered because samples submitted failed to meet specifications.
[c] Prices quoted only f.o.b. destination; f.o.b. shipping-point prices shown were estimated for purposes of comparison.

specification. By 1950 five manufacturers whose products met specification requirements were bidding for contracts apparently independently and competitively. Some of these were still unwilling to commit themselves to supply the entire demand of the government, and dual and multiple awards were necessary to insure procurement of all requirements. Purchases of filing cabinets in the fiscal year 1949 totaled $4,150,000.

Wood furniture.—Furniture has utility because of those characteristics which make it pleasing and acceptable in appearance as well as those which make it durable, comfortable, and convenient in use. Its salability depends more upon appearance than on other features. Because it is ordinarily sold to store buyers who are interested in its salability, there is a heavy emphasis on appearance; durability and convenience in use are secondary, although still important, factors.

One result of this emphasis on salability is periodic style changes. The most important period for selling furniture in primary markets is during the yearly furniture shows at which all manufacturers display their lines. Manufacturers feel the need of making an impression each year at the shows by displaying and promoting some new designs, regardless of how materially different they are from previous ones. This has led to a strong emphasis on superficial differentiation and an occasional tendency to save in costs by skimping on hidden construction details which affect durability.

The wood-furniture industry is able to make changes to meet particular specifications and design requirements for relatively small quantities. The cost of special designs and patterns can be absorbed in the total costs of perhaps 100 pieces without bringing such costs out of line with those of standard designs.

Manufacturers are numerous and geographically widely scattered, although there are centers, such as High Point, North Carolina; Grand Rapids, Michigan; and Chicago where plants cluster heavily. Many specialize in case goods or upholstered furniture, high quality or lower grades, or in modern, period, or traditional styles. All sell their output through department stores, retail furniture stores, or interior-decorating establishments. The products of each are differentiated by characteristics, which are significant or not from the government's viewpoint.

The government buys executive-type wood office furniture and household-and-quarters furniture from the manufacturers. In both instances specifications defining special products have been considered necessary in order to insure durability and functional interchangeability. In contrast with other products previously discussed, interchangeability in use is very important for furniture. Under the sealed-bids procedure different manufacturers may be awarded contracts over periods well within the life of the furniture previously procured, and the specifications must insure that the products of any contractor will be usable in combination with the products of former and future contractors. In addition, the products of different manufacturers vary so greatly in durability that minimum-quality requirements are necessary if the government is to have any chance of maximizing the utility per dollar in buying furniture. Executive office furniture and household-and-quarters furniture are alike in the respects just noted, but they differ considerably in other respects and can best be discussed separately.

The executive-type furniture and furnishings purchased by the government are constructed to special designs. This is necessary both for the reasons noted in the preceding paragraph and also to prevent competition among high-ranking government officials in furnishing offices. The needs of the officials who are entitled to use this type of furniture are common to all, and the government is, therefore, willing to eliminate personal preferences entirely and to make a common decision as to the appropriate design. The Federal Specifications include design drawings and define a style of furniture that is comparable with the best offered through regular market channels for the same use and specify construction features which give it maximum durability.

This kind of furniture is bought under federal-supply-schedule one-year term contracts let by sealed bids and normally with single awards to the low bidders for each item. The government reserves the right to make awards to other than low bidders and may require production samples to be submitted for examination and test before making awards. Thus, unusual considerations are permitted in making awards to insure delivery of the specified high-quality product. The procedure does, of course, tend to limit the number of competitive bidders, because a firm which has not supplied the product must expend much time and money to provide samples; and to assure the government that it is in a position to deliver the products according to the conditions of the contract. For the year ending April 30, 1950, contractors reported about $500,000 worth of sales under the contracts for furniture and furnishings of this type, with about 90 per cent of this amount accounted for by desks and chairs.

Price comparisons are not possible because (although the government does not prohibit it) the same items are not offered regularly to other buyers, the furniture sold by manufacturers generally is highly differentiated, and there is no information for comparing quality. Executive-type furniture varies greatly in design and sells at high prices. It is the opinion of government buyers and suppliers of this type of furniture that the government buys at prices much lower than it would pay if it, like most industrial firms, considered the furnishing of the offices of high-ranking officials to be individual decorating problems, and if it therefore bought furniture in small quantities.

There are usually a dozen or more bidders for contracts for executive-type furniture, half a dozen of whom have supplied these items in the past and bid competitively. Other firms from time to time bid for contracts, but their bids often run double or more than those of firms which have had experience with this business. Thus, while the government does obtain a measure of competition, the entry of new competitors is made very difficult by the required investment in patterns, designs, samples, and sales effort to assure the government that the company will be a reliable source of supply. A large part of this expense must be incurred before the award, and the uncertainty of bidding in competition with firms which have already absorbed this initial expense discourages many firms from bidding for contracts.

The buying of household-and-quarters furniture differs from the procurement of executive-type furniture in that the personal preferences of individuals who must use the furniture are considered to be important. In order to satisfy individual preferences and at the same time buy furniture that will be interchangeable with past and future purchases, a similar technique is used as in the purchase of rugs and carpets. Styles and patterns produced in quantity by the industry are specified by drawings, but minor variations not affecting interchangeable use of the item are permitted. Quality is defined by a specification which is in part a performance and in part a construction specification. Where fabrics are involved, the number of patterns and kinds and grades of fabrics which must be offered is specified, and bidders are required to furnish samples of the selection they will offer before contracts are awarded. These samples then become the standard selection for government purchases, and sets of them are made available to the ordering agencies. The resulting furniture is of a quality and design that may not be standard in the regular production of any manufacturer, but which can be produced by any well-equipped firm in relatively small quantities.

To a lesser degree than in executive-type office furniture, investment required in designs, patterns, samples, and sales work together with the uncertainty of being the low bidder, restrict the number of firms which find it profitable to bid. An indication of this situation is given in Table 31 which shows the number of firms submitting bids in comparison with the number invited to bid.

Each class of furniture shown in the table includes a large number of items on which separate prices were quoted. For many items only one or two bidders submitted offers. There are some jobbers and agents among the bidders, but most of them are manufacturers. Contractors are almost without exception manufacturers. If prices are considered not to be excessive, multiple awards are made in order to reduce delivery costs (which are rarely included in the price) and to insure satisfactory supply.

TABLE 31

HOUSEHOLD AND QUARTERS FURNITURE: NUMBER OF BIDDERS RESPONDING TO INVITATION TO BID

Term of contract	Class of furniture	Number of firms invited to bid	Number of bids received
8-1-1950 through 7-31-1951	Early American design....	272	8
5-1-1950 through 4-30-1951	Upholstered living room..	241	14
10-1-1950 through 9-30-1951....................	Traditional and modern...	440	25
11-1-1950 through 10-31-1951....................	Rattan..................	65	3

SOURCE: Files of the Federal Supply Service, Washington, D.C.

Post Office trucks.—An inappropriate specification can call for special production operations that substantially increase costs without adding utility that could be obtained by less costly operations. An outstanding example of such unwisely developed specifications may be found in the specifications by which Post Office Department trucks were purchased in the past.

Post Office trucks are subjected to exceptionally hard service because of the frequent stops and starts, the heavy traffic in which they must be driven, and the loads which must be carried. Because of this heavy service as well as the demands for safety of mails in transit, the trucks must be made to government specification.

The specification employed up to 1948 called for a sturdy truck that had been proved durable and efficient in service, but was very costly because of the many special features required by the specification. The specification was, in fact, outmoded, and manufacturers disliked bidding for contracts to supply the trucks. At one time, only one supplier bid to furnish trucks as complete units. After the close of World War II when the Federal Supply Service centralized the purchase of automotive vehicles, purchasing officials

TABLE 32

POST-OFFICE TRUCKS: GOVERNMENT-CONTRACT PRICES

Date of invitation to bid	Number of trucks purchased	Contractor	Price per truck (dollars)	Index
January 9, 1948......	1,480	Internat. Harvester Co.......	2,220	100.0
December 10, 1948...	1,200	Fargo Motor Co.............	2,178	98.1
September 12, 1949..	1,800	Ford Motor Co..............	1,515	68.2
June 12, 1950........	250	Ford Motor Co..............	1,542	69.9
July 11, 1950........	3,750	Fargo Motor Co.............	1,443	65.0

SOURCE: Federal Supply Service, Washington, D.C. All prices are average delivered prices for comparable light-class trucks purchased for the same use.

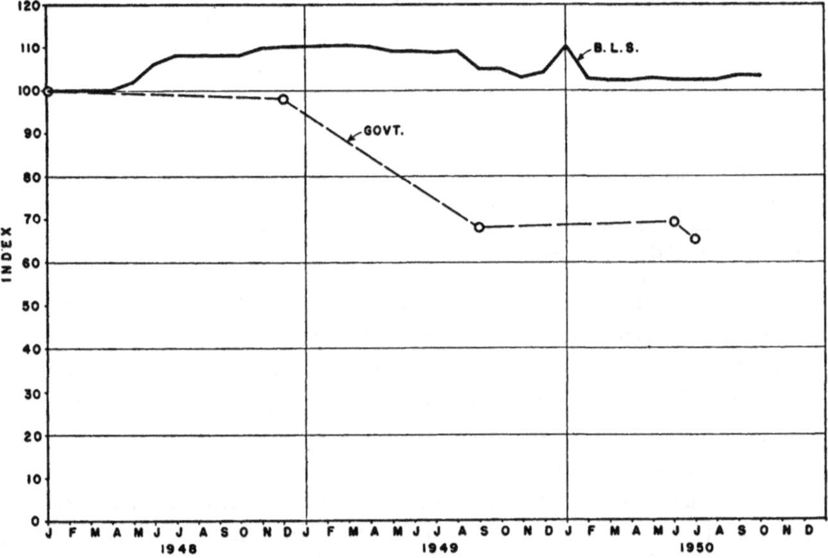

Fig. 14. Indexes of Government-Contract Prices for Post-Office Trucks and Bureau of Labor Statistics Average Wholesale Prices for Trucks (January, 1948 = 100).

Source: Index of government-contract prices calculated from prices in the files of the Federal Supply Service; index of B.L.S. average wholesale prices from *Average Wholesale Prices and Index Numbers of Individual Commodities,* Bureau of Labor Statistics.

together with the Post Office authorities and representatives of the industry, gradually brought the specification in line with industry's practice without sacrificing the serviceability or efficiency of the trucks.

Beginning with the 1948 purchases, changes were introduced as they were proved to be wise, until by 1950 the truck specified was as nearly in conformity with the production methods commonly used by manufacturers as the special nature of the use permitted. The results were an increase in the number of bidders until all major truck manufacturers were bidding, and a drop in the contract price from $2,220 in January, 1948, to $1,443 in July, 1950. These and the prices for intermediate periods are shown in Table 32. This marked downward trend in contract prices was obtained at a time when the trend in wholesale truck prices was slightly upward (Figure 14).

IX

Buying When the Sealed-Bids Device Is Ineffective

Characteristics of the Markets

In all markets discussed thus far the sealed-bids device results in some degree of direct price competition either because it fits government buying into existing market practice; or because, in combination with large-order quantities, it induces sellers to depart from those policies which lead to the quotation of stable prices, backed by sales promotion, and causes them to quote competitively for government contracts. The markets for government-specification products, discussed in the preceding chapter, are unique because sellers do not find it profitable to promote the sale of such products widely. In those markets, however, sealed bids do evoke a degree of price competition.

There are two significantly different types of markets in which the sealed-bids device does not prompt direct price competition: (1) those in which this may be explained by reference to the price policies of sellers, and (2) those in which it may be explained by reference to the product policies of the sellers. In these markets the government, in an effort to obtain price concessions from sellers, either supplements the sealed-bids device with other measures, or abandons it in favor of direct negotiation with suppliers.

In the first group of markets, sellers quote to the government either from their established price lists or in accordance with uniform price policies which eliminate active price competition. The government considers the products of competing sellers in some of these markets to be homogeneous, in others to be materially differentiated. In all markets, however, when contracting, it ignores any material differences and treats competing products as though they were homogeneous. Frequently buyers other than the government consider all these products to be differentiated. Except for the character of sellers' price policies these markets are similar to those previously discussed. They are not numerous, but they are quantitatively important. Included are markets for electric light bulbs, automobile tires and tubes, and steel office furniture.

In the second group are markets in which the products are sufficiently different from the nearest substitutes so that the government finds it profitable to buy them without attempting to produce direct price competition. The government is willing to pay a higher price rather than to accept a remote substitute. Multiple awards are made to all bidders offering makes which are demanded by the using agencies and which are considered to be priced fairly in relation to close substitutes. The products are very important in government purchasing. They include business machines, scientific equipment, pharmaceuticals, and various kinds of repair parts.

Evidence When Sellers' Price Policies Make Sealed Bids Ineffective

Electric lamps.—The markets for electric lamps are dominated by the General Electric Company and the Westinghouse Electric Corporation, which are the only companies producing complete lines of lamps. Sylvania Electric Products, Incorporated, is a large company, but it occupies a position subsidiary to the two major producers in the industry. In addition to these three, there are smaller companies which, although they produce limited lines of lamps, are important in the markets for specialized kinds, such as miniature lamps, fluorescent lamps, flash bulbs, silver-bowl lamps, or projection lamps.

Electric lamps of competing manufacturers are dimensionally and functionally interchangeable in use. Lamp bases and threads are standardized for the industry, and shapes and general over-all dimensions are substantially the same. Lamps of most manufacturers meet the minimum requirements of Federal Specifications, but they are to some degree materially differentiated in length of life. The standard kinds and sizes of lamps which are sold in volume are made by highly mechanized methods, and the investment required for tooling is high.

The two dominant firms pursue identical price policies. These consist of selling through authorized distributors and quoting list prices less discounts which vary for different classes of trade and for different yearly total values of purchases. A distinction is firmly maintained between buyers who purchase for use and those who purchase for resale.

Small-quantity users purchase at the retail list price. Contract users buy at discounts which depend on the yearly net value of their purchases. These discounts range from 26 per cent for annual purchases totaling $300 to a maximum discount of 40 per cent for annual purchases totaling $200,000. Information is not available to show what prices are paid by large-quantity buyers, such as those in the automobile industry, who buy lamps for resale as parts of their product, but prices are presumably lower than the most favorable ones quoted to users.

The smaller companies quote the same list prices as the large ones, but sometimes greater discounts. For Sylvania Electric Products, Incorporated, the maximum discount for users is 41 per cent compared with 40 per cent for the two largest companies, while the smaller companies quote as high as 42.5 per cent. The General Electric Company and the Westinghouse Electric Corporation tolerate this price competition relying upon their more adequate distribution facilities, completeness of line, and engineering service on special lamps to make their contracts attractive to users. The discount for distributors is not made known to users, but the Federal Supply Service officials believe it is from 3 to 5 per cent more than the maximum discount for users, and that it varies with volume, perhaps reaching as much as 47 per cent. These discounts apply to incandescent, tungsten-filament, general-lighting-type lamps. The discounts vary for different types of lamps, but within each type the competitive pattern is similar to that described above.

The government buys lamps on one-year federal-supply-schedule term contracts technically awarded by the sealed-bids procedure. In fact, however, awards are made to all qualified bidders. Electric lamps are among the few products for which bidding is restricted to firms whose products have been qualified by test before bidding. Any manufacturer may have his lamps tested for qualification to bid but must make the request six months in advance of the invitation to bid. The National Bureau of Standards draws samples from the manufacturer's production and conducts the tests. The products of contractors are also tested periodically during the life of the contract to insure continued compliance with specifications. Because many state and city governments will accept bids only from those lamp manufacturers who are qualified to bid for federal-government contracts, most manufacturers request the government to test their lamps, even if they do not bid for federal-government contracts. Partly as a result of some 30 years' experience with Federal Specifications, quality control is well established, and only very occasionally does a product fail to pass the qualifying tests.

The total purchases of lamps under such contracts during the period from September 1, 1948, through August 31, 1949, were reported by contractors to amount to $7,145,000 for all kinds of lamps. Manufacturers have informed the Federal Supply Service that this is approximately 3 per cent of the total lamp production of the largest manufacturer, the General Electric Company, and much larger percentages of the production of other companies. Because of the default provisions of government contracts, together with the possibility of work stoppages because of strikes or for other reasons, no one company is anxious to be committed for all the business. Although the contracts of the two large companies are not limited as to the quantity they will deliver, they have intimated to the Federal Supply Service that they would prefer not to bid for unlimited amounts of business if single awards were to be made.

On the invitation to bid issued in June, 1950, 11 bidders responded. One bidder failed to submit lamps for qualification tests and one submitted lamps which failed to meet the test requirements; the remaining 9 were awarded contracts. All bidders, with the exception of the General Electric Company and the Westinghouse Electric Corporation, were unwilling to commit themselves to accept more than a stated maximum amount of business per year. Furthermore, none of the companies, aside from the two leaders, are able to quote on all 400 kinds and sizes of lamps listed for common government use. Awards are made to the smaller companies to take advantage of the lower prices they offer and to the larger companies both to insure adequate supplies of lamps and to take advantage of the engineering service which they are in a position to offer on the many hundreds of kinds of special-application lamps the government requires.

The conditions of the contracts call for prices which include the cost of delivery of any quantity of lamps to any point in the United States. They also require contractors to furnish to the government 2,000 copies of a price list which includes item descriptions of the lamps they contract to furnish. These are distributed to the government agencies which purchase lamps under the contracts.

The discounts quoted to the government are the maximum discounts to contract users offered in the standard list and discount schedules. For the ordinary tungsten-filament lamps for general-lighting purposes these were, in 1950, 40 per cent for the General Electric Company and the Westinghouse Electric Corporation, 41 per cent for Sylvania Electric Products, Incorporated, 42 per cent for Kenrad, which is a subsidiary of Westinghouse, and 42.5 per cent for the Champion Lamp Works of the Consolidated Electric Lamp Company. All these are the published discounts for contract users whose yearly dollar volume of purchases at net prices totals $200,000 or more.

Although the purchasing policy of the government has not induced sellers to depart from their established price policies, it has brought to all agencies the advantage of the maximum discount for contract users. If agencies contracted separately for lamps, only the Department of Defense could obtain the maximum discount; others, according to estimates made by the Federal Supply Service, would receive on the average a 35 per cent discount. The centralization of contracting and the consequent use of single contracts for all agencies extend the maximum discount to all. In the year ending August 31, 1949, the nonmilitary agencies purchased lamps for $3,929,750, which was 55 per cent of the total of $7,145,000. This is equivalent to $6,549,583 list which at 35 per cent discount would bring the cost to $4,257,229, if purchases were made separately by agencies. Centralized contracting in this case resulted in a saving of $327,479 to the government.

Repeated attempts have been made to induce manufacturers to quote better prices for government contracts, but none have been successful. Plans to purchase lamps for definite large-quantity deliveries and distribute them through supply centers have been explored, but the manufacturers claim that this would not change the government's status as a user and in any event would not reduce costs to the manufacturers who must maintain local stocks to supply other customers. Kenrad, wholly owned by Westinghouse, at times quotes to local governments a larger discount than it offers to the federal government. Attempts to persuade Westinghouse to permit Kenrad to quote equally favorable discounts to the federal government have failed.

The costs of selling to the government in this case are no less than of selling to private users. Since most lamp manufacturers have received contracts they must compete for each order placed by the using agencies. In fact, the selling costs under the present scheme of centralized contracting and multiple awards are sometimes higher than if the agencies purchased separately, because many would buy under yearly contracts with single manufacturers. The necessity for multiple awards thus eliminates one of the advantages of the sealed-bids procedure which normally requires single awards to be made to the low bidder.

Automobile tires and tubes.—The markets for tires and tubes are similar in many respects to those for electric lamps, but the government's attempts to induce sellers to depart from established policies have been more successful for tires and tubes.

The tire-and-tube industry is composed of three types of companies: the major companies—such as the Goodyear Tire and Rubber Company, the B. F. Goodrich Company, the United States Rubber Company, and the Firestone Tire and Rubber Company—which dominate the industry in production volume and distribute tires nationally through factory outlets and authorized dealers; the smaller companies with national distribution; and the smaller companies with regional distribution.

Tires are products which can easily be varied in quality by substitution of different compounds and by changes in the kind of cords used in building the carcasses. Production equipment is specialized and requires a relatively heavy investment of capital, but production techniques are known by all companies and any company regardless of size—if it is adequately tooled—is able to produce a high-quality tire.

The quality of tires has improved a great deal in the past 30 years, but at any given time the quality of competitively priced tires of different manufacturers varies considerably as does the quality of the brands of any one producer and of different sizes within the same brand of the same manufacturer.[1] Competitive products are, therefore, substantially differentiated in wearing qualities even though they are dimensionally and functionally interchangeable in use.

Adequate laboratory tests for measuring the expected life of tires have not been developed, and the only certain method of measuring tire life is by controlled tests in use. Federal Specifications, during the period for which purchasing data were gathered, were composed of requirements which could insure the purchase of a tire which would give good service, but could not be used to measure tire life with sufficient precision to evaluate it in making con-

[1] See data presented in chap. iv, tables 12 and 14.

tract awards. The specifications called for qualification tests as a requirement for bidding, but this served only to eliminate bids from manufacturers who were not capable of making a satisfactory tire.

Tires are sold according to price lines, and the highest-quality tires of manufacturers, which are those purchased by the government, are identified by the term "first line" tires. This is really not an objective measure of quality but only an identification of the brand each manufacturer considers to be competitive in quality at the price line. The tire industry quotes to users and dealers prices which reflect price advantages in the following sequence: retail, contract dealer, national account, large dealer, state government, and original-equipment manufacturer.

The government has for years bought tires on federal-supply-schedule term contracts usually covering purchases of tires for periods of six months. Until 1938 these contracts were let by the sealed-bids procedure. Bids of manufacturers have never reflected active price competition and before 1938 appeared to the government to result from collusive action to eliminate price competition.

In response to the invitation to bid for contracts to cover the six-month period beginning October 1, 1937, the bids of 14 different companies with main offices in 6 states were identical to the cent for all but 15 items of the 129 for which prices were quoted. In these 15 instances one company was responsible for 13 of the different prices, and in 14 of them the prices were higher than the remaining identical bids. The purchasing officials understood from trade sources that tire companies filed with a trade association the prices at which they proposed to sell to dealers and other users including the government, the implication being that this device was used to effect identical bids to the government. The same situation had existed for the bids of previous years, and in this instance the government decided to take remedial action.[2]

All bids were rejected and invitations reissued. When the second set of bids turned out to be a precise duplicate of the first, the secretary of the Treasury formally asked the attorney general if under these conditions all bids could be rejected and the contract negotiated. The opinion of the attorney general was that the evidence of bidding warranted the conclusion that the bids were prima facie the result of collusive action and of a combination in

[2] *Government Purchasing—An Economic Commentary,* T.N.E.C. Monograph No. 19 (Washington: Government Printing Office, 1940). Pp. 37–38.

restraint of trade and that, therefore, the bids could be rejected and negotiation undertaken. The attorney general also suggested that the secretary of the Treasury might find it advisable to refer the matter to the Department of Justice for possible proceedings under the antitrust laws.[3]

The bids were then rejected, and a contract was negotiated with Sears Roebuck and Company at lower prices than those which had been offered by the tire manufacturers. This action, together with the possibility of antitrust action by the Department of Justice, was effective in inducing the tire companies to change their policy. On later invitations bids were not identical and offered tires at lower prices than previously quoted by manufacturers.[4] Since that time the government has been able to buy tires at prices which are the same as those paid by all but the largest original-equipment manufacturers.

At present the federal-supply-schedule contracts are required to be used by all executive departments and agencies of the government, and the prices cover delivery to any point in the United States for orders of two or more tires. Contracts for the six-month period beginning July 1, 1950, were in effect with 26 companies. Many of these companies were equipped to furnish only certain kinds and sizes of tires and tubes; 8 would deliver to any point in the United States including Alaska, 13 would deliver to any point in the Continental United States, while 6 would deliver only into specified zones within the United States.

Contracts are not let by the sealed-bids procedure but by negotiation. Proposals are solicited from all manufacturers, and the resulting bids are tabulated. Bids, as they are received, are not identical but those from the major companies cluster around one price, with the bids of some smaller companies ranging into lower prices. After the bids are tabulated, target prices are decided upon, and bidders whose prices are higher than these are called in and given the opportunity to lower their prices to one of the target levels. The highest of these levels is established at the lowest bid offered by a major company for each item.

As a result of the negotiation the major companies, together with many smaller ones, sign contracts at the target level of prices, with some of the smaller ones signing contracts at the lower prices they bid or down to which they have adjusted. For example, in the

[3] *Duty of Director of Procurement to Reject Collusive Bids* (1937), 39 Att. Gen., 93.

[4] *Government Purchasing—An Economic Commentary*, pp. 37–38.

schedule for six months beginning July 1, 1950, sixteen companies offer the 6 by 16 tire at $8.99, two at $8.93, one at $8.82, and one at $8.29. A comparison of government contract prices with those offered to other classes of purchasers in 1949 is shown in Table 33.

TABLE 33

AUTOMOBILE TIRES AND TUBES: GOVERNMENT-CONTRACT AND TRADE PRICES

(Prices delivered. Government-contract prices are for delivery to any point in U. S. in lots of two or more tires, for term contract May 1, 1949–August 31, 1949.)

Kind of tire or tube	Price in dollars			
	Government contract price	Special state price	National account price	Published retail price
6.00 x 16 4-ply passenger-car tire	8.51	8.62	10.01	14.75
Tube	1.52	1.60	1.80	2.65
6.50 x 16 4-ply passenger-car tire	9.85	10.61	12.32	18.15
Tube	1.85	1.85	2.07	3.05
7.00 x 20 10-ply truck tire	26.34	27.32	32.92	48.50
Tube	2.25	2.76	3.80	5.60
7.50 x 20 10-ply truck tire	30.85	32.42	39.06	57.55
Tube	3.12	3.20	4.41	6.50
8.25 x 20 10-ply truck tire	34.10	36.03	43.40	63.95
Tube	3.35	3.77	5.19	7.65

SOURCE: From information supplied to the Federal Supply Service by tire manufacturers.

The sequel to the decision that the bids of the tire companies in 1937 were collusive is of interest, because it led to a verdict by the courts that the government cannot collect damages suffered from payment of high prices resulting from collusion in violation of the Sherman Act. In 1939 the Department of Justice brought action against 18 identical bidders for government tire contracts to recover treble damages, exceeding $1,000,000 resulting from the high prices paid by the government for tires. The decision of the case turned on the point of whether or not the government was a "person" within the meaning of the act.[5] The district court before

[5] Section 7 of the Sherman Act provides: "Any person who shall be injured by reason of anything forbidden or declared to be unlawful by this act, may sue therefor . . . without respect to the amount in controversy, and shall recover threefold the damages by him sustained, and the costs of suit, including a reasonable attorney's fee." In Sec-

which the case was argued decided that the federal government was not a "person" within the meaning of the law, and this opinion was upheld by the Circuit Court of Appeals and by the Supreme Court.[6] Therefore, as matters stand, the government cannot sue for damages under the Sherman Act. In 1949 the attorney general recommended to a congressional committee studying monopoly power that the law should be amended to permit the government to sue for treble damages, but no action has been taken to amend the law.[7]

Cement.—At present, prices offered for cement contracts reflect apparently competitive bidding and, in view of this, cement could have been discussed in Chapter VI. It is included here because prices bid for cement contracts were remarkably uniform before the basing-point system of pricing was outlawed by the Supreme Court decision in 1948 and the attempts made by the government to obtain competition are of particular interest for the present discussion.

As in bids for tires and tubes, identical bids reflecting uniform prices of sellers have been an acute problem in the government's purchases of cement. The products of sellers are generally considered homogeneous by buyers of cement, and purchases are characteristically made on the basis of nationally standardized specifications. This establishes a definite basis for price competition uncomplicated by differences in the physical product, and doubtless has been a contributing factor in the decisions of sellers to adopt uniform pricing systems. In any event, prices quoted to the government commonly were identical for all bidders, sometimes to the sixth decimal place.[8]

The extent of identical bidding is indicated by the fact that

---

tion 8 "person" is defined "to include corporations and associations existing under or authorized by the laws of either the United States, the laws of any of the Territories, the laws of any State, or the laws of any foreign country."

[6] *Government Purchasing—An Economic Commentary,* pp. 101–102.

[7] Testimony of Attorney General Clark in the U.S. Congress, House, Subcommittee on Study of Monopoly Power of the Committee on the Judiciary, *Study of Monopoly Power,* Hearings, 81st Cong., 1st sess., Serial 14, Part 1; July and Aug., 1949 (Washington: 1949), pp. 86–87.

[8] The detailed evidence on identical bids for government cement contracts is voluminous and well known so it is not reproduced here. Tabulations of many bids for state and federal government contracts, both before and after the basing-point system was ruled to be illegal, are given in U.S. Congress, House, Select Committee on Small Business, *Small Business Objections on Basing Point Legislation, Particularly S. 1008,* Hearings, 81st Cong., 1st sess., pursuant to H. Res. 22, June 28–July 5, 1949 (Washington: 1949).

during the period from July 1, 1937, to May 1, 1939, for which data are available, two or more identical low bids occurred in the bidding for 910 federal-government cement contracts. For 351 contracts, bids other than the low bids were tied. This number of contracts was not related to the total contracts let for cement during the period, but all procuring agencies reported that the practice of submitting identical low bids was either invariable or common.[9]

The government was of the opinion that the prices were not only uniform, but were unnecessarily high,[10] and in effect this was admitted by representatives of the industry who stated that the prices charged to the government were often the same as those charged to small dealers in spite of the fact that the government often bought in very large quantities.[11]

The government tried in many ways to induce cement manufacturers to quote competitively for contracts. A method often attempted was to reject all bids and readvertise for new bids. For some commodities sellers bid competitively on the second invitation, but in bids for cement the second set most frequently was a replica of the first. In any event the process was time consuming and often impracticable because it could result in delays in the construction of needed projects.

On various occasions the Reclamation Bureau of the Department of the Interior—which purchases the largest volume of cement of any government agency—as well as other agencies, requested in invitations that bids be submitted f.o.b. mill instead of on a delivered basis. This attempt met with limited success; in some instances quotations were received on that basis, but later, companies refused to quote any but delivered prices.

In one instance invitations for large cement contracts were the occasion for the entry of a competitor into the industry. On May 1, 1939, bids were invited on 5,800,000 barrels of cement for the construction of Shasta Dam. Delivery of the cement was scheduled in amounts of 290,000 barrels per month for the first six months beginning September, 1941, and 200,000 barrels a month thereafter with deliveries to be completed in about two-and-a-quarter

[9] *Government Purchasing—An Economic Commentary,* p. 33.

[10] See for example, testimony of Secretary of Interior Ickes in U.S. Congress, Senate, Committee on Interstate Commerce, *To Prevent Uniform Delivered Prices,* Hearings, 74th Cong., 2d sess., on S. 4055, March 9 to April 10, 1936 (Washington: 1936), p. 286.

[11] Testimony of B. F. Affleck, president of the Universal Atlas Cement Company, *ibid.,* p. 474.

years. The successful bidder was to be required to post a performance bond of $3,451,000.

A group of men who had been active with companies which participated in the construction of Boulder Dam and who were familiar with the price policies of cement companies, organized the Permanente Cement Company for the purpose of entering the cement manufacturing business. This company bid for the contracts and was low bidder. Although the company had produced no cement at the time, it posted the bond and was awarded the entire contract. This was sufficient to enable the company to construct a plant and enter the cement business. Subsequently, however, the firm found that its interests were the same as those of other manufacturers in the industry, and the bids for government contracts submitted by it were soon identical with those of competitive firms.

Strong attempts were made to persuade the cement manufacturers to bid on an f.o.b. basis. In addition to public statements made by Secretary Ickes of the Department of the Interior on the subject, various high officials of the government had tried to persuade the industry to abandon the use of the basing-point system. This included a request from President Roosevelt to the industry. That the president's appeal caused a stirring in the industry is testified to by a letter from the chairman of the marketing committee of the Cement Institute to another director of the Institute. It read in part: "If we were a generally well regarded industry, we might be justified in taking a stiff trading position on the President's request. However, we are anything but popular, we have a very difficult position to maneuver out of; and we should not gamble unnecessarily, running as we do the risk of a blast from the President's office that may be ruinous. The f.o.b. mill price on Federal business is of no real importance; is entirely practical to grant; can, and I think will, be forced out of us. Therefore, good trading would have been to give in without any trading. Now, when it comes to the larger question of mill price on commercial business, much as I would like to think otherwise, I am convinced that we will have to maintain our basing point position and refuse the President's request . . ."[12]

The industry, however, ignored the attempts at moral suasion

[12] Reproduced in U.S. Congress, House, Select Committee on Small Business, *Small Business Objections on Basing Point Legislation, Particularly S. 1008,* Hearings, pp. 301–302.

and continued to quote to the government delivered prices figured by the basing-point system.

In the tire and tube industry the implied threat of court action, combined with the fact that one seller was willing to quote prices lower than those which firms generally quoted, was sufficient to cause the industry to revise its price policy. The basic conditions of the cement market as compared with those for tires in some respects favored the government's chances of obtaining competition—there was a fair number of producers of a homogeneous product who were in a position to bid for each contract, the government's demand was sufficiently large on individual contracts to offer an incentive to bid competitively, the quantities demanded were not so large as to prohibit the use of single awards to low bidders, and the nature of the demand was such that definite large-quantity deliveries to specified locations were possible. The cement industry, however, is characterized by high overhead costs, a high proportion of transportation costs in the total delivered price, and widely scattered demand and production. The temptation to cut prices is, therefore, strong, and the low prices feared from active price competition loom as a distinct possibility if uniform price policies are not observed. The fear that abandoning the basing-point system in quoting to the government would lead to a general breakdown of uniform pricing policy in the industry was apparently sufficient to prevent any measures, short of successful court action, from causing the industry to change the common price policy.

Steel office furniture.—Markets for sectional steel furniture and steel office desks differ from the markets for other types of furniture and steel filing cabinets discussed in Chapter VIII in that sellers are few and adhere to price policies which are sufficiently uniform to eliminate active direct price competition for government contracts.

Sectional steel furniture consists of various types of standardized sections: letter-size files, document files, card-index files, shallow drawers for documents and forms, compartments for books and stationery, and other units. These can be assembled in many compact combinations to fit the needs of a particular office. An active interest in obtaining this type of equipment was shown by certain members of the General Supply Committee in the early 1920's, and the designs were subsequently developed by the Globe Wernicke Company working with these government officials. In 1951 this company was still the only manufacturer.

The government's purchases of the 82 sectional items which compose this line of furniture totaled about $160,000 for the year ending April 30, 1950, and some sales were made to other users. The government bought by the sealed-bids method, but would consider only bids which included offers for the entire line because it believed the volume on individual pieces was insufficient to attract bidders.

Up to 1951, however, the Globe Wernicke Company had been the only bidder. The investment required in tooling was believed to be far in excess of the yearly purchases by the government. In view of this fact and the uncertainty of being the low bidder, other firms were not attracted by the government business alone. The total demand apparently was also insufficent to encourage the entry of additional firms at the prices established for the product by the Globe Wernicke Company. Prices were limited by the prices of other kinds of office furniture which are not sectional, and the limited and elastic demand appeared to permit the Globe Wernicke Company to retain a monopoly of the market at the prices it had established.

The company sold to the government at prices which were equivalent to its prices to dealers. Because there were no other suppliers, the only alternative the government had to accepting the prices was to reject the bids and purchase other kinds of furniture. The government considered the prices in relation to the utility of sectional furniture to be reasonable compared with the same ratio for substitute products.

The market for steel desks presents the government with problems similar in some respects to those for steel files. Desks made for private users are sold at list prices which vary somewhat for different manufacturers, but the discounts for dealers also vary, and the net prices to dealers are approximately the same throughout the market. Competition for sales takes the form of product differentiation, and in recent years the practice of periodic model changes has become important with the changes consisting largely of differences in appearance.

The government buys a government-specification desk which is also purchased by a few other large-quantity buyers. Differences in design and color of the standard desks of the industry make them unsuitable for government use, but a more important reason for specifying a nonstandard desk is that the commercial desks are not considered by the government to be sufficiently durable to yield the maximum wear per dollar of purchase price. In comparison with steel filing cases, however, the investment for tools and production line equipment to manufacture desks is substantially greater. As a result only a few manufacturers produce the Federal Specification desk. The dominant firm in the government market is the General Fireproofing Company which is also a leading firm in the nongovernment market.

The development of the postwar market for Federal Specification desks took the same form as for steel filing cases. It was known that agencies were paying very high prices locally for desks and often were able to buy only the "streamlined" models which were not so durable as the specification desk. The government attempted to interest airplane and other war-material manufacturers, who were facing conversion to the manufacture of civilian products, in bidding on government specification desks, but none of them were attracted by the possibilities of entering the steel office furniture business. In 1948, however, the General Fireproofing Company agreed to quote for government contracts for limited quantities of desks. The government then used the same technique as it applied in procuring filing cabinets. The Federal Supply Service issued an order that all requisitions for desks be sent to Washington for centralized purchasing.

For the first contract under this arrangement let in August, 1948, the only bidder was the General Fireproofing Company; for the second contract in April, 1949, the Security Steel Equipment Company also bid, but the bid was high and the government was unwilling to award a contract at that price. Both companies, however, were awarded contracts on the following three invitations (Table 34). On one of these invitations three additional firms bid, but their offers were about 60 per cent higher than the price of the General Fireproofing Company, and this apparently discouraged them from bidding on subsequent contracts. In the summer of 1950 the Art Metal Construction Company also bid, but received no contract because its quotation was considered to be high. These bids gave the appearance of price competition, but were very close to dealers' net prices. In the summer of 1950 the government was still in the position of buying at prices set by the price policies of sellers for the market as a whole. The fact that it buys in far larger quantities than any other purchaser had not induced manufacturers to bid in active direct competition for government contracts. The few suppliers in the market apparently found it advantageous to follow uniform policies. The shortage of steel was offered as an explanation of the lack of direct competition, but this did not deter more active competition in the market for filing cabinets which also require steel of similar qualities. The heavy investment required to manufacture desks deterred entry and left the few firms undisturbed in pursuing their established price policies.

TABLE 34

OFFICE DESKS:[a] BIDDERS' PRICES AND CONTRACTS AWARDED

(Prices per desk, f.o.b. shipping point. Prices of successful bidders in bold face.)

Bidders	Term of contract				
	8-9-1948 through 2-9-1949	4-1-1949 through 7-19-1949	8-3-1949 through 12-31-1949	1-1-1950 through 6-30-1950	7-1-1950 through 12-31-1950
The General Fireproofing Co....	**77.61**	**62.15**	**61.00**	**61.00**	**63.75**
Security Steel Equipment Co...	.....	72.30	**60.50**[b]	**62.35**	**65.06**
Kanrickjon, Inc..............	.....	.....	106.00	.....	.....
National Office Furniture Co....	.....	.....	100.00	.....	.....
Penny and Gordon...........	.....	.....	100.00	.....	.....
Art Metal Construction Co.....	.....	.....	.....	.....	69.30

SOURCE: Based on data in the contract files of the Federal Supply Service, Washington, D.C.
[a] Desks, office, steel, flat top, 30½ inches high, 60 inches long, 34 inches wide, double pedestal. Item no. 26-D-2205.
[b] F.o.b. shipping point prices not quoted. Estimated from f.o.b. destination prices.

EVIDENCE WHEN PRODUCT DIFFERENTIATION MAKES SEALED BIDS INEFFECTIVE

Business machines and scientific equipment.—Business machines and scientific equipment are materially differentiated for the government's use in three ways: (1) by their different suitability for performing particular kinds of operations, (2) by their different suitability for the acquired skills of particular operators, and (3) by their different suitability for satisfying the personal preferences of particular operators (which is only psychologically related to the first two kinds of differences).

The differences in the ability of machines to perform different kinds of operations are obvious. Simple calculating machines and bookkeeping machines both can be used to perform arithmetical calculations, but the former cannot be used to write them on accounting forms. Many machines considered different in kind in this respect are substitutes to some degree for a given use. Manufacturers, however, have successfully developed a wide variety of specialized machines which justify their purchase costs because small savings in repetitive operations add up to a large sum. The government requires many different machines for this reason.

Different machines may perform exactly the same operation but be materially differentiated with respect to the acquired skills of particular operators and to the cost of performing the operation. Comptometers and Monroe calculating machines both can be used for arithmetical calculations, but the usefulness of a Monroe calculator to an operator trained to use a Comptometer is very small. The competition of substitute products in these machines, however, is generally closer than competition between machines which perform different operations, and the price differences between them are likely to be smaller.

Because of the differences in such machines with respect to operators' efficiency, the government finds it profitable to purchase the makes of machines which fit the skills of the operators. The government has, at least conceptually, the alternative of hiring employees trained to use the least costly machines, but the costs involved in such a personnel program would ordinarily far outweigh the gains which could be expected from buying the lowest-cost machines suitable for the operations. Where machines are significantly more efficient in performing operations, however, the government, like other employers, does hire specially trained operators.

Operators of many kinds of machines which are interchangeable with regard to the operations they will perform and the training required to use them have strong preferences for the machine of a particular manufacturer. This is especially pronounced in certain types of scientific equipment and typewriters. Different makes of microscopes or typewriters may be identical by any objective measurements of performance and may require practically insignificant adaptations of existing skills for operators to reach the same efficiency using the different makes, but still preferences may be very strong for one make. Equally efficient scientists or stenographers insist that different makes are the best.

These preferences are sufficiently important to make the government unwilling to risk the possible loss of efficiency to gain the advantage of any possible price reduction which might follow grouping several makes and awarding contracts to the low bidder. This decision is reinforced by the fact that the cost per year of the machines is very small compared to the salary cost per year of the operator.

In view of this high degree of material differentiation the government buys business machines and scientific equipment on federal-supply-schedule one-year term contracts awarded without direct price competition to all manufacturers whose products are demanded by government employees.

The only method the government has for obtaining price concessions from suppliers is persuasion backed by the possibility of refusal to sign a contract under which the using agencies can order equipment from the supplier.[13] The government argues that because it uses large quantities of equipment and is willing to contract directly with the manufacturer, it should be offered a lower price than a small-quantity purchaser pays when buying through dealers. Many manufacturers sell to the government at some slight price concession, but some charge the government the same price as any individual would pay if he walked into a store and purchased one machine. The price concession may be a 10 or 20 per cent discount from the retail price which also may be offered by dealers to certain classes of buyers, or the concession may be the granting of a quantity discount directly on orders for any quantity which is normally rebated to large-quantity users if their yearly purchases justify it. Also, the rentals of machines required for peak work loads are credited on the purchase of new machines.

On occasion the government has refused to sign a contract with a supplier who would grant no concession. In that event, however, the government finds it against its own interest to shut off purchases altogether, and must allow machines to be bought after the requisitioning agency certifies that the purchase is necessary for efficiency and cannot be postponed. For two years, on one occasion, no contract was signed with the Felt and Tarrant Manufacturing Company for Comptometers, at the end of which the company agreed to credit rentals of machines required for peak work loads to the purchase of new machines. It refused, however, to extend the 15 per cent discount applied to government purchases by the Marchant Calculating Machine Company and the Friden Calculat-

[13] A notice is included in the invitations to bid for office equipment contracts which reads as follows: "Special Notice. Bidders are advised that the acceptance or the rejection of the bids received will give consideration to possible benefits accruing by reason of making multiple awards. When there is no showing in a particular bid that the Government derives any benefit in price or otherwise by acceptance thereof, the right is reserved to make no contract with that particular bidder for the article involved. Any information the bidder may desire to submit in this respect should be attached to and made a part of his bid."

ing Machine Company which supply the closest substitutes for the Comptometer.

No method so far used by the government has been successful in obtaining prices for these types of equipment which could be expected from direct price competition for contracts.

The market for typewriters presents the same problems of multiple awards in the face of manufacturers' uniform price policies as the markets for other business machines. About thirty years ago the uniform prices of manufacturers were considered to be unreasonably high, in view of the large-quantity purchases by the government, and Congress placed a price ceiling of $70 on typewriters for government purchase. Although manufacturers repeatedly claimed they were losing money at the price of $70, they continued to sell to the government even when this price was about $20 less than the price to educational institutions which receive the lowest price of any customer of the industry. After World War II, however, they refused to bid on government invitations except at higher than ceiling prices. For a time no contracts were awarded and finally Congress was persuaded to lift the ceiling.

At the present time federal agencies are authorized to pay no more for a typewriter than 90 per cent of the price offered to the most-favored customer of the company. The "most-favored customer" is interpreted to mean the most-favored commercial customer, which is any large commercial user. The discount to such users is 19 per cent off the retail list price and the government's price is 90 per cent of that, or a discount of slightly over 27 per cent. When the government buys for instructional use in the public schools of the District of Columbia and institutions of instruction of the government, the standard educational institution discount of 33⅓ per cent is extended to it.

Repair parts.—The buying of various repair parts illustrates the effect on prices of a high degree of product differentiation in the form of inspection service and prompt delivery. The purchase of automobile repair parts is a good case in point.

The cost of repair parts is typically small compared either with the investment in an automobile or the cost of inefficiency which can result from the vehicle's being out of service for any length of time. Dimensional interchangeability and durability are the important characteristics sought in buying parts.

All manufacturers of automobiles offer complete lines of repair parts for the yearly models still in use through their authorized distributors and dealers. These are sold at list prices less discounts to classes of trade. The maximum discount is to dealers with a smaller discount off list for garages and repairmen who are not authorized dealers. The government negotiates term contracts with manufacturers under which agencies throughout the country can obtain parts from the nearest authorized dealers at prices which are substantially lower than those offered to garages and repairmen, but are 5 to 10 per cent higher than the net prices to dealers.

The bulk of repair parts is purchased by the automobile manufacturers from independent parts manufacturers. It would be possible for the government to buy directly from the parts manufacturers at prices much lower than present contract prices. If it did so, however, the only appropriate method of purchase would be through yearly contracts let to bidders on qualified-products lists with periodic checks on the quality of the manufacturers' output. Such a program would involve the costs of preparing many specifications, of testing to qualify products, and of stocking thousands of parts in many locations throughout the country. The question is whether or not the saving through buying from primary sources in open competition would offset these expenses plus the risk of receiving poor-quality parts which such a program would involve. To date it has been judged to be advisable to pay "an extra layer of profit," as the purchasing officials put it, which results from buying a highly differentiated product without direct competition, rather than incur the expenses and risks involved in the alternative program. The possibility of direct purchase, however, must act as a limiting factor in the price decisions of the present contractors.

Pharmaceutical preparations.—Pharmaceuticals provide an interesting example of products which are well defined by nationally accepted objective standards, those of the United States Pharmacopoeia, and yet are highly differentiated by the personal preferences of the doctors who prescribe their use. The government, so far as the civilian agencies are concerned, accepts these preferences as material because it takes the position that the doctors, in government service as elsewhere, who must accept personally the burden of the responsibility for the health of their patients, should be permitted to choose the pharmaceuticals necessary for their treatment of the patients.

The manufacturers of pharmaceuticals, of course, differentiate their products highly by advertised claims of superiority and spend a great deal of promotional effort to win the loyalty of doctors.

The sales in the industry are distributed among well over 100 firms, and each of these has among its customers physicians of equal competence and integrity who have faith that its products are better than those of its competitors. At the same time the Food and Drug Administration enforces a rigorous control over the quality of the pharmaceutical preparations to insure that they meet the standards of the United States Pharmacopoeia. These standards in turn have been developed by the most capable doctors and by medical research scientists to define products which are homogeneous from the viewpoint of their intended physiological therapeutic effect.

In view of the fact that pharmaceuticals are considered to be substantially materially differentiated, the government buys them without direct price competition on federal-supply-schedule term contracts entered into with all bidders who are considered responsible. As a result there are 103 contractors from whom the requisitioning agencies may order pharmaceutical preparations. Not all of them offer complete lines of the products but all major manufacturers are included among the contractors.

Contractors furnish government agencies lists and descriptions of the products they offer for sale with net prices shown for each item. Although all contractors receive awards and there is no direct price competition for contracts, price reductions are obtained. The published prices of different manufacturers established for the general market vary considerably for comparable items. In preparing their special price lists for distribution to government agencies the contractors adjust prices to bring them more nearly in line with the prices of rival firms. This results in prices which are estimated to be 13 per cent below dealers' prices which the using agencies would ordinarily pay if they purchased individually.

There is little doubt that the government could procure pharmaceutical preparations at more substantial price reductions than at present if it considered the differences between the products of manufacturers to be immaterial. A measure of this possibility is available for aspirin (Table 35).

The Federal Supply Service provides two methods for agencies to procure aspirin: by ordering supplies under federal-supply-schedule term contracts which cover entire catalog lines of pharmaceuticals, or by ordering from the federal supply centers which purchase it in large quantities and stock it for distribution to the agencies. In December, 1950, agencies paid about 25 cents for a

100-tablet bottle if they bought it under the supply-schedule contracts, compared with 9 cents for the same item if they bought it from the supply centers. These prices compared with the fair-trade retail minimums ranging from 30 to 49 cents (Table 35). In addition to showing the variation of prices when aspirin is procured by alternative methods of contracting, the figures illustrate the indirect competition resulting from the probability that agencies

TABLE 35

ASPIRIN: GOVERNMENT-CONTRACT, RETAIL, AND WHOLESALE PRICES
(Prices per 100-tablet bottle, December, 1950)

Manufacturer or source of supply	Price in dollars			
	Retail		Whole-salers' net	Govern-ment
	List	Fair trade		
E. R. Squibb and Sons	...	.49	.325	.25
Parke, Davis and Co.	.54	.45	.30	.25
Sharpe and Dohme, Inc.	...	.30	.24	.24
Federal Supply Service supply centers (stores)	...	...	...	.09
Government large-quantity contract	...	...	...	.08

SOURCE: The retail and wholesale prices are from the *American Druggist Bluebook, 1950;* the government-contract prices are from the price lists of the pharmaceutical manufacturer contractors under Federal Supply Schedule for Class 51, item no. 51-P-365 for the period September 15, 1950, through September 14, 1951; the stores-issue price is from the *Store Stock Catalog* price list for Zone 1, October, 1950, through December, 1950; and the definite-quantity contract price is from the contract files of the Federal Supply Service, Washington, D.C.

when ordering will compare the prices offered by rival suppliers under the schedule. Sharpe and Dohme quoted 24 cents to the government—the same price at which it sold to wholesalers. Squibb and Parke Davis quoted 25 cents, which was close to the Sharpe and Dohme price but well below their established wholesalers' net prices. The differences between supply-schedule prices paid and those which could be obtained by consolidating requirements and purchasing large quantities from low bidders might not be so pronounced for all pharmaceuticals as for aspirin, but they would doubtless be substantial.

Cigarettes and tobacco.—Like scientists for their instruments, stenographers for their typewriters, and doctors for their drugs, smokers have strong preferences for particular brands of cigarettes. The government considers these as material; hence the same technique for purchasing them is used as with the products discussed above, and with the same results in purchase prices. The prices are uniform and stable, and the government, ordering in minimum quantities of from 10 to 60 cartons depending on the brand, paid in 1950 identical prices of slightly over 14 cents a package for 11 brands including all the most popular ones. This was the price including federal tax. Provisions are also made in the contracts for the purchase of tax-free cigarettes by agencies which are entitled to buy them. The advantages of the contract result from the savings in administrative costs of contracting, not from price reductions through centralized purchasing.

X

The Effectiveness of Sealed Bids and Negotiation in Evoking Competition

The evidence concerning contracting for commodities in different types of markets has been presented in Chapters VI through IX. The operation of the contracting devices used by the government has been analyzed in comparison with alternative devices which might be used. In the following pages a summary evaluation is attempted of the effectiveness with which the contracting devices call forth competition from prospective suppliers. This evaluation is focused on the operation of the devices used in bidding, negotiating, and awarding contracts; in Chapter XI the end results of the operation of the government's purchasing policies, including the internal and contracting policies, are evaluated.

Homogeneous Products in Markets Where Sellers Compete on Price

In markets for homogeneous products all elements of the sealed-bids device are consistently applied by the government. The relevant comparison is with limited competitive bids based on specifications, because specifications are used generally to define the homogeneous product.[1] For purposes of analysis it is assumed that, where sealed bids are used (1) invitations reach all potentially competitive bidders, (2) all prospective bidders are informed of past bid and contract prices, and (3) unit costs of supplying goods do not include any amounts to cover sales and advertising promotion attributable to efforts to be included in the bidders' lists or to influence awards of contracts. For limited competitive bids it is assumed that (1) no more than six firms are invited to bid, (2) bidders are not informed about past bid and contract prices of

[1] The elements of the sealed-bids and limited-competitive-bids devices are compared in chap. v, fig. 3.

rivals, and (3) unit costs include the usual amounts to cover sales and advertising promotion. Although these assumptions accentuate the differences between the devices, they are in general accord with the facts.

The government specifies, in addition to the physical product, all services such as delivery and installation, and competition in these markets is therefore concentrated on price. The price quoted by a seller is determined by three factors: (1) his estimate of the highest price the government would pay if he were the only bidder, (2) his marginal cost of supplying the goods specified in the invitation to bid, and (3) his estimate of the prices which his competitors will bid. His estimate of what the government would pay will set his upper limit, his marginal costs will set the lower limit, and his estimate of the price his competitors will quote will determine the price which he will bid. He will attempt to set his price just low enough to secure the business so long as it covers his marginal costs. In arriving at this judgment the bidder has available his own and his competitors' past bid and contract prices, a knowledge of his own sales and plant capacity, and some idea of the trend of sales and capacity of his competitors and of the industry as a whole.

The significant differences in prices quoted when sealed bids and limited competitive bids are used, result from (1) open bidding compared with limited competitive bidding, (2) single awards compared with multiple or rotating awards, (3) lower costs of sales and advertising promotion when quoting by sealed bids compared with limited competitive bids, and (4) public availability of bid and contract information compared with unavailability of such information. The effect of each of these elements varies depending on whether there is a buyers' or a sellers' market at the time bids are made.

Open bidding and single awards in a buyers' market.—In a buyers' market—that is, when sales in the industry are declining or are constant at levels which result in unused capacity in some plants in the industry—a seller can expect competitors to be worried about excess capacity in their plants and to quote prices lower than those at which previous contracts were awarded. Any seller in the industry could be the one whose calculation of marginal costs led him to bid the lowest price at the time of a particular invitation to bid. After a succession of contracts, prices would approach a level determined by the lowest cost calculation of the bidders.[2] This appears to have occurred in the bids for white enamel paint and toilet tissue during 1949 and the first half of 1950 when sellers stated that contract prices were below average costs which included a reasonable amount of overhead.

If the government limited the number of bidders, say to six, as private purchasers generally do, but still made single awards, prices would similarly be expected to reach levels below which none of the six suppliers would be willing to quote. The lack of knowledge of competitors' past bid and contract prices (assumed as an element of the limited-competitive-bids device) would introduce an element of uncertainty in bidders' calculations but would not affect the result.

The cost calculations of firms composing the industry, however, are different at any time and vary for individual firms. The open-bidding feature of sealed bids, therefore, would bring lower prices than would result from limited bidding. This would occur because the seller whose cost calculations are lowest is free to bid while he might not be among the six whose bids are invited. In most cases open bidding should bring the lowest prices on this score.

If the government made multiple or rotating awards in place of single awards to insure continuity of supply, higher prices would be expected for two reasons. First, assuming awards were made to two suppliers, bidders need to quote only low enough to underbid the third-lowest bidder. Second, the practice of alternating awards among the six bidders could lead to an award to the third-lowest bidder even though his price was slightly higher but was not considered to be "out of line." In considering present contract prices the government would, in this instance, be discounting the utility it expected to receive in the future from continuous supply. Under sealed bids each contract is awarded independently of previous or future supply relationships to the single bidder offering the lowest price.

It is interesting to note that the assumed advantages of continuity

[2] The sealed-bids device has been compared in its effect with a "Dutch auction." In a "Dutch auction" bidders can revise their price offers for each contract as often as they wish in the light of the knowledge of competitors' price offers. If bidders act independently and rationally, the price for each contract would be just below the marginal costs as calculated by the last bidder to drop out. When sealed bids are used, each bidder can make only one price offer, and must arrive at it by using data that are usually a month old or older. All competitors are more likely to be influenced by considerations of demand, and the price on any one contract might be well above the price reached had the bidding been conducted in the manner of a "Dutch auction."

of supply must be illusory to many buyers. If the shortage of supply is general in the industry, suppliers must ration their short supplies among their customers. By the nature of the supply situation, if all buyers practice making multiple awards, there must still be some who are not favored by their suppliers. The advantages are more certain where shortages occur in the plants of particular suppliers but not in those of others. Even where suppliers are unable to meet delivery promises, it is usually possible for the government to find alternative sources before the shortage is acute.

Open bidding and single awards in a sellers' market.—In a sellers' market—that is, when sales in relation to capacity are rising in the industry or are stable at levels which leave no excess capacity in plants—the effect of the two devices on prices is quite different depending on whether contracts are let independently of one another (single awards) or whether continuity of supply is considered (multiple awards) when limited competitive bids are used.

In a sellers' market, if single awards are made, contract prices resulting from the use of either device will be higher on each succeeding contract. The rise might be very substantial and be maintained until added production capacity or the reduction of demand cause the reappearance of some excess capacity in the industry. The same situation would exist whether bidding was open or limited. During the price rise, however, the prices for each contract will be determined by the estimates sellers make of the price their competitors will quote, and these estimates will vary among bidders if there is no previous agreement among them. Open bidding during this period will bring lower prices than limited bidding because the seller whose estimate is lowest is free to bid.

The effect is quite different if multiple or alternating awards are made. Prices quoted when sealed bids (single awards) are used, result from calculations related to the current contract alone and reflect the full increase made possible by the rise in demand. Sellers would be expected to be more hesitant to raise prices to buyers who, in view of their past loyalty, could be counted on to give them orders when sales again declined. The evidence on toilet-tissue prices illustrates the fact that prices obtained from sealed bids can rise to levels substantially higher than those at which the same physical products are sold to buyers using other devices. This is not uncommon in government purchasing in strong sellers' markets.

Sales costs.—Selling costs are lower under the sealed-bids procedure than under limited competitive bids. The open-bidding feature permits any seller to bid without solicitation beyond a simple request to have his name placed on a mailing list. Automatic award to the low bidder and prohibition against negotiation eliminate any chance for sales and advertising expenditures to influence awards of contracts. Some initial expense is required to become familiar with government contracting procedure, but that is all.

The fact that contracting with the government requires small outlay for sales expense may or may not affect prices. Costs would not be noticeably changed for sellers who obtain government contracts only occasionally, but those sellers who obtain a substantial volume of government business would be very conscious of the lower costs. During periods when business is so slack that particular sellers in competitive markets exclude sales costs from their price calculations, the lower costs of doing business with the government would have no effect on prices. Neither would cost differences have any effect when prices are calculated purely on demand considerations. During periods when sellers include sales costs in their price calculations, however, sealed bids would bring lower prices than limited competitive bids because those sellers who do a sizable amount of government business would quote on the basis of lower costs.

Public availability of bid information.—In markets where price competition for government contracts is accepted practice, access to the past bid and contract prices of competitors provides pertinent facts for price calculations on current bids and doubtless sharpens price competition. This is particularly true in view of the fact that the Robinson-Patman Act does not apply when sellers bid to the federal government, and also the fact that bids to the government, which is looked upon as a special customer, have little influence on the prices quoted to other customers.

Long-run effectiveness of sealed bids.—The analysis thus far indicates that sealed bids evoke lower prices from rival suppliers during buyers' markets because (1) bidding is open to all responsible sellers, (2) single awards take advantage of the lowest prices quoted, and (3) on occasion, the lower costs of selling to the government result in lower bids. During sellers' markets, when demand and prices are increasing, however, a point may be reached where the prices yielded by sealed bids are substantially higher than those obtained from limited competitive bids.

It is the opinion of buyers who use the sealed-bids device that the periods during which prices are higher than those obtained by other devices are of short duration compared with the periods during which the prices are lower, and are, of course, confined largely to periods when there is no excess capacity. The point at which the prices obtained by the two devices cross is not precisely determinable. It depends on the judgment of the sellers as to the desirability of the contracts being offered by the sealed-bids device, the sellers' judgment as to what prices their competitors will quote, and the importance of continued supply relations with buyers using the limited-bids device. The evidence suggests that during 1949 and the first half of 1950 prices were lower when sealed bids were used than when limited competitive bids were used. This was a period of high business activity, but one when firms had had a chance to adjust capacity to production demands. The indication, therefore, is that sealed bids result in higher prices only when sales in the industry are pressing very heavily on capacity. Some amount of excess capacity usually exists in at least some firms in an industry. In view of these considerations it is reasonable to conclude that, aside from periods such as wartime when firms are not free to adjust production capacity to sales volume, sealed bids bring lower prices than limited competitive bids.

Homogeneous Products in Markets Where Sellers Quote Stable Prices

Oligopolistic markets with a competitive fringe.—In many markets which are ordinarily characterized by stable or uniform prices some sellers, if given the incentive, will depart from their customary policies and attempt to obtain contracts through price competition. The open-bidding and single-award features of sealed bids are very effective in calling forth price competition in such oligopolistic markets with a competitive fringe. Often such price competition initiated by the smaller "fringe" sellers is contagious, with the result that the majority of sellers will bid competitively for government contracts. An example is the market for stencil paper in which most sellers, although there are not many in the industry, bid actively for contracts. Sealed bids are more effective than limited competitive bids in these markets because the open-bidding feature increases the chances that the fringe sellers will offer bids.

In some markets, of which cement is an outstanding example, sellers adhere to their price policies so strongly that sealed bids are ineffective, and it is doubtful whether any negotiating device would offer sufficient incentive to cause departures from established price policies. In some markets, however, the fact that bid and contract information is kept confidential under limited competitive bids may make that device the more effective.

Public availability of bid information.—In the opinion of the editors of the National Association of Purchasing Agents *Handbook,* public availability of bidders' prices would prevent buyers from obtaining price concessions, which could be expected if they kept the information confidential.[3] Some direct evidence of the effect of this policy in raising prices to the government was given by officials of steel companies before a congressional committee. The president of the Continental Steel Company testified that in bidding to the government his company quoted published prices, but that these were only the starting point for negotiation with many private buyers. When asked by a committee member for an explanation for not using the same policy when selling to the government as when selling to private buyers, he said, "Well, you ought to buy like some of the other buyers. . . . You should not advertise your price."[4] The president of the Bethlehem Steel Corporation testified that his company pursued the same policy when selling to the government, apparently for the same reason.[5]

For the government, keeping prices confidential is not a practicable alternative to making them public. The nature of government budgeting and accounting requires that contract prices resulting from centralized purchasing be known by hundreds and sometimes thousands of persons. An indication of the extent to which price information must be diffused is given by the fact that 2,000 copies of suppliers' price lists are required to inform the ordering agencies throughout the country of prices under federal-supply-schedule contracts which are mandatory for use by all agencies of the executive branch of the government. Also, the public nature of government contracting prevents keeping prices confidential except where for security reasons this is necessary. Suppliers who are dissatisfied with awards could be expected to complain either to the General Accounting Office or to their con-

[3] See chap. v, p. 88.

[4] U.S. Congress, Senate, Committee on Interstate Commerce, *To Prevent Uniform Delivered Prices,* Hearings, 74th Cong., 2d sess., on S. 4055, March 9 to April 10, 1936 (Washington: 1936), p. 67.

[5] *Verbatim Record of the Proceedings of the U.S. Temporary National Economic Committee* (Steel Industry), IX (Oct. 26–Dec. 8, 1939), 10596.

gressmen or both, and the result would be interminable investigations and justifications of awards. On political grounds alone a policy of withholding information on bids and awards would be unworkable.

Negotiation.—Negotiation, based on arguments that selling to the government directly rather than through wholesalers justifies manufacturers to quote the same price to the government as they do to wholesalers, is often an effective method of reducing prices. This is especially so when the negotiation is backed by the possibility of refusing to award contracts to sellers who offer no price concessions. This is possible only where demand is postponable for sufficiently long periods to make the loss of business induce firms to sell directly at a price concession, or where substitute products can be used for a time without too great a loss in efficiency. Negotiation has been used with very good effect in buying many types of office equipment, steel desks, and steel filing cabinets. The possibility of purchasing substitute products must also be a strong factor in granting the government a favorable trade status in the scheme of discounts for many other commodities, such as pharmaceutical preparations and repair parts.

Antitrust actions.—Where collusive agreements are the cause of stable or uniform prices, action under the antitrust laws and the statute making conspiracy to defraud the government an offense, has been effective in reducing prices to the government in a few important cases.

It was noted in Chapter IX in the discussion of automobile tires and tubes that the federal government cannot sue for damages under the Sherman Act. Similarly it cannot take action against sellers under the Robinson-Patman Act if there is evidence that sellers are quoting discriminatory high prices to the government, because this law has been interpreted by the attorney general as not applying to federal-government purchases. This interpretation has been accepted by the Federal Trade Commission.[6] Suits for

[6] *Applicability of Robinson-Patman Act to Government Contracts for Supplies* (1936), 38 Att. Gen., 539. The attorney general reasoned that the act merely amends the Clayton Act which has not been regarded as applicable to government contracts. He further stated that if the amended statute did apply, lower prices to the government in all likelihood would not violate the law as they probably reflected lower estimated costs of doing business with the government because of quantity purchases, the absence of credit risk, solicitation expense, and the like. The attorney general gave his opinion in answer to the question of whether or not under the law a seller could discriminate in favor of the government by quoting lower prices. Although he made no statement on higher prices, it would appear that the law would also be inapplicable when sellers quote higher prices to the federal government.

damages under the antitrust laws, such as were effective in reducing tire prices to the government, are no longer available as a method of combatting collusive bidding.

The government may, however, sue for damages under the statute concerning conspiracy to defraud the government.[7] Such suits have been used successfully to prevent collusive bidding in a few instances.[8]

Such direct action is seldom a practicable measure for purchasing officers. The evidence in the bids alone is insufficient to establish a case or even to provide adequate indication that grounds exist for a suit. Each purchasing officer must buy many commodities, and the impersonal nature of most government contracting does not bring them in sufficiently intimate touch with an industry to obtain the additional information which is necessary for such action.

The Federal Property and Administrative Services Act of 1949 directs the administrator of General Services to report to the attorney general for appropriate action any bids received after advertising which in his opinion evidence any violation of the antitrust laws.[9] In the three years following the establishment of the General Services Administration, however, the administrator found no occasion to refer any bids to the attorney general.

Differentiated Products in Markets Where Sellers Compete on Price

In the markets for differentiated products, discussed in Chapters VII and IX, buyers ordinarily purchase at whatever point in the channel of distribution their trade status assigns them, most often through distributors, and receive quotations of prices which are usually selected from a predetermined schedule of stable prices. Purchases are frequently based on brand names, but specifications are used for many types of equipment. Price competition is largely avoided, and sellers rely principally on other methods for obtaining contracts.

When buying in these markets in the past, the government pursued policies very similar to those now used by most private buyers. The difference was that bidding was not limited, and awards

[7] 18 *U.S. Code* (1946), sec. 88.

[8] For example, see *United States v. William F. Hess et al*, U.S. District Court for the Western District of Pennsylvania, No. 10462 criminal (Washington: 1939).

[9] 63 *U.S. Stat. at L.* (1949), 394, sec. 302 d.

were made to single low bidders. When purchases were made on the basis of a brand name, the government specified the brand name "or equal" and thus, technically, any supplier could bid and claim that his brand was the equal of the one specified.

With the development of Federal Specifications and centralized purchasing programs, however, the government has fashioned policies intended to offset the effectiveness of product differentiation and provide manufacturers with incentives to depart from their policies of quoting stable prices. One incentive offered by the government is a clear statement that all products meeting Federal Specifications will be considered equivalent for purchase and that the low bidder will receive the contract; the other has been the offer of a substantial volume of business on each contract. Neither of the policies is sufficient alone to be completely successful. When quantities are small, the policy of product homogeneity is unlikely to be sufficient to persuade manufacturers to quote special prices either directly or through their wholesalers, and when large quantities are purchased on a brand-name "or equal" basis manufacturers are likely to quote prices close to their established ones and rely on the vagueness of the product definition to limit or exclude competition. As when selling to private buyers, they may then promote the idea to the awarding officer that the products of their rivals are not equal. Both the government's internal purchasing policy and the use of sealed-bids device are thus required to create a new market. In the markets here considered these incentives have been sufficient to induce manufacturers to quote directly and competitively for government contracts.

The relevant comparison is sealed bids with limited competitive bids, but with different methods of product definition. The effects of open bidding, of single awards, of making bid and contract information publicly available, and of lower selling costs, are all qualitatively the same in markets for differentiated products as they are in markets for homogeneous products. These effects have been analyzed above and need not be repeated here. The effect of using specifications instead of brand names or, in some cases, of the different methods of using specifications requires analysis. How well these policies serve the interests of the government varies greatly depending on whether the ignored product differentiation is immaterial or material in the government's judgment.

Products judged by the government to be homogeneous.—In markets for products which are considered by some sellers to be differentiated but by the government to be homogeneous, it is relevant to compare buying on specification with buying on approved lists of brand-name products. The evidence on resin emulsion paint, stencil paper, carbon paper, liquid type cleaner, and breakfast cereals, demonstrates that the price advantages to the government which result from buying on specification rather than on brand-names "or equal" basis are very substantial. When the government, through its commodity research, has learned that the differences claimed for their products by rival suppliers are immaterial, there is no loss of utility to offset the price advantage gained.

In general the price advantages are derived from buying from manufacturers instead of from wholesalers or jobbers, and from direct price competition among the supplying manufacturers. More specifically, the lower prices would logically be expected for several reasons: (1) stripping competitive products of immaterial differentiation permits requirements for different makes of products to be consolidated and purchased on a single contract, thus providing an incentive for suppliers to quote low prices; (2) the larger quantities and direct competition often induce manufacturers to bid directly to the government rather than through the irregular wholesalers; (3) sometimes when the product design can economically be adjusted (as for stencil paper), cost savings are obtained through the elimination of qualities not required by Federal Specification; (4) sales and advertising costs attributable to establishing effective product differentiation, which for this class of products are substantial, can have no effect in persuading the government to buy and may be eliminated from price calculations; and (5) the use of specifications, single awards, and open bidding often induces sellers to abandon their policies of quoting established stable prices and to engage in active price competition.

Products judged by the government to reflect real utility differences.—For many materially differentiated products, particularly machinery and equipment, private buyers using limited competitive bids evaluate differences between competitive products. Specifications are used as standards against which to measure the quality differences. For the few commodities where the government also uses this technique—dry batteries are an example—the product-definition policy is the same as when limited competitive bids are used and sealed bids yield gains from the increased competition resulting from the other features.

It may be noted in this connection, that a homogeneous product is not a necessary condition for a competitive market. It is often assumed to be a necessary condition, because when the products of rivals are perfectly interchangeable in use. prices can be compared quantitatively and a rational choice can be made. When competitive products are not homogeneous, but are functionally interchangeable; and when the material differences can be quantitatively measured and combined with the bid prices to form utility–price ratios, comparisons of such ratios calculated for each of the competitive products permits competition just as direct as that among suppliers of homogeneous products.

The fact that the data of bidders' quotations and calculations determining awards are made public, acts to limit the government's use of evaluation factors. The basis for evaluation must be objective and clearly defensible, because it may be questioned by unsuccessful bidders either directly or through the General Accounting Office or Congress. Often it is difficult to work out a formula that is not subject to criticism. Private purchasers do not make the basis for award known to bidders or the public and are able to avoid time-consuming discussions regarding the validity of their decisions. Often a sound technical decision can be made even though it involves some degree of error caused by inevitable differences in the judgment of experts.

For these reasons the government, when making awards, seldom uses specifications as standards against which to evaluate quality differences. Instead, it ignores any differences between rival products in spite of the fact that it recognizes that such differences are material and may substantially affect the utility–price ratios of the goods it buys. The evidence discussed both in Chapter IV and Chapter VII demonstrates that the differences so ignored can be very substantial. Awards are sometimes made to low bidders when the prices of other bidders are only slightly higher and are clearly more than offset by added utility. In such cases the government loses by failing to evaluate material product differences.

Sealed bids may also be compared with limited competitive bids based on approved products lists where the evaluation of differences rests upon opinions about the quality of the brands. Evaluation of quality by brand names causes two sources of loss to buyers: one involving the decisions of the sellers and the other the decisions of the buyers.

In markets for differentiated products sellers aim to persuade buyers to make their evaluation on the basis of brand names; of course, each seller aims to convince buyers that his brand is the best. His price calculations normally must include costs of sales promotion, and if he believes his product to be successfully differentiated in the minds of buyers he may refuse to quote other than his prices established for the trade in general regardless of the quantity. If the seller is a manufacturer who deviates from his policy by quoting directly to the buyer, he may bid no lower than the prices at which he sells to distributors.[10]

If the seller of a differentiated product believes that the products of his competitors have been more successfully differentiated than his own, he may attempt to underbid them. In this case the amount by which he cuts his price will be influenced by his opinion of his competitors' action. If he believes they will quote their established prices, he will need only to cut low enough to offset the buyer's evaluation of the lower utility of his product and thus bring the price–quality ratio for his product above that of his competitors. Compared with the use of specifications to reduce rival products to homogeneity, the most likely results of the use of brand names in buying would be: (1) all sellers would quote higher prices, (2) prices would approach costs more slowly during periods when the industry is operating at low sales volume in relation to plant capacity, and (3) costs used in setting prices would be higher by the extra sales costs unless the situation was reached where these were eliminated from calculations of marginal costs.

The use of brand names also introduces an element of uncertainty in the calculations of buyers. As pointed out in Chapter IV brand names cannot be universally relied upon as consistently trustworthy definitions of product quality, and they provide no objective basis for comparing quality of different brands. The quality of different brands can be compared only by reference to some standard, and the moment an objective standard is used the basis for comparison is a specification and not brand names. All other methods known for comparing quality introduce some unknown amount of error caused by lack of objective facts and the influence of sellers' claims based on the salability rather than the utility of the products.

The use of sealed bids in buying products which are considered by other buyers to be differentiated but by the government to be

[10] Cf. chap. ix in which this is shown to happen frequently for products which are successfully differentiated in the government's judgment.

homogeneous, therefore, results in lower prices than the use of limited competitive bids based on approved products lists, for several reasons: it reduces the sales-promotion costs of sellers; it eliminates considerations of product differentiation from sellers' price calculations and focuses their attention on direct price competition; and it increases the precision of product definition and comparison of the quality of products.

The failure to evaluate material differences where they exist may more than offset the errors resulting from irrational judgments of product quality which occur when approved products lists are used. The irrational judgment of material differences may, in other words, be more in accord with the facts than the deliberate ignoring of such differences.

Differentiated Products in Markets Where Sellers Quote Stable Prices

In the markets for differentiated products, discussed in Chapter IX, the price policies of sellers are strongly supported by the fact that their products are materially differentiated to a high degree. The government has no way to obtain direct price competition because no competitors exist who furnish a product sufficiently similar to be economically interchangeable with the product of the one seller. Competition of substitutes does, of course, limit the level to which the prices of these differentiated products can rise.

The government's problems of how to negotiate for the most favorable price are parallel to those it meets in homogeneous products where sellers quote stable prices. As in those instances, public availability of bid and contract information reinforces sellers' determination to maintain their established prices, although the incentive to cut prices, even secretly, is much less for differentiated than for homogeneous products.

Negotiation at times induces the manufacturers to sell to the government at dealers' prices. However, the argument that there are cost savings in doing business with the government does not apply. The products are purchased on term contracts with all major competitors, and each firm must incur the same sales costs to influence government agencies as to influence other buyers. There is unlikely to be any basis for antitrust actions. The products are highly differentiated, and the stable prices are usually different for products of different firms. Bidding, therefore, does not provide any direct indication of collusive price agreements, if they do exist.

The most important barrier to direct price competition is the absence of competitive firms for the same product. The corrective is the entry of more firms into the market, and the bar to this is either patent protection or investment in relation to profitability of the business. There is little the government can do to encourage the entry of new firms aside from the action it has already taken in consolidating demand and ordering in large quantities which may attract them.

The government faces many of its most difficult buying problems in these markets, and the effectiveness of its methods is limited. This does not mean, however, that it does not buy advantageously from the viewpoint of the taxpayer. Although its buying devices may be less effective in some markets than the devices which private buyers may use, the operation of its internal purchasing policy results in substantial advantages. These are discussed in the following chapter.

XI

The Effectiveness of Centralized Policy Determination

In addition to the legal requirement that sealed bids be used in contracting—evaluated in the preceding chapter—the dominant feature of congressional policy with regard to purchasing is the delegation of authority to the GSA for centralizing purchases and for unifying the purchasing policies of all agencies. The effectiveness of the policies established by the Federal Supply Service in the exercise of this grant of authority is evaluated in the present chapter.

METHOD AND CRITERIA FOR EVALUATION

The Federal Supply Service programs can be judged by comparing them with the uncentralized purchasing by each agency which would replace the centralized programs if they were abandoned. Such a comparison permits a judgment whether the Federal Supply Service pays its way by the savings which result from its programs. The comparison, however, will differ for different types of programs.

Degree of centralization.—The Federal Supply Service has spent a substantial part of its effort in formulating uniform policies to guide and reduce costs of the purchasing performed by the agencies. It has proceeded slowly with centralized purchasing programs. In the fiscal year 1951, through its federal supply schedules, federal-supply-center stores, and direct-delivery programs, the Federal Supply Service contracted for about $310,000,000 worth of goods used by the civilian and military agencies.[1] A substantial part of this amount was procured by the military agencies through all three types of Federal Supply Service programs, although there is

[1] Table 37.

no way to estimate the amount accurately. The centralized purchasing programs, therefore, accounted for a substantially smaller part of the $865,000,000 of civilian agency purchases[2] than a comparison of that figure with the $310,000,000 would indicate. It was estimated by the Federal Supply Service that its predecessor, the Bureau of Federal Supply, had contracted in the fiscal year 1948 for 20 per cent of the requirements of the civilian agencies.[3] The degree of centralization appears to have increased between 1948 and 1952, but it is unlikely that the increase was substantial.

Furthermore, each of the Federal Supply Service programs involves a significantly different kind of centralization. It is therefore desirable to evaluate separately (1) centralized guidance of product choice, (2) centralized guidance of agency purchasing, (3) centralized purchasing at agencies' request, (4) centralized purchasing with uncentralized ordering (federal supply-center stores), (5) centralized contracting with uncentralized (federal supply schedules), and (6) centralized purchasing of consolidated requirements of agencies for direct delivery to them.

Criteria for evaluation.—As stated in Chapter I, the objective of supply, and of purchasing, is to help minimize the costs of government by maximizing the utility received for the dollars spent in procuring and consuming the goods it needs, and by minimizing any losses resulting from shortages caused by untimely deliveries. The supply programs closely related to purchasing which have been considered in this study directly affect the magnitude of the utility-per-dollar ratios by influencing (1) the choice of the products to buy, (2) the price paid, and (3) the administrative costs of standardizing demands, purchasing, and distributing the products.[4] The effect of these three factors, together with timeliness of supply, on the utility-per-dollar ratio are the criteria by which the effectiveness of each Federal Supply Service program must be judged. The programs affecting choice are applied to agency as well as centralized purchasing, and can best be discussed first.

Centralized Guidance of Product Choice

The agency employees decide what will be bought when they initiate requisitions, but they cannot choose freely from the full range

[2] Chap. i, table 1.

[3] Testimony of C. E. Mack in U.S. Congress, House, Committee on Appropriations, *Treasury Department Appropriation Bill for 1950,* Hearings, 81st Cong., 1st sess. (Washington: 1949).

[4] Cf. chap. i, "Objectives and functions of supply."

of goods offered in markets. Limitations on choice are imposed principally by the Federal Standard Stock Catalog and Federal Specifications. As a practical matter the catalog and specifications serve to facilitate wise choice by forcing the selection, from the range of close substitute products commonly considered to be equally suitable for a given use, the one which the government believes can be purchased at the most favorable utility-per-dollar ratio.

Such centrally determined limitations on choice are a practical alternative to free choice by the agency personnel because their needs are common for large numbers of items. The programs by which choice is limited, however, must be justified in terms of their effect on administrative costs and on the utility–price ratios, both of which are determinants of the utility received per dollar spent. The following discussion centers on the effect the program has on the utility–price ratios. The effect on administrative costs is discussed later.

Quantitative importance of choice.—The choice of the commodity to buy is undoubtedly a major determinant of the magnitude of the utility–price ratios. The evidence in the earlier chapters of this study shows that the gains from rational choice among close substitute products can easily exceed those obtained from price competition. The choice of the reinforced-link tire chain, discussed in Chapter IV, for example, tripled the utility–price ratio for those agencies which previously used the heavy-duty chain although, before the tests were made which resulted in the specification, the reinforced-link chain was considered to be inferior by many users who based their judgment on the best prevailing information offered by market sources.[5] This 200 per cent increase in the utility–price ratio compares with the 30 per cent increase from the 23 per cent reduction in price resulting from centralized contracting and competitive bidding compared with the previous uncentralized purchasing by the agencies.[6]

Other evidence shows the importance of choice. The tire-testing program showed a variation of about 60 per cent[7] in the wear of tires which sold in the same price line; while the tests of dry batteries showed that equally well-accepted brands selling in the same

[5] Chap. iv, p. 58.

[6] Table 36.

[7] Chap. iv, table 12.

price lines varied in life by as much as 90 per cent.[8] Although the evidence on the government-specification products is not quantitative in form, it also supports the conclusion that rational choice is important.

Savings in price and serviceability.—Granted the importance of the specification and catalog programs, the question remains whether central determination of them is more effective than leaving the job to be done by the individual agencies.

Centralized guidance of product choice is valuable because (1) only if the work is centralized can the most highly qualified commodity experts among all agencies be mustered for each specification project, and (2) commodity research and testing programs are frequently economical only if the potential savings from the purchases of many agencies are in prospect.

A substantial part of the more than 700 experts who have contributed to the development of Federal Specifications have been drawn from a relatively few agencies such as the National Bureau of Standards, the Department of Defense, and the Department of Agriculture, while the rest have been employed throughout the remaining agencies. It would be obviously impracticable for each of the several dozen agencies to call on the services of these men for the development of many duplicate systems of specifications. In the absence of the Federal-Specifications program the agencies would be forced to develop specifications with less highly qualified people.

The advantages of centralized commodity testing is illustrated by the tire-testing program which also provides quantitative evidence of savings.[9] Information from use tests made by the Post Office Department indicated that an adequate testing program for automobile tires and the development of new specifications and qualified-products lists would increase the serviceability of tires purchased by the government by 20 per cent with no increase in price.

An appropriation of $150,000 for the fiscal year 1951 permitted the Federal Supply Service to finance a test program conducted by the Bureau of Standards which confirmed the Post Office De-

[8] For No. 6 dry cells, manufacturer E's brand showed an expected life of 163 per cent of that required by the Federal Specification while manufacturer J's brand showed 85 per cent, a variation of 90 per cent. Chap. iv, table 13.

[9] The tire-test results are shown in chap. iv, table 12. The rest of the data are from the files of the Federal Supply Service, Washington, D.C.

partment's tests and resulted in the development of a performance specification for tires. The new specifications were applied to the federal-supply-schedule contracting procedure early in 1952, and, as a result, by the winter of 1953 the average servicability of tires purchased by the government had increased 8 per cent, according to Federal Supply Service estimates. The results up to that date also indicated that continued testing would lead to the 20 per cent increase in serviceability originally expected.

According to these estimates tires for a year would cost $20,000,000—using the spring of 1953 rate of purchase—and these would last as long as $21,600,000 worth of the tires which would have been purchased had the new specifications not been used. The potential yearly savings, if the 20 per cent increase is achieved, will be correspondingly greater. With the exception of the Department of Defense, no single agency could justify the expenditure of $150,000 required to develop the performance requirements of the tire specification, nor could each agency acting individually expect to be successful in financing the yearly costs of qualification testing which amount to about $128,000. All civilian agencies and the Department of Defense procure tires under the federal supply schedules.

On both counts—the ability to muster special competence and the economy of commodity research and testing—centralization of cataloging and the development of Federal Specifications appear to lead to more rational product choice than would the uncentralized development of such programs. The experience of private industry also supports this conclusion. The centralized research and specification-development programs of some 450 societies and associations are supported financially and through participation in committee work by private firms of many kinds.[10]

Centralized Guidance of Agency Purchasing

Central determination of policies to guide local purchasing, as in product choice, is a practical alternative to policy determination by individual agencies because, to a large degree, all agencies have the same supply problems; not only are most items purchased for exactly the same purposes, but the purchasing of all agencies must

[10] The activities of more than 450 American societies and associations in which standardization was a major or important activity are outlined in National Bureau of Standards, *Standardization Activities of National Technical and Trade Organizations* (Washington: 1941).

conform to laws enacted by Congress and centrally interpreted and elaborated by the General Accounting Office, the Attorney General's Office, the Treasury, and the Bureau of the Budget.

The Federal Supply Service has worked to reduce the administrative costs of local purchasing by providing all agencies with standard procedures and forms, as a part of the General Services *Regulations* and with Federal Specifications which each agency otherwise would have to prepare separately. The advantages result both from the simple elimination of duplication of effort and from the selection of the most economical of the alternative procedures which could be used for a given purpose.

The programs which affect local purchasing have no decisive effect on the prices paid for goods. The use of Federal Specifications doubtless does have an effect on prices, but central policies do not greatly influence such important determinants of price as sources of supply, the number of bidders, or contract quantities. The important influences of such policies are on the choice of products to buy, discussed in the preceding section, and the administrative costs of local purchasing.

Requisitioning and contracting costs.—In 1948 the Bureau of the Budget calculated that the cost of salaries alone directly allocable to requisitioning of supplies by an agency was $7.99 per transaction, and the cost allocable to contracting by sealed bids for direct-delivery purchases was $15.28 per transaction.[11] An estimate of the Federal Supply Service placed the minimum costs of contracting for small purchases when sealed bids are not used at from $4 to $5 per transaction.[12] At the time the studies were made, in 1948 before the establishment of the Federal Supply Service, the steps taken in requisitioning goods and in contracting for them were the same for centralized, uncentralized, small-value, or large-value transactions.[13]

When these partial costs of requisitioning and contracting are considered together with the data on the number and size of purchase orders placed by the government, it is clear that the reduction of administrative costs has offered great possibilities for savings. In 1948 the number of contracts placed by all agencies, military and civilian, was estimated to be more than 3,000,000.[14]

[11] *Detailed Report on the Federal Supply System* (as identified in chap. ii, n. 14), table 6, and text pp. 79–82.

[12] Files of the Federal Supply Service.

[13] *Detailed Report on the Federal Supply System,* p. 79.

[14] *Ibid.,* p. 77.

Even if allowance is made for the large number of contracts placed by the military agencies, the administrative costs of requisitioning and contracting incurred by the civilian agencies must have amounted to many millions of dollars each year. Since almost 90 per cent of the total number of orders placed by the agencies were for $100 or less, administrative costs are of prime importance in uncentralized purchasing.

GSA regulations.—Before the establishment of the Federal Supply Service in 1949, no effective program was in existence for reducing administrative costs of the uncentralized purchasing of the agencies. A few agencies had been successful in simplifying particular procedures in their own purchasing, but no means existed to extend their use to all agencies or to study systematically purchasing procedures and devise more effective ones.[15] By the spring of 1953, the *Regulations of the General Services Administration* provided simplified standard procedures and forms for contracting, for bonding of suppliers, and for making small purchases. No estimates of the savings from the use of the *Regulations* were available, although the Federal Supply Service and the agencies expected the savings to be significant, particularly from the simplified procedures for handling small purchases.

Specification development costs.—The Hoover Commission in 1948 stated that "the cost of preparing the average Federal Specification probably exceeds $1,000 in salaries alone."[16] During the fiscal year 1952, approximately 614 Federal Specifications were completed. Dividing this number into the Federal Supply Service operating expenses for work on commodity specifications of $526,907 for the same year[17] gives a figure of about $860 per specification. A part of the time of the Specifications Branch personnel is spent on commodity problems other than the development of specifications, but the greater part of the cost of development is contributed by the agencies which provide the time of their commodity experts. The cost of salaries of Federal Supply Service and agency personnel must be substantially higher than $1,000 per specification. For particular specifications requiring elaborate commodity research and testing programs, the tire specification for example, the costs are many thousands of dollars higher.

Administrative costs of specifications and catalogs.—The Federal

[15] *Ibid.*, p. 79.
[16] *Ibid.*, p. 275.
[17] Table F, Appendix.

Specifications program probably results in greater savings in administrative expense to the agencies than any other program of the Federal Supply Service. The use of objective commodity specifications is required by law, and each agency would find it necessary to develop its own specifications if Federal Specifications were not available. The total administrative costs which would be required if each agency developed and maintained currently its own versions of a substantial part of the 2,719 Federal Specifications which it needs in its purchasing, would be many times the present cost of doing the job once for all agencies. Not only would the administrative costs be increased if this function were decentralized, but, as pointed out earlier in this chapter, the quality of the specifications would probably be seriously deteriorated.

During the fiscal year 1953 the cataloging program of the Federal Supply Service for the civilian agencies came to a standstill because Congress cut the funds requested for the program. The work which had been done up to the end of the fiscal year 1952 which was of value to the agencies consisted principally of keeping the old Federal Standard Stock Catalog up to date for use by the Federal Supply Service in its centralized purchasing programs and by a few important agencies for procurement of selected items. The cataloging program at present does not make possible any significant savings in administrative costs of purchasing to the civilian agencies.

Centralized Purchasing at Agencies' Request

In the year ending June 30, 1952, the Federal Supply Service purchased more than $44,000,000 worth of goods for direct delivery to agencies.[18] The greater part of this was for purchases made at the request of agencies which believed the Federal Supply Service could contract for them more efficiently than they could, and the rest was conversion of large-quantity orders placed by the agencies against the federal-supply-center stores to orders for direct delivery from suppliers to the agencies.

Many agencies are not equipped to purchase unusually large quantities or specialized kinds of goods which they occasionally require. They may, however, take advantage of the provision of the law that the Federal Supply Service shall, on request, extend purchasing services to any agency. Such purchases, together with the orders on stores which are converted to direct delivery,

[18] Table 37.

amounted to about $32,000,000 in the fiscal year 1952. Federal Supply Service officials estimate that the savings to the government amount to 5 per cent of the value of purchases, or $1,600,000, largely because of reductions in price. No charge is made to the agencies for this service, and the purchases are handled by the regular purchasing staff of the regional offices of the Federal Supply Service. The fact that the agencies requested the service supports the claim of savings; it is reasonable to conclude in such cases that the specialized staff of the Federal Supply Service obtains somewhat more favorable contracts than the unspecialized staffs of the agencies.

The balance of the $44,000,000—about $12,000,000—included several million dollars worth of household furniture for living quarters purchased for direct delivery to the Departments of the Army and the Air Force at the request of these agencies; and purchases made under a standing agreement with the Department of the Interior providing that the Seattle office of the Federal Supply Service procure all requirements for the Alaska Native Service, the Alaska Railroad, and the Alaska Road Commission. Under the Department of the Interior agreement, the Federal Supply Service was reimbursed by slightly more than $300,000 for the purchasing service. No claims of savings in price or administrative costs are made by the Federal Supply Service for these purchases, although the decision of the agencies to use the Federal Supply Service facilities implies some advantage to the government. These programs apparently offer no embarrassment to the agencies because of slow deliveries. If they did, the agencies would doubtless make other purchasing arrangements.

Centralized Purchasing with Uncentralized Ordering (Supply-Center Stores)

The stores program is an attempt to combine the advantages of lower prices from large orders with local availability of supplies.

Normally substantial price advantages are extended to the agencies by the stores' program.[19] According to Federal Supply Service estimates, during the fiscal year 1952 the $63,800,000 worth of goods issued by the supply centers represented savings of $17,200,000 as compared with what the agencies would have paid if they had purchased them independently—an estimated saving of 27 per cent. The comparable figures for the fiscal year 1951 were $44,800,000 worth of stores' issues with savings of $7,900,000, or

[19] Files of the Federal Supply Service.

17.6 per cent.[20] The savings fluctuate from year to year depending on the trend in mill and other wholesale prices and the inventory policy of the Federal Supply Service. The high savings in 1952 compared with those in 1951 were in part the result of heavy purchases of goods for stock late in 1951 which were issued in 1952 after prices had risen. No estimates of aggregate savings are available for other years.

These estimates are based on a comparison of stores-issue prices with retail prices obtained for a sample of items by comparative shopping in Washington, D.C. An estimate was then made of the average discounts from retail prices which the agencies would have been able to obtain if they had made the purchases. For all classes of goods handled by the stores this was judged to average 75 per cent of the discount obtained by the Federal Supply Service on its consolidated purchases for stores, or a saving to the agencies of 25 per cent of the difference between the estimated retail prices and the stores-issue prices. Thus the comparative shopping data indicated that the goods issued from the supply centers were selling at retail at 52 per cent higher than stores-issue prices in 1952, and about 41 per cent higher in 1951. Comparative shopping lists for November, 1948, and December, 1949, from which aggregate savings were not estimated, show retail prices which were 40 per cent and 55 per cent higher than the prices paid by the Federal Supply Service.[21]

The administrative costs of the agencies are less when supplies are procured from the supply centers than they would be if the agencies purchased independently. Either way the supplies must be requisitioned, but, if the agencies were to purchase the goods, they would incur the additional administrative costs of contracting. The savings are substantial because more than 172,000 requisitions were placed by the agencies on the supply centers in the fiscal year 1951,[22] and the costs of contracting are estimated to exceed $15 per transaction when sealed bids are used, and $4 to $5 for small purchases exempted from the sealed-bids requirement. No accurate estimate can be made because there is not a one-to-one ratio between requisitions and contracts; left to their own devices the agencies would doubtless install central stores, as they did be-

[20] Table 37.

[21] Tables C and D, Appendix.

[22] U.S. General Services Administration, *Report of the Administrator of General Services for the Year Ending June 30, 1951* (Washington: 1952), p. 56.

fore the advent of the Bureau of Federal Supply, and consolidate requisitions to reduce contracting costs.

In evaluating the effectiveness of the supply centers the administrative costs of the centralized program must also be considered. Two comparisons are useful; one, the total administrative costs compared with the savings in price and administrative costs to the agencies under present conditions and, two, the administrative costs of the centralized stores with the costs which would be incurred by the agencies if they provided their own stores facilities.

Before the fiscal year 1951 the Federal Supply Service was obliged by law to include a markup in the stores-issue prices to cover the administrative costs of purchasing, storage, and issue. A markup of 10 per cent was used. Cost studies by the Federal Supply Service indicated that this markup amply covered the administrative expenses, and the figure was accepted by the Bureau of the Budget and congressional appropriation committees as being adequate. In the fiscal year 1952 the total expended directly for stores operations was $5,800,000 (Table E, Appendix)—9.5 per cent of the $63,800,000 worth of issues. This is substantially less than the Federal Supply Service estimate of $17,200,000 savings in prices paid by the agencies which does not include the savings in administrative costs of contracting.

The Federal Supply Service has taken steps to reduce the administrative costs of storage and issue. In 1950, after a study of the storage facilities and practices of several executive agencies, the Federal Supply Service made recommendations to improve the scheduling of requisitions. As a result the average number of line items per requisition—a convenient index of economical requisitions—was increased by 28 per cent in the fiscal year 1951 compared with 1950.[23] This amounts to a corresponding reduction in the number of requisitions and in the administrative expense incurred by the agencies in processing them and by the Federal Supply Service in supplying the goods requisitioned.

If the Federal Supply Service stores program were discontinued, it would be reasonable to expect that the administrative costs of purchasing to the government would be increased rather than reduced. The present program was installed as a result of a census of government purchasing taken by the Bureau of Federal Supply after the outbreak of war in 1941. The census showed that there were more than 400 warehouses operated by the civilian agencies.

[23] *Ibid.*, p. 56.

Many of these were liquidated and others consolidated to form the present twelve supply centers.[24] In evaluating the effectiveness of the present system it must be kept in mind that a multiplicity of stores would replace the present centralized stores. It is obviously impossible, however, to estimate the comparative administrative costs.

Centralized Contracting with Uncentralized Ordering (Federal Supply Schedules)

The federal supply schedules are similar to the stores program because they both use centralized contracting and local ordering. The price advantages, however, are generally smaller because the quantities are indefinite at the time the contracts are awarded. Also, agencies must allow more time for deliveries when ordering under the federal supply schedules than when ordering from stores.

The Federal Supply Service estimates that the agencies benefited in the fiscal year 1951 by price savings of $15,000,000 or 7.5 per cent of the estimated purchases of $200,000,000 made under the contracts. For the fiscal year 1952 the savings were estimated at $26,000,000 or 8.7 per cent of the estimated purchases of $300,000,000.[25]

These estimates were based on the judgment of the buyers of the Federal Supply Service and checked by consultation with the supplying contractors and agencies which use the contracts. For each of the approximately 100 schedules, estimates were made of the percentage by which the schedule contract prices were less than retail prices, and the percentage off retail at which the agencies could have bought if they had contracted individually for the goods. From these figures the savings for each schedule and the total for all schedules were calculated. The contract prices were estimated to range from retail prices to 50 per cent less; and the estimated savings to agencies on purchases under individual contracts ranged from nothing to 12.5 per cent.[26] No completely independent check of these estimates is available, but checks made with suppliers, trade association representatives, and a few government agencies in Washington on the accuracy of similar estimates of savings on seven schedules in January, 1951, lend support to the

[24] Testimony of C. E. Mack in *Treasury Department Appropriation Bill for 1950*, Hearings, p. 389.

[25] Table 37.

[26] Files of the Federal Supply Service.

opinion that the estimates are reasonably correct. The estimated savings in price for these schedules ranged from 8 per cent for electric lamps, to 33 per cent for ready-to-eat cereals (Table 36).

In making its estimates the Federal Supply Service assumed that the large agencies, such as the Veterans Administration would be able to buy as favorably as the Federal Supply Service and that the benefits of centralized contracting are derived principally from the price savings extended to the smaller agencies.

The operating expenses obligated in the fiscal year 1952 for federal supply schedules contracting totaled $1,100,000.[27] This is small compared with the claimed savings of $26,000,000. It is probably less than the administrative costs would be if these purchases were decentralized and made by agencies.

TABLE 36

ESTIMATED PRICE SAVINGS ON PURCHASES UNDER SELECTED FEDERAL SUPPLY SCHEDULES

(January, 1951)

Supply schedule	Average price reduction (per cent)
Electric lamps	8
Automobile tires and tubes	10
Pharmaceutical and biological preparations	13
Carpets and rugs	17
Pyrex glassware	17
Tire chains	23
Ready-to-eat cereals	33

SOURCE: Files of the Federal Supply Service, Washington, D.C.

CENTRALIZED PURCHASING OF CONSOLIDATED REQUIREMENTS FOR DIRECT DELIVERY

Centralized purchasing of the consolidated requirements for delivery directly to all agencies on the one hand offers the greatest prospect of price reductions, and on the other hand requires the agencies to determine their needs well in advance of the time the goods are wanted. For these reasons such purchases are confined to durable goods of relatively high unit cost for which price competition among prospective suppliers can be expected. Automotive vehicles, refrigerators, and water coolers are the important items.

The Federal Supply Service estimates that the following price

[27] Table F, Appendix.

savings were obtained for the agencies through the consolidated requirement programs: $2,500,000 or 7 per cent of the total purchases of $35,800,000 during the fiscal year 1951, and $2,300,000 or 6.5 per cent of the total purchases of $35,200,000 during the fiscal year 1952.[28]

The task of estimating the savings on these consolidated-requirements purchases is comparatively simple because few items are involved and the personnel operating the programs are in a position to know. The estimates are made for individual items. Automobiles, for example, were purchased under the centralized program at an average discount off list prices of 25 per cent in the fiscal year 1952, and it was estimated that the agencies could have, on the average, purchased them at 20 per cent off list, a saving of about 6 per cent. Purchase prices for the commodities included in the programs ranged from 24 per cent to 45 per cent off the retail prices, and it was estimated that the agencies obtained price savings by using the programs which ranged from 4 per cent to 14 per cent for the different commodities.

Some extra administrative costs are expended in consolidating the requirements and there are some savings in contracting expenses by letting contracts centrally. It is difficult to make any useful quantitative estimates of the administrative costs because the process of consolidating demands is, for some commodities, tied in with the process of proving essentiality of the items for the programs of the agencies. The latter is considered to be needed independently of the central-purchasing program to provide a curb on unwise procurement of such high-value items.

Summary

In summarizing the evaluation of the Federal Supply Service programs, presented in the foregoing pages, it is useful to compare the claimed savings with the total expenditures made by the Federal Supply Service to operate the programs. This is possible for the fiscal year 1952 but not for earlier years because the method of reporting expenditures then does not permit detailed comparisons. The price savings claimed in Table 37 for the four centralized-purchasing programs totaled $47,100,000 in the fiscal year 1952 during which $17,400,000[29] were obligated for operating expenses by the agency.

[28] Table 37.

[29] Sum of totals in tables E and F, Appendix.

The comparison of the $47,100,000 of price savings with the $17,400,000 of obligations for operating expenses is inadequate on two counts. It does not consider any savings in the price paid for the increase of *serviceability* or *utility* of the procured goods resulting from the centralized programs of federal specifications, cataloging, property utilization, inspection, and traffic management, although the *expense* of these programs is included; and it does not include any savings in the operating expenses of the agencies resulting from the functions performed by the Federal Supply Service—expenses which would have to be assumed if the Federal Supply Service did not exist.

TABLE 37

ESTIMATED PRICE SAVINGS TO AGENCIES FROM FEDERAL SUPPLY SERVICE CENTRALIZED CONTRACTING PROGRAMS

(Fiscal years ending June 30, 1951, and June 30, 1952)

Program	Fiscal year 1951			Fiscal year 1952		
	Volume (millions of dollars)	Savings in purchase prices		Volume (millions of dollars)	Savings in purchase prices	
		Millions of dollars	Per cent		Millions of dollars	Per cent
Federal supply schedules	200.0	15.0	7.5	300.0	26.0	8.7
Consolidated direct delivery	35.8	2.5	7.0	35.2	2.3	6.5
Unconsolidated direct delivery	29.9	0.5	1.7	44.3	1.6	3.6
Stores issues	44.8	7.9	17.6	63.8	17.2	27.0
Total	310.5	25.9	9.6	443.3	47.1	10.6

SOURCE: *Annual Report of the Administrator of General Services*, for the years ending June 30, 1951, and June 30, 1952.

The price savings were calculated on the assumption that the agencies would have procured goods meeting the same Federal Specifications used by the Federal Supply Service. Thus in claiming price savings on the federal supply schedule for tires, the $1,600,000 claimed to have been saved by the 8 per cent increase in serviceability was not included. This would raise the estimated savings to $48,700,000 for the fiscal year 1952. As was pointed out earlier, no over-all quantitative estimates of such savings can be obtained, but clearly the specialized talent available for centralized commodity testing and specification development frequently results in a better choice of products than could result from uncentralized development by each agency.

The obligations incurred under the budget classifications headed "personal property utilization and disposal," "commodity cataloging," "supply schedule and excess property inspection," and "traffic management" total $1,800,000. If this amount is deducted from the total obligations, the remaining amount of $15,600,000 better represents the administrative expenses of the supply functions immediately connected with purchasing, which have been considered in this study.

A fair comparison would also include an estimate of the savings in administrative expenses to the agencies. Two types of savings have been discussed in this chapter. One type is the saving from simplified agency purchasing. This is gained because the Federal Supply Service (1) from its central position discovers the best method currently used by any agency and extends its use to all agencies, (2) employs specialized personnel to devise simplified methods, and (3) provides expert representation for all agencies in dealings with Congress, the General Accounting Office, the Treasury, and the Bureau of the Budget.

The other type of saving is the administrative expenses which the agencies need not incur because of functions currently performed for them by the Federal Supply Service. These functions are specifications development, centralization of purchase programs (to the extent agencies would have their own central purchasing programs), invitation of bids and award of contracts, and storage and issue. So far as the present degree of centralization is concerned, the analysis in the foregoing pages leads to the conclusion that the administrative costs of performing these functions on an uncentralized basis would be substantially greater than the present expenditures of the Federal Supply Service. The specifications and storage-and-issue programs in particular would rapidly multiply in cost if performed adequately on an uncentralized basis.

There are, therefore, the following estimated economies: (1) $47,100,000 of price savings, (2) savings from the increased life of products, such as the $1,600,000 for tires, (3) savings in administrative costs due to simplification of uncentralized purchasing, and (4) savings to the agencies in administrative costs resulting from the performance of supply functions for the agencies by the Federal Supply Service. It seems to be clear that the actual savings, although they cannot be estimated quantitatively, must have heavily overweighed the $15,600,000 of operating expenses incurred by the Federal Supply Service in the fiscal year 1952. The comparison would probably be somewhat less favorable for periods of declining prices. During periods of rising prices the term contracts of the federal supply schedules, and the stores program which involves issuing goods some time after the award of contracts, increase the price savings shown by such centralized-purchasing programs. To some extent the opposite would be true in times of declining prices. All government term contracts, however, include clauses which require the vendors to extend price reductions they make to others to the government, regardless of the prices at which contracts were awarded. This would ameliorate the unfavorable effect as would any hand-to-mouth buying policies instituted by the Federal Supply Service. Still, the program has yet to be tested in such a period. Throughout the life of the Bureau of Federal Supply and the Federal Supply Service the price level has been rising.

XII

Conclusions

Two major conclusions have been drawn from the study thus far: (1) the use of sealed bids, guided by the present legal requirements and permitted exceptions, generally evokes greater competition and results in lower prices than the government could expect from alternative devices commonly used in private purchasing, and (2) the congressional policy of assigning to a single agency the authority to determine the purchasing policies and programs for all civilian agencies has increased the utility per dollar received by the government.

To say this does not mean that government purchasing cannot be improved. A comparison of the various programs with alternatives other than those used to form the above judgments reveals some of the ways in which the programs could be made more effective for the federal government and also more useful to other large-quantity purchasers.

Federal Government

Federal Supply Catalog.—The decision of Congress not to appropriate funds for the fiscal year 1953 cataloging programs has not only suspended progress on the civilian part of the prospective federal catalog system, but has made it difficult, if not impossible, to keep current the parts of the old Federal Standard Stock Catalog which are used in the centralized-purchasing programs.

If funds are not obtained to maintain the Federal Standard Stock Catalog, the federal supply schedules and the federal-supply-center stock catalogs—by means of which about 48,000 of the most important supply items are procured—will gradually become obsolete. The large potential benefits to the civilian agencies from the proposed new Federal Supply Catalog system must await the time when Congress is willing to invest funds in its development over the period of several years required to complete the task. If the military agencies complete their part of the Federal Supply Catalog system the task of the civilian agencies will be somewhat simplified, but the greater part of the work will remain to be done.

Commodity research.—The commodity-research and testing programs conducted in the interest of purchasing by the Bureau of Standards and other agencies have amply demonstrated their value. They have provided methods of test and commodity data for constructing a substantial part of the Federal Specifications. The amount of research, however, falls far short of covering the needs. This fact is recognized by the Federal Supply Service, but failure to obtain appropriations has prevented the launching of programs which hold promise of being self-liquidating over a very brief period.

The lack of sufficient commodity research underlies certain deficiencies in the Federal Specification system and the failure to evaluate quality in awarding contracts. This is discussed below.

Federal Specifications.—In recent years substantial progress has been made in the development of Federal Specifications. The 2,712 Federal Specifications available as of the beginning of 1953 constitute almost half of the 6,000 which are estimated to be required to complete the system. The present number provides the basis for a good deal more than half the volume of the civilian purchases and for the substantial volume of the same items which are purchased by the military agencies.

The full benefits of purchasing by means of adequate specifications will be realized only after the completion of the Federal Specifications system and the commodity-research programs required to improve existing specifications. To make the program fully effective, the government should intensify and broaden its efforts to bring Federal Specifications into accord with the specifications of national standards agencies such as the American Standards Association.

Qualified-products lists.—For many items inconsistencies in the quality of products from various sources of supply combined with relatively small orders which makes inspection uneconomical, prevent the use of federal supply schedules, which otherwise would be profitable. Qualified-products lists, which provide the answer to this problem, are available for only a few products. The use of such lists for many additional products is needed, but is prevented by the lack of the commodity research required to develop them. Since, in government practice, the basis for qualification is included in a Federal Specification for the commodity, the want of qualified-products lists is an added reflection of the present inadequacy of Federal Specifications.

Evaluation of quality differences.—A major deficiency in government contracting procedure is the general failure to evaluate the material quality differences of competitive products offered in response to invitations to bid, and to use such evaluations in awarding contracts. The Federal Property and Administrative Services Act of 1949 specifically permits such evaluations, and standard contract forms prepared by the Federal Supply Service now include the statement that contracts "shall be awarded to that responsible bidder whose bid, conforming to the Invitation for Bids, will be most advantageous to the Government, price and other factors considered." Despite this legal encouragement, neither the Federal Supply Service nor the other agencies evaluate quality above that specified when making awards excepting in the very few cases of commodities for which evaluation formulas based on test results have been established.

Broadening the use of evaluation methods in government contracting is difficult because the basis for evaluation must be stated in invitations to bid, and awards must be defensible if questioned by unsuccessful bidders either directly, through the General Accounting Office, or through their congressmen. Therefore, specific methods for evaluating quality differences with a defensible degree of quantitative accuracy must be worked out, commodity by commodity. Such evaluation methods can only be evolved through commodity-research programs which, as previously noted, have been insufficient to cover the need.

Purchasing-program research.—For many years Congress struck out from appropriation bills budget requests for the establishment of purchasing-program research. Such research is urgently required to tailor federal-supply-schedule and other contracts to the price and market structures of particular industries; to take advantage of any regular seasonal price movements; to develop the information required for simplification of forms and procedures; to decentralize purchasing assignments to regional offices or to other agencies best situated to perform them; to determine the relative advantages of centralized compared with agency purchasing; and to substantiate requests for funds for needed programs. Research is also needed to complement the commodity-research and testing programs.

Since the establishment of the General Services Administration in 1949, the Federal Supply Service has been able to conduct a limited amount of such purchasing-program research. As a result, a substantial part of the purchasing previously performed in Washington has been assigned to regional offices, many federal supply schedules have been improved, industry consultants were hired to improve the purchase of furniture, the size of orders submitted by the agencies to the federal supply centers have been increased, and substantial progress has been made in standardizing forms and simplifying the procedures for making small purchases. Much more research which leads to such improvements is needed, and as yet only a start has been made to develop the information needed to support requests for funds.

Centralized purchasing.—Government decisions to extend the federal-supply-schedule, federal-supply-center, and centralized-requirements purchase programs will make necessary increasingly more adequate information than has been available in the past. The present degree of centralization of purchasing appears to be amply justified in terms of savings, but if the programs are extended they will approach the margin of their usefulness, and more refined data than has been available on comparative prices and administrative costs will be needed to make wise decisions.

Simplified procedures.—The simplified procedures for making small purchases; the exemptions from the sealed-bids procedure of contracts below $500 for some agencies and $1,000 for others; the standard contracting forms—all promise important savings in the administrative expenses of contracting without corresponding increases in purchase prices or sacrifices in product quality. These procedures and forms require administrative adaptations by the individual agencies before they will be fully applied to purchasing operations. Agencies are slow to make such adaptations and continued pressure will be required to obtain the full benefits which these innovations make possible.

Implications for Other Large-Quantity Purchasers

Federal-government purchasing is of interest to other large-quantity purchasers for two reasons: first, the data developed by the government are either immediately or potentially useful for other types of purchasing; and secondly, the experience of the government with the operations of its purchasing policies raises questions regarding the effectiveness of private purchasing policies which are worthy of consideration.

Purchasing specifications.—All purchasers who buy in relatively large quantities for use or for resale under their own brands, have a need for purchase specifications. Federal specifications are among the most important sources of such information, and they are widely used, particularly by state and local government buyers, but also by institutional and other private buyers.

Federal Specifications often differ in significant respects from the specifications available for the same commodities from other sources such as the American Standards Association and the American Society for Testing Materials. Such differences in widely used specifications are confusing to purchasers who must select one to use, and are often costly to sellers who may have to supply differently designed products to meet the different requirements demanded by their customers. There would be widespread benefit if the purchase specifications promulgated by nationally recognized agencies, including the government, were unified into a single consistent system which met all real needs of purchasers. Such a unified system is technically feasible and has been achieved in part, although for economic reasons it is difficult to complete. A degree of such unification has been brought about through the government's policy of using the standards of nationally recognized agencies wherever such standards meet the government's needs, and by the use of Federal Specifications as data for the development of national standards.

It has already been suggested that the government can profit by intensifying its efforts to bring Federal Specifications in accord with generally accepted national standards. Private standards agencies also have a major responsibility for such unification. The primary responsibility rests with the American Standards Association which is organized to unify the standards of technical societies and trade associations, that is, of industry generally. The ASA has promulgated only about 1,300 standards of which the greatest number are not intended for use as purchase specifications. These obviously cannot meet the needs of the government which requires some 6,000 Federal Specifications for its purchasing. Standards of other agencies are used by the government, but they are often difficult for the government to adopt because they do not have the same degree of national acceptance as American Standards developed by the ASA. Improved coördination of standards development by all interested agencies, not only the government, but also the ASA and other private agencies, can speed unification to the benefit of all concerned.

Purchasing information.—Much additional information developed by the government for its purchasing has concrete value for state and local governments, institutional and other private buyers. Such information includes facts concerning the kinds and grades of commodities which are available for purchase to meet a given need, the uses for which each kind and grade are best adapted, the most efficient methods of using and maintaining the commodities, description of the normal channels of distribution and types of sellers, a listing and evaluation of the specifications which are available for use in buying, an explanation of alternative methods of inviting bids, whether or not submittal of samples should be required, the most appropriate methods of evaluating competitive offers when awarding contracts, and methods of inspection and testing of goods.

The General Services Administration does not attempt to make such information available for the good reason that it is responsible only for government purchasing and not for supplying information to other buyers. Some agency, such as the Department of Commerce which has a responsibility for aiding business—and particularly small business—might well consider the advisability of undertaking to compile and maintain a handbook which would make the commodity and purchasing data gathered for federal-government use available to the business community generally.

Purchasing policy.—Although the problems of private purchasing differ in important respects from those of the federal government, the experience of the government has implications for private purchasing which are worth exploring.

The internal policies of the government under which a single agency determines the policies to be followed by all agencies and conducts central-contracting, purchasing, and stores programs, were adopted by the government after their worth had been demonstrated by large-scale private buyers. Although such centralized policies could undoubtedly be used to better advantage by many private buyers, they have been investigated and discussed in the purchasing literature.

The use of standard commodity catalogs and purchase specifications is also common in private purchasing, although much more reliance is placed on sellers' identifications and less on the consistent use of specifications than in government purchasing. It is noteworthy that the National Association of Purchasing Agents within the past few years has taken an increased interest in promoting the use of national standard purchase specifications. For various types of commodities purchased by private buyers, it would be useful to have further studies of the price savings and administrative costs which result from using catalogs and specifications to concentrate demands on fewer items and widen markets, and particularly of the advantages of coöperative commodity research through private and government agencies.

Challenging implications for private buying are raised by the success with which the federal government has used sealed bids. It is the consistent use of all elements of sealed bids that is unique. Bidding open to all qualified suppliers; the use of objective commodity specifications; prohibition of negotiation after submittal of bids; single awards to low bidders—each of these elements of sealed bids is used to some extent by private purchasers, but practice among them varies greatly, and few use all these policies consistently.

Private purchasers generally operate on the assumption that they can evoke sufficient competition by limiting their invitations to bid to a relatively few potentially successful sources of supply. The experience of the government and analysis of the operation of limited compared with open bidding indicates that such a policy fails to take full advantage of the possibilities of price competition. Research into private contracting might well reveal that purchasers could gain by opening their bidding to much larger groups of suppliers than is now the practice.

Similarly, private buyers place heavy reliance on multiple and rotating awards to insure continuity of supply. Research might indicate that in many important instances the presumed advantages of continuity of supply are illusory, and single awards to low bidders would sharpen competition without in fact increasing the danger of embarrassing shortages.

Negotiation after submittal of bids; reciprocity; holding price and contract information in confidence—all bear further investigation in comparison with alternative policies which might be adopted.

Buyers along with sellers are responsible for the effective operation of markets. Research into and consequent reappraisal of the elements of purchasing policy suggested above could lead to a tightening of contracting procedures which would increase competition with benefit not only to the purchasers but to the economy as a whole.

APPENDIX

Standard Form 33
Prescribed by General Services Administration, Nov. 1949 Edition

INVITATION, BID, AND AWARD

(SUPPLY CONTRACT)

CONTRACT NO.	PAGE NO.	NUMBER OF PAGES
ORDER NO. *(If any)*	1	

ISSUED BY	ADDRESS

INVITATION FOR BIDS

DATE ISSUED	INVITATION NO.

Sealed bids in ____________, SUBJECT TO THE TERMS AND CONDITIONS OF THIS INVITATION, ITS SCHEDULE AND THE ATTACHED GENERAL PROVISIONS, will be received at the above office until ______ o'clock ____ m., ____________ Time ____________ *(date)*, and at that time publicly opened, for furnishing the following supplies or services, at the time specified in the Schedule, for delivery f. o. b. ____________

General information and instructions to bidders are contained in the terms and conditions on the reverse hereof.

SCHEDULE

ITEM NO.	SUPPLIES OR SERVICES	QUANTITY *(Number of units)*	UNIT	UNIT PRICE	AMOUNT

BID | DATE

In compliance with the above, the undersigned offers and agrees, if this Bid be accepted within ________ calendar days (*60 calendar days unless a different period be inserted by the bidder*) from the date of the opening, to furnish any or all of the items upon which prices are quoted, at the price set opposite each item, delivered at the designated point(s) and within the time specified in the Schedule of the Invitation for Bids. Discounts will be allowed for prompt payment as follows:

________ percent, 10 calendar days; ________ percent, 20 calendar days; ________ percent, 30 calendar days.

BIDDER REPRESENTS: (*Check appropriate boxes*)

(*1*) That the aggregate number of employees of the bidder and its affiliates is ☐ 500 or more, ☐ less than 500.

(*2*) That he is a ☐ regular dealer in, ☐ manufacturer of, the supplies bid upon.

(*3*) That he ☐ has, ☐ has not, employed or retained a company or person (*other than a full-time employee*) to solicit or secure this contract, and agrees to furnish information relating thereto as requested by the contracting officer.

INDICATE WHETHER ☐ INDIVIDUAL; ☐ PARTNERSHIP; ☐ CORPORATION. INCORPORATED IN THE STATE OF

NAME AND ADDRESS OF BIDDER (*Street, city, zone, and State. Type or print*)	SIGNATURE AND TITLE OF PERSON AUTHORIZED TO SIGN THIS BID (*Type or print name and title under signature*)

AWARD | DATE

ACCEPTED AS TO ITEMS NUMBERED	AMOUNT	UNITED STATES OF AMERICA
	$	BY ________________ CONTRACTING OFFICER
INVOICE FOR PAYMENT SHOULD BE MAILED TO		ACCOUNTING AND APPROPRIATION DATA
PAYMENT WILL BE MADE BY		

Standard Form 33
Nov. 1949 Edition

16—60682-1

TABLE A

Bidders' Prices for White Enamel Paint[a] Contracts, Responses to 11 Invitations to Bid Dated April 1, 1948–May 10, 1950

(Net prices per gallon, f.o.b. Washington, D.C., for definite delivery of specified quantities. Prices of successful bidders in bold face.)

Bidders	Date of invitation to bid and quantity										
	1948			1949						1950	
	4-1 2,500 gal.	5-13 6,000 gal.	12-16 3,150 gal.	3-1 1,500 gal.	4-27 1,750 gal.	7-11 1,450 gal.	10-17 4,500 gal.	11-4 1,500 gal.	12-27 2,500 gal.	2-28 1,500 gal.	5-4 2,800 gal.
Vita-Var Corp.	2.90	2.31	2.35	2.15	2.20	1.95	4.95	3.70	2.95	1.95	1.75
Atlantic Varnish and Paint Co., Inc.	1.89	1.78[b]	2.09	2.24	1.95	....	1.75	1.81	1.89	1.75	1.84
Central Paint and Varnish Works, Inc.	1.70	2.06[b]	2.26	2.04	1.92	**1.78**	1.66	**1.50**	1.54	1.61	....
Thomas C. Mee Co.	3.51	....	3.13	2.22	2.44	2.14	1.94	2.04	1.85	2.01	2.00
Pur-All Paint Products Co., Inc.	....	3.35	2.75	1.89	1.89	1.88	1.79	1.65	1.63	1.63	1.67
Standard Enamel and Paint Corp.	....	3.71	2.60	2.61	2.88	3.60	2.83	2.82	2.64	2.87	3.65
Chilton Paint Co.	2.67	2.42	2.23	1.93	1.87	....	1.76	1.73	....	1.78	1.88
Rose Diehl Paint Corp.	....	2.21	**1.98**	2.05	1.96	1.79	1.76	1.79	1.76	1.91	....
The Sherwin Williams Co.	....	....	2.77	2.14	2.07	2.07	1.95	1.94	1.97	2.12	2.14
M. A. Bruder and Sons, Inc.	2.20	....	2.54	2.49	1.84	1.82	1.83	1.79	....	1.70	....
R. L. Carlisle Chemical and Mfg. Co.	2.47	2.11[b]	....	2.17	2.68	....	....	2.06	1.84	1.61	2.21
Dixie Paint and Varnish Co.	....	....	2.41	2.57	....	2.03	2.22	1.95	1.82	1.85	1.84
Franklin Paint Co., Inc.	....	....	2.49	2.48	2.08	2.10	1.94	2.04	2.23	2.26	....
Jaegle Paint and Varnish Co.	2.00	....	2.00	1.90	....	2.00	1.60	1.57	**1.50**	1.50[c]	....
W. J. Sutcliffe Co.	....	....	2.76	2.52	1.98	1.86	1.88	1.89	1.91	1.86	....
Bruning Bros.	**1.59**	**2.17**	2.00	2.19	1.86	....	....	1.67	1.57	....	....
Color Craft Corp.	2.69	2.73	2.79	2.24	....	2.49	2.47	....	....	2.46	....
Felton Sibley and Co., Inc.	....	....	2.67	2.87	....	2.38	2.40	2.38	2.50	2.28	....
The Glidden Co.	....	....	2.54	2.15	2.24	2.21	....	1.97	2.10	....	2.05
Hoboken White Lead and Color Works	....	....	2.82	1.96	....	1.93	....	2.05	1.75	1.65	1.92
Hub Paint and Varnish Co., Inc.	....	....	2.06	1.94	....	....	**1.52**	1.62	1.54	1.54	**1.54**
Lasting Products	3.38	....	....	2.45	1.79	....	1.82	1.62	1.85	....	1.95
Lilly Paint Products	3.10	....	2.90	2.45	2.10	....	....	1.85	1.80	1.75	....
Purity Paint Products Corp.	....	....	2.15	1.97	....	....	1.76	1.77	1.70	1.66	1.73
William Armstrong Smith Co.	....	....	2.29	2.01	....	2.30	....	1.91	1.88	1.82	1.59

The C. M. Athey Paint Co.	....	....	2.03	1.87	....	....	....	1.67	1.53	**1.51**	1.64
Baltimore Paint and Color Works	....	....	....	3.35	....	1.90	3.00	1.64	1.57	1.56	....
C. E. Bradley Laboratories, Inc.	....	....	....	2.18	....	....	1.94	1.83	1.86	1.77	1.81
Capital Paint and Varnish Wks., N.Y.	2.32	2.01[b]	2.78	**1.82**	**1.68**	2.69	....	....	....	....	....
Casein and Oil Products Co.	....	....	2.57	2.47	2.47	....	2.33	1.88	....	1.73	....
Hock Paint and Chemical Works, Inc.	....	....	....	2.21	....	1.97	....	1.80	1.81	1.67	1.70
S. C. Johnson and Son, Inc.	....	....	....	3.78	4.32	4.32	4.48	4.32	4.32	....	....
M. J. Merkin Paint Co., Inc.	....	....	....	1.90	1.82	....	....	1.72	1.82	1.77	1.62
Payson Corp.	....	2.38	2.05	2.03	1.85	1.85	....	....	....	....	1.83
Southport Paint Co., Inc.	....	....	....	2.42	2.37	....	2.36	2.38	2.23	....	2.23
The White Co.	....	3.56	2.92	....	....	....	....	1.92	2.57	2.65	2.67
Yarnall Paint Co.	....	....	2.51	2.15	1.97	....	....	2.07	2.07	....	2.02
Capital Paint and Varnish Wks., Chi.	2.25	2.29	....	2.69	2.65	....	2.69	....	....	....	....
20th Century Paint and Varnish Corp.	....	....	2.51	2.46	1.92	1.94	1.85	....	....	....	....
Allied Paint and Color Works, Inc.	....	....	....	....	....	....	1.66	1.65	....	1.70	1.74
Atlas Paint and Varnish Co., Inc.	....	....	2.42	....	2.04	1.80	....	1.63	....	....	....
Carpenter-Morton Co.	....	....	2.23	....	2.23	2.18	....	1.83	....	....	....
Bradley Paint Engineers, Inc.	2.28	2.47	....	2.66	....	....	....	....	2.18	....	....
Everseal Mfg. Co., Inc.	1.90	....	....	2.52	....	....	....	....	....	1.57	1.86
A. C. Horn Division of Sun Chemical	....	....	....	....	....	....	2.27	2.33	3.25	2.02	....
Marvelite Paint Co.	....	....	2.46	2.20	2.41	2.10	....	....	....	....	....
Pavinoleum, Inc.	....	....	3.25	....	2.94	....	....	2.45	2.94	....	....
The Acorn Refining Co.	....	....	....	....	....	....	....	2.35	2.32	....	4.49
H. B. Davis Co.	....	....	2.78	2.20	....	....	....	1.75	....	....	....
Goodyear Paint and Varnish Co.	3.04	2.73	....	....	....	....	....	2.59	....	....	....
Hudson Paint and Varnish, Inc.	....	....	....	2.70	2.57	....	....	2.72	....	....	....
Keystone Varnish Co.	....	....	....	2.05	1.84	....	....	1.84	....	....	....
Paint Engineers, Inc.	1.76	....	....	1.93	1.75	....	....	....	....	....	....
The Parr Paint and Color Co.	2.89	....	2.61	2.67	....	....	....	....	....	....	....
F. O. Pierce	....	....	3.35	2.59	....	....	....	....	....	....	2.10
McDougall-Butler Co., Inc.	....	....	3.56	3.40	3.27	....	....	....	....	....	....
Varcraft Works, Inc.	....	....	....	2.20	1.90	....	....	1.80	....	....	....

SOURCE: Compiled from data in the contract files of the Federal Supply Service, Washington, D.C. This table includes only those firms which bid on three or more contracts.

[a] Enamel, interior, gloss, white, in 5-gallon containers, in accordance with Federal Specification no. TT-E-506a dated 12-16-1949 and Amendment 1, dated 6-13-1949. Item no. 52-E-6021.

[b] Bids rejected because paint offered failed to meet specifications.

[c] This bidder bid on additional items of paint on the same invitation and qualified his bid on an "all or none" basis. As he was not the low bidder on other items, the price on this item was not a firm offer.

TABLE B

BIDDERS' PRICES FOR TIOLET-TISSUE[a] CONTRACTS, RESPONSES TO 23 INVITATIONS TO BID DATED MARCH 22, 1948–NOVEMBER 30, 1950
(Net prices per carton of 100 rolls, f.o.b. Washington, D.C., for definite delivery of specified quantities.
Prices of successful bidders in bold face.)

Bidders	Date of invitation to bid, and quantity																						
	1948						1949									1950							
	3–22 2,400 cart.	4–26 3,000 cart.	5–27 3,800 cart.	7–2 5,000 cart.	8–24 1,900 cart.	10–22 2,000 cart.	1–5 2,000 cart.	1–27 2,000 cart.	3–4 3,000 cart.	6–24 3,000 cart.	7–29 3,100 cart.	8–25 3,300 cart.	10–5 2,400 cart.	11–1 1,500 cart.	12–5 1,200 cart.	1–5 1,000 cart.	1–31 3,000 cart.	4–3 1,000 cart.	5–3 1,000 cart.	6–29 1,500 cart.	11–1 1,500 cart.	11–17 1,200 cart.	11–30 1,500 cart.
Ashland Paper Mills, Inc.[b]	11.47	**10.63**	9.80[c]	**9.19**[d]	9.55	8.79	6.08	6.18	**5.17**	**4.57**	4.84	**4.69**	5.40	5.40	5.40	5.40	5.35	**4.98**	4.92	**4.59**	9.15	....	**9.15**
International Cellucotton Products Co.	11.23[c]	11.23	11.23	11.23	11.23	11.23	11.23	9.90	9.90	9.90	9.90	9.90	....	9.90	9.90	9.90	9.46	9.46	9.46	9.46	9.90	....	....
Park Tissue Mills, Inc.	8.00[c]	8.20	11.09	....	8.25	**7.50**	**5.82**	5.84	5.56	4.63	4.63	6.06	....	4.96	**4.72**	**4.72**	**4.72**	....	4.98	5.37	**8.99**	**9.05**	10.84
Resolute Paper Products Corp.[e]	**11.27**	11.30	....	8.83[c]	....	....	6.20	6.31	5.77	4.97	5.94	5.94	5.94	5.52	5.03	4.83	4.83	5.29	5.18	5.66	9.29	9.07	10.03
Arlington Sales Agency[f]	....	....	....	....	....	7.95	7.10	6.70	6.70	5.10	5.10	....	5.50	5.50	5.50	4.95	4.95	4.75[c]	4.75	4.95	....	....	....
Walker Goulard Plehn Co., Inc.[f]	....	10.94	**9.89**	10.29	8.83	7.91	5.92	5.60	5.46	6.17	....	....	6.18	....	....	6.19	6.19	6.20	....	6.50	....	....	....
Raycarr Sales Co.[f]	11.48	10.78	9.19[c]	10.34	**8.18**	8.12	6.14	5.56[c]	....	4.90	....	....	....	....	....	5.15	....	....	....	....	9.85	9.95	11.58
Hudson Pulp and Paper Corp.	....	....	....	....	....	....	6.32	6.17	5.48	4.99	5.01	5.20	....	5.46	5.22	5.22	....	5.19	4.94	4.83	....	....	....
Paper Service Co., Inc.	....	....	9.85[c]	**9.25**[d]	....	....	....	5.93	5.44	....	4.57	5.16	4.72[c]	4.74	5.03	....	....	....	**4.63**	4.63	....	....	....
Green View Tissue Mills, Inc.[f]	....	....	....	....	....	....	....	....	....	....	4.80	....	5.71	....	5.59	5.43	5.51	5.58	5.72	5.45	10.81	....	....
Wheeler Paper Corp.	....	....	....	9.33	8.98	7.87	....	....	6.83	5.38	5.32	5.43	....	5.72	....	5.18	....	....	....	....	....	....	....
Peerless Paper Mills, Inc.	....	....	....	....	....	....	....	6.57	....	....	....	....	5.31	5.40	7.18	....	6.47	6.04	6.03	6.29	....	....	....

APW Products Co., Inc.	....	....	....	....	....	....	6.78	6.76	....	4.61	....	5.03	....	5.63	....	....	5.29	....	5.17	....	....	....	....
Leonard Tissue Co.	....	....	....	....	....	....	....	6.08	5.88	....	....	5.13	....	5.63	5.15	5.25	5.39	....	....	....	....	....	....
Winchester Paper Co.	....	....	10.20	....	....	....	5.81[c]	....	....	....	**4.55**	....	4.90	....	5.03	5.15	5.47	....	....	....	....	....	....
Morgan Paper Co., Inc.	....	....	....	....	....	7.99	....	....	....	5.18	4.79	....	**4.79**	....	....	5.37	5.37	....	....	....	....	....	....
Wexler Paper Products[f]	....	11.93	....	9.60	9.20	....	8.20	7.78	7.56	....	....	....	....	....	....	....	....	....	....	....	....	....	....
Empire Paper Co.[f]	....	....	....	9.15[c]	9.27	....	7.16	7.24	6.25	....	....	....	....	....	....	....	....	....	....	....	....	....	....
Groveton Papers Co.	....	....	....	....	....	....	....	....	....	4.55[c]	....	....	....	**4.65**	....	....	5.08	....	5.15	....	9.71	....	....
The Old Dominion Paper Co.[f]	16.74	....	....	10.27	8.37	8.65	7.20	....	....	....	....	....	....	....	....	....	....	....	....	....	....	....	....
Sterling Pulp and Paper Co.	....	....	....	....	....	....	....	6.40	6.27	5.20	4.90	....	....	....	....	....	5.39	....	....	....	....	....	....
Falls Paper and Power Co.	....	....	....	....	....	....	....	....	....	....	....	6.69	6.62	....	....	....	....	....	6.50	6.52	....	....	....
S. Freedman and Sons[f]	12.50	....	11.38	....	....	....	7.63	7.42	....	....	....	....	....	....	....	....	....	....	....	....	....	....	....
Rushmore Paper Mills, Inc.	....	....	....	....	....	....	6.62	**5.58**	5.10[c]	....	....	5.34	....	....	....	....	....	....	....	....	....	....	....
Woodland Paper Products	....	....	....	....	9.25	....	....	....	....	5.50	6.65	....	....	....	....	....	....	....	....	....	....	9.75	....
Hanover Paper Corp.[f]	....	....	10.90	....	....	....	....	7.20	6.65	....	....	....	....	....	....	....	....	....	....	....	....	....	....
National Paper and Twine Co.	....	....	....	....	....	....	7.35	....	....	5.12	....	....	....	....	....	....	4.90	....	....	....	....	....	....
National Paper Corp. of Pennsylvania	....	....	....	8.46	....	....	6.47	6.05	....	....	....	....	....	....	....	....	....	....	....	....	....	....	....
Sales International Co.	....	....	....	....	....	....	7.84	6.93	8.91	....	....	....	....	....	....	....	....	....	....	....	....	....	....
Charles S. Sher Co., Inc.	....	....	....	....	....	....	....	....	6.78	5.14	4.36[c]	....	....	....	....	....	....	....	....	....	....	....	....
Stevens and Thompson Paper Co.	....	....	....	....	....	....	....	....	....	5.63	....	....	....	....	....	7.91	7.91	....	....	....	....	....	....

Source: Compiled from data in the contract files of the Federal Supply Service. This table includes only those firms which bid on three or more contracts.

[a] Toilet tissue in rolls, 1000 sheets to the roll, 100 rolls to the carton, in accordance with Federal Specification UU-P-556b and Amendment 1, Type I. Item no. 29-P-1020.

[b] The bids shown for this firm include those of its subsidiary company, White-Washburne Co., Inc.

[c] Bid rejected because it failed to meet product or other specifications of the invitation.

[d] Partial award, as the lowest bidder bid only on 500 cartons.

[e] The bids shown for this firm include those of its subsidiary company, Windsor Locks Paper Corp.

[f] Jobber.

TABLE C

Federal Supply Service Stores-Issue Prices to Agencies Compared with Retail Prices November 19, 1948

Stock-catalog item number	Item description	Unit	Stores-issue price per unit[a] (dollars)	Typical retail price per unit[b] (dollars)	Percentage by which retail exceeds stores prices	Annual sales (units)	Value of annual sales at stores-issue prices (dollars)	Value of annual sales at typical retail prices (dollars)
5-F-4033	Flags, no. 7, 5′2″ x 9′9″	each	6.32	9.75	35.2	2,985	18,865	29,104
17-B-7210	Batteries, flashlight	each	0.06	0.10	40.0	425,418	25,525	42,550
17-L-535-300	Tubes, fluorescent, electric, 48″, 40 watt	each	0.83	1.10	24.5	36,154	30,008	39,764
17-L-7068	Lamps, desk, fluorescent, 14½″ high, 18″ shade	each	4.30	8.00	46.3	3,418	14,697	27,344
17-T-805	Tape, friction, ¾″ wide ½-lb. roll	roll	0.31	0.43	27.9	92,378	28,637	39,720
21-C-272-90	Cord, venetian blind, drab	100 feet	0.75	1.65	54.5	16,809	12,607	27,735
21-R-365	Rope, manila, ⅜″ diameter, 500 ft. to coil	coil	9.20	13.45	31.5	2,174	19,999	29,240
26-S-16030	Sections, filing, steel 4-drawer, letter size	each	53.26	69.75	23.6	5,064	269,722	353,336
27-B-630	Blankets, 80% wool, gray, 66″ x 84″	each	5.04	7.75	34.9	1,496	7,540	11,594
27-C-310	Cheesecloth, bleached, 36″ wide, 75-yd. bolt	bolt	7.50	9.75	23.1	18,196	136,468	177,409
27-C-2675	Cloths, wash, turkish, 12″ x 12″	dozen	1.29	1.80	28.3	19,413	25,043	34,943
27-M-178-525	Mats, floor, composition, 48″ x 54″	each	4.29	8.00	46.4	4,850	20,807	38,800
27-P-610	Pillowcases, cotton, 36½″ x 45″	each	0.57	0.69	17.4	61,736	35,190	42,598
27-S-7080	Sheets, cotton, bleached, 63″ x 99″	each	2.15	2.59	17.0	61,954	133,200	160,507
27-S-7110	Sheets, cotton, bleached, 72″ x 108″	each	2.45	3.20	23.4	11,915	29,193	39,200
27-S-7570	Sheeting, cotton, bleached, 72″ wide, 50-yd. bolt	bolt	45.00	50.00	10.0	519	23,360	25,950
27-T-3428	Towels, bath, turkish, 22″ x 44″	each	0.56	0.62	9.7	108,655	60,847	67,366
27-T-3450	Towels, cotton, crash, 17″ x 36″	each	0.21	0.27	22.2	272,977	57,325	73,720
27-T-3455	Towels, dish, 36″ x 36″	each	0.31	0.35	11.4	55,132	17,091	19,296
29-P-1023	Paper, toilet, 800 sheets per pkg., 125 pkgs. to carton	carton	13.17	14.50	9.2	14,178	194,660	214,320
29-T-300	Tissues, cleansing, 9″ x 10″, 500 to box	box	0.27	0.40	32.5	211,711	57,162	84,657
34-S-500	Skins, chamois, appr. 488 sq. inches	each	2.40	3.98	39.7	10,309	24,743	41,030
38-B-100	Brooms, corn, lightweight	each	0.91	1.27	28.3	18,374	16,720	23,335

38-B-4580	Brushes, floor, sweeping, 18″	each	3.75	5.40	30.6	13,430	50,363	72,522
38-B-4585	Brushes, floor, sweeping, 24″	each	5.02	7.15	29.8	5,348	26,847	38,238
38-H-235	Handles, brush, floor, sweeping	each	0.24	0.35	31.4	69,680	16,723	24,388
41-S-188	Saws, hand, crosscut, 26″	each	2.69	5.75	53.2	2,346	6,313	13,490
41-S-3220	Shovels, round, point, long handle	each	1.80	2.95	38.9	7,280	13,104	21,476
42-C-1740	Cans, ash or garbage, 24-gal.	each	5.34	8.85	39.7	8,195	43,762	72,514
42-C-20720-635	Cloth, wire screen, bronze, 36″, 100-ft. roll	roll	26.44	36.00	26.6	796	21,051	28,656
42-N-25808	Nails, common, flat heads, 6-penny, 2″	100 lbs.	8.92	11.30	21.1	612	5,464	6,916
51-C-1554-15	Compound, antifreeze, nonvolatile, 1-gal. can	gallon	2.01	3.25	38.2	219,040	440,270	711,917
51-D-109	Developer, photo-copying, dark development	package	0.38	0.45	15.6	59,093	22,455	26,592
51-S-1655	Soap, laundry, floating, 6-oz. cake, 100 to case	case	6.26	8.40	25.5	8,008	50,130	67,275
51-T-5963	Trisodium phosphate, 100-lb. container	container	4.75	5.75	17.4	5,944	28,237	34,178
52-P-4505	Paint, exterior, oil, white, 1-gal. can	can	3.54	5.70	37.9	3,498	12,383	19,939
52-T-891	Turpentine, gum spirits, 1-gal. can	can	1.10	1.50	26.7	9,669	10,636	14,504
52-V-2965	Varnish, spar, water resisting, 1-gal. can	can	1.91	6.00	68.2	6,768	12,927	40,608
52-W-400	Wax, floor, liquid, 1-gal. container	container	0.75	2.35	68.1	10,004	7,503	23,509
53-B-2110	Bands, rubber, no. 18, ⅛-lb. box	box	0.12	0.20	40.0	29,601	3,552	5,920
53-B-11362	Binders, 3-ring, imitation leather, 11″ x 8½″, stiff cover	each	0.73	1.40	47.9	18,245	13,319	25,546
53-C-12344	Clips, wire, Gem pattern, large, 100 to box	box	0.04	0.08	50.0	1,693,314	67,733	126,999
53-E-5808	Erasers, typewriter, circular, with brush	dozen	0.76	1.50	49.3	22,986	17,469	34,479
53-F-1222	Fasteners, paper, flexible, 1″, 50 sets to box	box	0.40	0.95	57.9	86,222	34,489	81,911
53-P-412	Pads, calender, folding type, 3¾″ x 5⅞″	each	0.35	0.63	44.4	191,647	67,076	120,738
53-P-520	Pads, desk, cardboard, stiff back	each	0.38	0.60	36.7	23,033	8,753	13,820
53-P-1244	Pads, memo, white, ruled both sides, 8″ 10½″, 12 pads to package	package	1.94	2.40	19.2	43,080	83,575	103,383

For explanation of references "a" and "b" see the following page.

TABLE C—*Continued*

Stock-catalog item number	Item description	Unit	Stores-issue price per unit[a] (dollars)	Typical retail price per unit[b] (dollars)	Percentage by which retail exceeds stores prices	Annual sales (units)	Value of annual sales at stores-issue prices (dollars)	Value of annual sales at typical retail prices (dollars)
53-P-7980	Paper, carbon, executive, 8″ x 11″, 100 sheets to box	box	1.18	2.25	47.6	2,376	2,804	5,346
53-P-30015-10	Pencils, wood cased, lead, general writing, superthin	dozen	0.27	0.34	20.6	2,946	795	1,010
53-P-35950	Perforators, paper, adjustable, with 3¼″ heads	each	6.96	13.72	49.3	1,864	12,973	25,571
53-T-265-10 through 53-T-282	Tabs, transparent, 10 6″ strips to box	box	0.28	0.43	34.1	290,000	81,200	123,262
54-M-31590	Machines, paper fastening, wire spool type	each	3.65	6.51	43.9	7,416	27,067	48,278
54-M-31630	Machines, paper fastening, light duty	each	2.51	4.50	44.2	42,421	106,476	190,895
54-R-1870	Receptacles, wastebasket, metal, round	each	0.71	1.50	52.7	17,627	12,515	26,441
54-S-13000	Sharpeners, pencil, office	each	1.22	2.50	51.2	21,250	25,925	53,125
57-P-3170	Plasters, adhesive, surgical, 3″, 5-yd. spool	spool	0.48	0.80	40.0	38,429	18,446	30,743
58-E-202	Extinguishers, fire, carbon tetrachloride, 1-qt.	each	5.84	12.00	51.3	16,577	96,807	198,939
58-E-220	Extinguishers, fire, soda and acid, plain finish, 2½-gal. capacity	each	13.41	24.00	44.1	2,107	28,260	50,568
70-M-595	Mowers, lawn, hand operated, 18″ blades	each	17.00	19.95	14.8	2,632	44,745	52,508
	Total						2,837,021	4,246,886
	Average percentage by which retail exceeds stores prices				33.2			

SOURCE: Compiled from data in the files of the Federal Supply Service.

[a] Stores-issue prices are prices paid by requisitioning government agencies. Issue prices are firm for periods of two months and are calculated to yield an average markup of 10 per cent above purchase prices to cover administrative costs of purchase, storage, and issue. Actual percentages of markup will vary both over time and for different items because (1) contract prices differ and the timing of contracts does not coincide with the two-month periods during which issue prices are constant and (2) the percentage markup applied varies for different classes of items according to the administrative costs of storing and issuing.

TABLE D

FEDERAL SUPPLY SERVICE STORES-ISSUE PRICES TO AGENCIES COMPARED WITH RETAIL PRICES DECEMBER 12, 1949

Stock-catalog item number	Item description	Unit	Stores-issue price per unit[a] (dollars)	Typical retail price per unit[b] (dollars)	Percentage by which retail exceeds stores prices	Annual sales (units)	Value of annual sales at stores-issue prices (dollars)	Value of annual sales at typical retail prices (dollars)
17-B-7211	Battery, flashlight, size D, metal-clad	each	0.06	0.10	40.0	731,906	43,914	73,190
17-L-7067-10	Lamp, desk, swinging arm, 2 tube, 34″ ext.	each	8.63	26.75	67.7	5,296	45,704	141,668
27-B-467	Bedspreads, white, 63″ x 90″, cotton, bleached	each	1.95	2.25	13.3	28,200	54,990	63,450
42-C-1750	Cans, ash or garbage, galv. steel, 32-gallon	each	5.97	9.75	38.7	8,478	50,613	82,660
51-C-1554-15	Compound, antifreeze, nonvolatile, 1-gal. can	gallon	2.01	3.75	46.4	178,441	358,666	669,153
51-S-1910	Soap, milled, toilet, 2½ oz. cake, 144 to case	case	3.43	4.32	20.6	25,384	87,067	109,658
53-B-11700	Binder, 3-ring, 2″ capacity, 11 x 8½″	each	0.87	2.70	67.7	83,470	72,618	225,369
53-I-1724	Drawing ink, black, Higgins	bottle	0.15	0.25	40.0	26,604	3,990	6,651
53-N-203	Folded napkins, white, 1000 to package	package	0.78	1.50	48.0	68,192	53,189	102,288
53-P-1148	Memorandum pad, 8 x 10½″, white	package	1.14	1.44	20.8	12,938	14,749	18,630
53-P-30004	General writing pencil no. 2	dozen	0.14	0.55	74.5	675,677	94,594	371,622
53-R-908	Reinforcements, eyelet, ¼″ hole	box	0.03	0.10	70.0	239,479	7,184	23,947
53-S-1000	Shears, 6″ steel	pair	0.92	2.60	64.6	14,529	13,366	37,775
58-E-202	Extinguishers, fire	each	5.90	10.00	41.0	65,556	386,780	655,560
	Total						1,287,430	2,581,626
	Average percentage by which retail exceeds stores prices				50.1			

SOURCE: Compiled from data in the files of the Federal Supply Service.

[a] Stores-issue prices are prices paid by requisitioning government agencies. Issue prices are firm for periods of two months and are calculated to yield an average markup of 10 per cent above purchase prices to cover administrative costs of purchase, storage, and issue. Actual percentages of markup will vary both over time and for different items because (1) contract prices differ and the timing of contracts does not coincide with the two-month periods during which issue prices are constant and (2) the percentage markup applied varies for different classes of items according to the administrative costs of storing and issuing.

[b] Typical retail prices were collected by comparative shoppers and are prices for comparable items purchased in small quantities in Washington, D.C., retail outlets.

TABLE E

Expenses, General Supply Fund, General Services Administration

Obligations by activities
(in dollars)

Description	1952 Actual
Direct obligations	
Direct-order purchasing	2,031,393
Stores operations	5,813,715
Direct-order inspection	520,536
Space and related costs	1,589,124
Equipment maintenance	39,712
Administrative operations	2,611,292
Subtotal	12,605,772
Obligations of 1951 charged to 1952 under comptroller-general's decision 13—105234	749,511
Total direct obligations	13,355,283
Obligations payable out of reimbursements from other accounts	
Direct order purchasing	11,840
Stores operations	259,537
Direct order inspection	21,676
Equipment maintenance	1,300
Administrative operations	6,063
Total obligations payable out of reimbursements from other accounts	300,416
Total obligations	13,655,699

Source: *The Budget of the United States Government for the Fiscal Year Ending June 30, 1954* (Washington, D.C.: 1953), p. 276.

TABLE F

Operating Expenses, Federal Supply Service, General Services Administration

Obligations by activities
(in dollars)

Description	1952 Actual
Direct obligations	
Supply management	103,725
Supply-schedule contracting	1,102,753
Personal-property utilization and disposal	532,982
Commodity specifications	526,907
Commodity cataloging	954,569
Supply-schedule and excess-property inspection	163,708
Traffic management	305,939
Total direct obligations	3,690,583
Obligations payable out of reimbursements from other accounts	
Commodity cataloging	8,250
Total obligations	3,698,833

Source: *The Budget of the United States Government for the Fiscal Year Ending June 30, 1954* (Washington, D.C.: 1953), pp. 274–275.

www.ingramcontent.com/pod-product-compliance
Lightning Source LLC
Chambersburg PA
CBHW031128270326
41929CB00011B/1540

* 9 7 8 0 5 2 0 3 4 5 4 9 2 *